FILES

_____

MERIDIAN

Crossing Aesthetics

Werner Hamacher

Editor

Translated by Geoffrey Winthrop-Young

*Stanford
University
Press*

*Stanford
California
2008*

FILES

Law and Media Technology

Cornelia Vismann

Stanford University Press
Stanford, California

Files: Law and Media Technology was originally published in
German in 2000 under the title *Akten. Medientechnik und
Recht* © 2000, Fischer Taschenbuch GmbH,
Frankfurt am Main.

This book was published with the assistance of the Holcombe
Academic Translation Trust and the Editorial Committe of the
Modern Law Review.

Printed in the United States of America
on acid-free, archival-quality paper

Library of Congress Cataloging-in-Publication Data

Vismann, Cornelia.
[Akten. English]
Files : law and media technology / Cornelia Vismann ;
translated by Geoffrey Winthrop-Young.
p.   cm.—(Meridian)
Includes bibliographical references.
ISBN 978-0-8047-5150-6 (cloth : alk. paper)
ISBN 978-0-8047-5151-3 (pbk. : alk. paper)
1. Information storage and retrieval system—
Law.   2. Digital media—Law and legislation.   3. Files
(Records)—Technological innovations.   I. Title.
K87.V57 2008
343.0999—dc22
2007039414

Contents

Acknowledgments

This translation came about on the initiative of Werner Hamacher, whose unswerving commitment to making it part of the Meridian: Crossing Aesthetics series has my full gratitude. I am also grateful to Niki Lacey for securing financial support for the translation through the editorial committee of *The Modern Law Review*. My special thanks goes here to Hugh Collins, the general editor, as well as to Martin Loughlin and Tim Murphy. Further support was made available by the Holcombe Academic Translation Trust, for which I thank especially Michael King and Anton Schütz, who also offered valuable advice for rendering difficult passages into English. This translation resulted in a friendship with Geoffrey Winthrop-Young, whose speed I admire, whose witty e-mails I enjoyed, and whose tacit corrections of my negligence I shall need furthermore. To the German original, *Akten*, I owe the acquaintance of Raul Hilberg. The translation is dedicated to his memory.

Cornelia Vismann,
Frankfurt am Main, New Year's Eve, 2007

The following translation is an abridged version of the original text, *Akten: Medientechnik und Recht*. All deletions and editorial changes were undertaken in close consultation with the author.

I would like to thank Anton Schütz for reading the manuscript and offering valuable comments. I am especially grateful to Cornelia Vismann for her generous help and advice throughout the project.

G. Winthrop-Young,
University of British Columbia

Preface: Off the Record

Well then, dear colleague,
Into the registry with us. We need to stack
The files up. For they are toppled on
The floor like the Tower of Babel, everywhere.[1]

With these words Judge Adam in Heinrich von Kleist's comedy *The Broken Pitcher* invites his clerk into the registry of a Dutch village court near Utrecht around 1800. Once inside, they are confronted with Babylonian mounds of toppled files. Those who work with records are familiar with the problem: files pile up on desks, accumulate in offices, and fill attics and basements. Though registered, their order collapses time and again, though collected, quashed, dispatched, sold, shredded, or destroyed in some other way, they keep mushrooming. Their incessant proliferation seems a natural phenomenon. Masses of paper arise and merge into mountains that join together to form entire mountain ranges. Floods of paper empty into oceans; ravines flanked by shelves cut through impassable terrain. Those brave enough to traverse this paperscape measure the amount of files in meters, kilograms, or basket loads. As a rule, however, it is impossible to count the number of files, for unlike books, files are not discrete or enumerable units. They can appear in all shapes and forms: as loose pages, lying in little boxes, wrapped in packing paper, or enclosed in capsules; they may present themselves as bundles tied with a string or assume the shape of vertical folders ready to enfold anything that can fit between two paper covers. Reference may be to a single file, a procedure covering several files, or the entire content of an archive. Files are the variables in the universe of writing and the law.

When files or records are referred to in the plural, their content rarely seems to matter; it is buried underneath their materiality. And even when files are opened to reveal their contents, they are not simply read. Files are *processed*, just like stones and other such matter. The English language distinguishes between their materiality and their function. *Files*—derived from the thread or wire that binds the leaves together—refers to the former, but if the focus is not on their physicality, we speak of *records*, in correspondence with their function as *recording devices*.[2] The German term *Akten*, on the other hand, does not differentiate between readable corpora of texts and space-consuming convolutes of paper. From a media-technological perspective, this homonym, despite its terminological indifference to matter and function, is quite precise: *Akten* (records) generate *Akten* (files). Recording apparatuses produce loads of files. The quasi-natural phenomenon that more and more files come into being turns out to be a medial effect of records. Acting as recording machines, *Akten* / records promote the mushrooming, dissemination, and proliferation of *Akten* / files. The more user-friendly and accessible the recording technologies, the more files will be generated. The countless instructions issued by the upper administrative echelons to rigorously select and only put down what is most important are an attempt to stem the tide, but authorless recording machines do not obey such orders. They are designed to record whatever can be recorded and thus continue their space-consuming existence. For the administrations of the Western world, a life without files, without any recording, a life *off the record*, is simply unthinkable. Babylonian stacks of files, "floods of official paper,"[3] are the inevitable consequence.

This book focuses on the media-technological conditions of files and recording devices with a view to their largest area of application, the law. More precisely, it will investigate how files control the formalization and differentiation of the law. Consider, as a kind of vanishing point, the *Rechtsstaat*, the fully developed state governed by the rule of law composed of the abstract law on one side and the agencies that set down and enforce the law on the other. Files process the separation of the law into authority and administration. They contribute to the formation of the three major entities on which the law is based: truth, state, and subject. This inquiry is therefore not concerned with the content of the files stored in agencies, institutions, or enterprises, but with the part that official records have in the emergence of the notions of truth, the concepts of state, and the constructions of the subject in Western history.

Files cannot be defined. As variables in the universe of writing they elude any general, context-free determination. Beyond their varying historical concretions, they can only be defined in formal fashion as that which generates a certain type of law. Likewise, the *law* eludes any precise definition. In this book it is dealt with not as an instrument or medium for the arbitration of conflicts but as a repository of forms of authoritarian and administrative acts that assume concrete shape in files. Based on this reconstruction of their concurrence, law and files mutually determine each other. A given recording technology entails specific forms and instances of the law. A new way of binding or of writing things down, a change in the way data are collected, affects the legal framework. It is only in such a diachronic description that the discourse of the law assumes its specific appearances. Only then, by turning into parchment *codices*, string-tied convolutes, or standardized chrome folders, do files acquire face, form, and format.

While the choice of the following examples from the history of the law may be determined by chance or the logic of proximity, the focal points of the narrative are far less accidental. They are derived not from any history of administration but from literature. Literary fictions that deal with administrations highlight those media and realities of the law that nonfictional, scholarly self-presentations of the law and its history tend to overlook or even suppress. Hence Kafka's chancery fantasies can be used to write a genealogy of the law. In the same way, Bartleby's recording fictions mirror the facts of recording. Narratives by Kafka and Melville do not merely illustrate the machines and apparatuses of the law, or the logic of bureaucracy driven to its extreme. As narrative residues discarded by the grand tales of the origin and evolution of the law, they stand at the end of a process of differentiation that also entailed a removal of literature from the law. From these literary narratives the way leads back into chanceries in which jurists and poets once formed a productive unit.

The grand genealogical fiction that structures the development of Western law is called *Rome*. The reference to Rome models Western law as well as its historical representation. The Roman Empire, expanding alongside the circulation of its files and immortalizing itself by archiving them, prescribes the way in which Western law files turn from visible signs of power to their banishment in obscure offices. Initially poised to perform the medial reign of the law, files are increasingly put to the service of the law. This shift from central support to marginalization is repeated around 1200 AD. Initially the policies of the Staufer emperor Frederick II employ files as a medium to create presence, to blend and impress, but already in the chanceries of Emperor Maximilian I files are relegated to the administrative underbelly of the law and its representation. From there they proceed to trellised, inaccessible chanceries. They relieve the law from the quotidian, troublesome, and occasionally violent business of executing particular laws. What transcends the files from now on is the radiance of abstract law. At this stage of differentiation, files themselves become an object of legal regulation. They do not only administer, they are themselves administered, for example by a filing plan, the panacea of so many twentieth-century administrative reforms. As societies grow aware of the secret power of files, the latter become objects of federal legislation that governs the access to records. As the federal laws on the protection of data privacy indicate, files become the object of regulations designed to protect the self-determining and self-processing subject.

Files can also be distinguished along the lines of how they act on specific legal regulations and institutions. The two basic forms in which files act are *transmission* and *storage*. In between there is room for several other actions, scriptural operations and record manipulations. One of the actions is to delete concepts, that is, the far-reaching act of canceling that confers authority to files (chapters 1 and 2) and introduces the question of truth. Similarly, that specific recording technique known as *protocol* aims at authenticating files. The goal of combating forgeries—the very concept of which arose as a counterconcept to truth—introduces a set of formalizations (chapter 2, sections 1 and 2). And finally the two principal acts performed by files generate their own institutions by turning the chancery into a transmission device and the archive into a storage system. Once the archives grow out of bounds and more files are hoarded than circulate, files no longer control themselves. This requires an action in the realm of the real that is not restricted to the level of the signifier: the ordered segregation and destruction of files (chapter 5).

These acts—transmitting, storing, canceling, manipulating, and destroying—write the history of the law. They find a weak echo in the federal law for data projection, where they reoccur as *transfer, storage, cancellation, modification,* and *deletion.* The echo is weak because these activities now refer to the handling of *data*, the informational substrate of files. By virtue of this shift to the data dispositive, files are removed from the order of the visible. Their materiality is no longer of any concern, which is why data-protection laws can safely ignore all physical acts. The final chapter will reflect on this trend toward dematerialization. The appearance of files as stylized pictograms or icons on computer screens indicates the end of the epoch of files. When, in the very moment of their disappearance from the realm of the physically real, files once more appear in all their physical presence, when they unexpectedly emerge from the hiding places and archives in which they were locked up for decades and even centuries, then we are able to see how important they were for the institutions of the West.

This book is written for those who work with files, who know of their power and of the life they take on in agencies and archives. It is also written for those who no longer handle physical files, who may have forgotten all about files but who nonetheless use programs that derive from the technologies of file processing. Friedrich Kittler's media theory was instrumental for the media-archaeological understanding of the impact of those files that only appear in digital format. Another crucial contribution was the file-related work of Bernhard Siegert and Wolfgang Ernst on the *postal system* and the *archive*.[4] From the start Marie Theres Fögen offered important advice; she also brought about the contact with the most important creditor and referee of this project, Michael Stolleis, without whom it would never have matured into a doctoral thesis. Dieter Simon ensured that despite its content, the work did not remain unfinished. The writing was done during my time as an assistant to Anselm Haverkamp; I received a lot of input from the graduate colloquium on "Representation—Rhetoric—Knowledge" at the Europa University in Frankfurt/Oder. Residing in the other Frankfurt, Günter Frankenberg, my second supervisor, supported my work, as did Klaus Günther and Peter Goodrich. Peter Berz was the most consistent and original critic. To all I am very grateful.

FILES

§ 1 Law's Writing Lessons

A Short Grammatology of Files

Faced with Babylonian stacks of files, the question arises whether there can ever be a legal culture devoid of files. How are we to conceive of a state *off the record*? How is the law to function without record-keeping devices? Questions such as these have prompted an area of research that inquires into the origin of law and writing. It posits an initial "oral legal culture" that does not resort to legal texts but instead retrieves oral traditions from collective memory. Based on this hypothesis, researchers attempt to date the historic switch from oral to written law.

In chapter 28 of his autobiographical work *Tristes Tropiques*, the French ethnologist Claude Lévi-Strauss tells a different story of the encounter between writing and the law. He narrates an "incident" that took place during a small journey through the Brazilian jungle that he undertook with the Nambikwara tribe. The goal was a distant plateau where the Nambikwara were to meet up with other groups to whom they were related by kinship or marriage. Lévi-Strauss was planning to use the gathering to count the population. His account does not, as Jacques Derrida would have it, read like a "parable"[1] about the origin of writing, but rather like an experiment designed to show the emergence of writing from administration.

> It is unnecessary to point out that the Nambikwara have no written language. . . . Nevertheless, as I had done among the Caduveo, I handed out sheets of paper and pencils. At first they did nothing with them, then one day I saw that they were all busy drawing wavy, horizontal lines. I wondered what

they were trying to do, then it was suddenly borne upon me that they were writing or, to be more accurate, were trying to use their pencils in the same way as I did mine, which was the only way they could conceive of. . . . The majority did this and no more, but the chief had further ambitions. No doubt he was the only one who had grasped the purpose of writing. So he asked me for a writing-pad, and when we both had one, and were working together, if I asked for information on a given point, he did not supply it verbally but drew wavy lines on his paper and presented them to me, as if I could read his reply. He was half taken in by his own make-believe; each time he completed a line, he examined it anxiously as if expecting the meaning to leap from the page, and the same look of disappointment came over his face. But he never admitted this, and there was a tacit understanding between us to the effect that his unintelligible scribbling had a meaning which I pretended to decipher; his verbal commentary followed almost at once, relieving me of the need to ask for explanations.[2]

Lévi-Strauss's so-called writing lesson re-enacts in the shape of a comedy the European drama of writing. Following Rousseau's script, this drama begins with the fictitious equality of all. And for Lévi-Strauss all are indeed equal: equally illiterate, that is, in an innocent state of pure orality. This state is jeopardized once the members of the tribe are equipped with the white man's weapons, pencil and paper. Despite equal initial conditions, matters soon start to change: the drama of suppression by the power of writing takes its course. According to Lévi-Strauss, the majority soon lose interest in the writing utensils, with one exception. He writes because he is the chief; and he is the chief because he writes. His position of power is linked to writing—more precisely, to the act of writing. The latter is the crucial ingredient of his empowerment through writing, not the decipherability of his signs, since he draws nothing but wavy lines. Lévi-Strauss comments that the chief was probably the only one to have grasped the function of writing, which resides in the power of staging.

   "If I asked for information on a given point, he did not supply it verbally but drew wavy lines on his paper and presented them to me"—this is how the ethnologist introduces the writing scene. By executing the sequence *ask-draw-present-supply*, individual acts add up to a completed transaction. Translated into the discourse of civic law, *order-produce-offer-transfer* are the constituent elements of a contract. Their object is the physical act of handing something over. It is a *datum* in the word's most literal sense, hence Jacques Lacan's commentary on Lévi-Strauss that "the ritual gifts are already symbols in the sense that 'symbol' points toward a contract."[3] In other words, in contractually defined relationships, information and goods are treated alike. From the point of view of the transfer they are equivalent. The more the gaze of the ethnologist is focused on the factuality of the transaction, that is, on the act of handing over, the less it understands, or wants to understand. Instead it counts, that is to say: it formalizes.

Derrida's commentary on Lévi-Strauss's "Writing Lesson" in *Grammatology* also sidelines questions of understanding. He considers the writing of the Nambikwara to be made up of signs, *gramme*, without any fixed meaning. From a grammatological point of view, meaning arises in this small ethnological scene from the playfully honest agreement between the ethnologist and his informant that the communicated signs constitute information. These signs, however, are not fixed in writing but produced in a subsequent act; they are signifiers without a signified. Non-ethnologists tend to forget this tacit agreement; instead they reiterate the legend of a phonetic writing system that communicates the meaning of spoken words. As a result, wavy lines that do not correspond to meaning or speech do not fulfill the criteria of writing. A phonologically oriented approach to writing cannot but dismiss them as wavy signs, childish and meaningless.

The phonetic concept of writing is based on its opposition to spoken language, and it is this contrast between orality and literacy that usually shapes our research into the law. The alleged advantages of writing are emphasized to explain the transition from an oral to a written culture of law. "Preservation and duration," as well as improved control functions, are said to have prompted the passage of law into writing.[4] By contrast, an increased tendency toward establishing a framework of legality is said to have been fueled by a "more intensive and conscious stage of literacy."[5] The literal /oral binary entails a permanent comparison between media that eventually gives rise to the specific qualities of each form of transmission. According to this binary, the validity and security of the law belong to writing, whereas lack of duration, individual case law, and greater proximity to specific events are associated with orality. The evolution of the law finds its place in between the two, presenting itself as a history of progressive rationalization and intensified literacy.

But once law and literacy are so closely intertwined, researchers lose sight of those forms of writing that belong to the law, although they are geared neither toward preservation nor toward validity or security. Recognizing this gap, new approaches to writing have begun to examine precisely those texts that do not stress law, permanence, and authority. Niklas Luhmann distinguishes between sacral and pragmatic forms of writing to illuminate a legal culture that did not recognize written records "as a condition for legal validity";[6] in much the same way, this new approach has, under the heading of "pragmatic literacy," introduced a wealth of primarily administrative textual material that hitherto had been ignored by legal historians. But while this new approach is instrumental for our investigation, it is at least in one respect still tied to the old ideas concerning the evolution of literacy: it too is looking for factors that motivated a switch to literal transcription. Though it no longer centers on the advantageous durability of writing, but instead draws attention to specific goals by arguing, for instance, that the will to plan ahead and secure the future promoted a more intensive usage of writing, such explanations remain indebted to the notion of a pristine oral culture that chose, for rationally plausible reasons, to adopt writing. Guided by these assumptions, researchers discover hybrid formations within the dichotomy of orality and literacy, such as the quasi-oral usage of writing. The pragmatic conceptualization of writing, however, remains subject to cultural imprints that have characterized *writing* since Rousseau associated it with *voice*. What remains unknown is the rhetorical deployment of the voice in legal acts, as well as the internal logic of signs and their movements in administrative procedures.

In turn, Lévi-Strauss, who from an ethnologist's more distant vantage point tackled the issue of the coupling of orality and literacy, and Derrida, who added a historical perspective, have laid the foundation for a grammatological approach to files. It is concerned not with the reasons that may have persuaded other legal cultures to adopt written records, but with how these administrative forms of writing *function* precisely insofar as they are not subject to the logic of speech. A different history of the law emerges, one whose point of origin is not an oral culture. Rather, it has as its point of departure administrative records. The inquiry into the origin of the law leads not to a state of pure orality or to forms of writing that are more closely linked to an orally performed legal culture, but to administrative record keeping. Before such administrative texts turn into files, they are to be found in smaller, nonsyntactic units. To understand these basic forms, we must once again turn to the Nambikwara writing lesson. It is not about empowerment through an act of writing or the concurrence of meaning, speech, and writing, nor is it about what language philosophy calls a performative act. It is about *administration.* That is why Derrida furnishes no specific commentary. He views it simply as a continuation—this time in a social context—of the first writing lesson that centers on the power of writing. But it is necessary to observe the scene more closely to grasp the divide between authority and administration that sheds light on the processing of signs and thus on the early shapes of files. Lévi-Strauss continues his account:

> As soon as he had got the company together, he took from a basket a piece of paper covered with wavy lines and made a show of reading it, pretending to hesitate as he checked on it the list of objects I was to give in exchange for the presents offered to me: so-and-so was to have a chopper in exchange for a bow and arrows, someone else beads in exchange for his necklace. . . . This farce went on for two hours. Was he perhaps hoping to delude himself? More probably he wanted to astonish his companions, to convince them that he was acting as an intermediary agent for the exchange of the goods, that he was in alliance with the white man and shared his secrets. We were eager to be off, since the most dangerous point would obviously be reached when all the marvels I had brought had been transferred to native hands. So I did not try to explore the matter further, and we began the return journey with the Indians still acting as our guides.[7]

The chief does what from a genealogical point of view is an early form of writing and a basic administrative procedure: he compiles lists. Lists conform neither to orality nor to literacy. They represent nonphonetic writing; they are a nonsyntactic formation of items. Repeating or enumerating items is said to have produced the alphabet, that is, the alphanumerical writing system in which letters function as numerals. It is maybe no coincidence that Lévi-Strauss encountered such lists just when he was planning to conduct a census. The latter, after all, produced one of the oldest types of lists, the register of inhabitants, which is invoked every Christmas by ritual readings of Luke 2:1: "And it came to pass in those days, that there went out a decree from Caesar Augustus, that all the world should be taxed."

While the first transfer of written signs between the chief and the ethnologist took place as a dialogue, that is, within the classic framework of communication, the second scene revealed that the exchange was exclusively regulated by lists. Lists do not communicate, they control transfer operations. The ritualized features of the second writing scene highlight its function. The individual items are not put down in writing for the sake of memorizing spoken words, but in order to regulate goods, things, or people. Lists sort and engender circulation. Specifically, the chief's list governs the transfer of objects. The storage capacity of writing is hardly of any concern. The chief does not hold on to his list of gifts, it is only of use during the actual exchange. Items that would be completely uncoordinated without such a list are momentarily called to order; for a brief moment the act of exchanging and that of writing are fused, and things are translated into signs, *gramme*. The latter mark the passage that objects have to traverse before arriving as gifts. The list, then, becomes the medium of transfer; the gifts turn into transferable items. They become a symbol in Lacan's sense.

Once the wondrous items and the power that comes with their possession have been exchanged, the chief's list has served its purpose. Its function is restricted to the written ritual of transaction, after which the balance between the contractual partners and the equal distribution of goods and gifts is in danger of collapsing. The possibility of conflict between the two tribes that had been lurking in the background since the beginning of the first writing lesson now becomes imminent. The ethnologist responds to this danger with a hasty retreat, which, once again, may cause things to circulate. His writing lesson, according to which lists are an administrative form of literacy that stands in no relationship to speech, hints at the origins of the complicity of writing and the law. Archaeological evidence suggests that this complicity can be found in lists, especially in those featuring nonsyntactical sign systems.

The Babylonian Empire in the third millennium BC was suffused with lists: lists on the per-capita consumption of female workers, lists containing inventories of wheat and beer, lists with names of trees, shrubs, and administrative offices, lists for those training to become compilers of lists. For a long time they remained unread. Their deciphering was hampered by a phonological concept of writing that took the signs on shards to be narrative texts. Referring to Egyptian writing, Oswald Spengler rejected this hypothesis in 1935 by alluding to a nonsyntactic formation of signs: "The hope of deducing a language from such pictorial signs," he wrote, "is based . . . on the ignorance of the fact that they are not composed of sentences."[8] It was only after dropping the assumption that the strange signs conform to the logic of grammar, sentence, and line that they were revealed to be accounting lists based on a nonsyntactic order. In 1959 the philologist Leo Oppenheim was able to start deciphering Babylonian tablets by reading them as administrative notes rather than epical texts.

As already indicated by the list of the Nambikwara chief, lists have the sole task of controlling transactions. In other words, they facilitate the administration of supply inventories by means of written signs. Once the supplies have been used up or the gifts have been distributed, the list has performed its task as a temporary storage device. Its function consists solely in "delayed transfer."[9] Beyond their administrative usage, there is no need to preserve them for the future. Subsequently, the particulars inscribed on clay tablets are very concise; they are an abbreviated list of items devoid of syntax or explanatory comments, and hence of little use in any extra-administrative context. Hence we may formulate the rule: the more comprehensive the record, the more suited it is for long-term storage. Detailed narratives do not depend on the tacit knowledge of quotidian practice; they decouple information from the immediate usage of that information. The scarcity of signs in nonsyntactical lists, however, is indebted to the spatial logic of *place value systems*. With items that can be referred to each other, a topological economy of signs begins. Hence the in*forma*tion to be found on Mesopotamian lists is already contained in their "format." A virtual scheme determines where a sign will be impressed on wet clay. The left column, for instance, is for incoming items while the right is reserved for outgoing items. An item is determined by its placement on the list rather than by any outside reference. The position alone encodes the values of an entry.

What can be said about lists also applies to files, for lists are a "core set of files."[10] At their core, files are governed by lists; lists program the emergence of files, hence they predetermine the sequence of steps that make up a list. Lists with tasks to be performed govern the inside of the file world, from their initial compilation to their final storage. As algorithmic entities, files are after all not indebted to any author for their existence. Unlike books and other written documents, files are, in the terminology of archival sciences, "process-generated." The process generators are list-shaped control signs. Usually they are written in abbreviated form. As operative signs, they steer the progress of a file from inception to dismissal. Without *acc, exp, edivi,* or *f* that report on the various stages of the procedure, no draft can be passed on; without the annotation *cor,* which resembles a wavy line, no clear copy may be prepared; without a note of dispatch, no copy be so filed, and so on. Every file note indirectly contains a command. Reporting the execution of an order triggers the next one. In the secret language of administrations, *M, coll,* and *repr* are imperatives that set off chain reactions. They are the nonsyntactical signs or operators that send records into administrative orbit, always accompanied by *scratch file,* the bureaucratic formula for salvation. So when, against all intentions, records multiply and chart their own course through official corridors, when they start taking on a life of their own in filing rooms, this is an indication that lists or programs are at work.

Lists not only program the progress of files, they also document it *uno actu* by noting the procedure and execution of official acts. "After having fulfilled their control function, notes and underwritings become . . . an automatically generated protocol."[11] An executed command, then, has a double orientation: it generates the next command and notes its own execution. It is both imperative and information. In other words: the file contains its own progression. This remarkable effect—that control signs function as a self-protocol—explains a widely held misunderstanding that turns files into epistemic objects. Within the written-oral paradigm, it endows files with a presentist trait, as if records, unlike other forms of writing, were able to turn communicative acts into writing without loss, thus guaranteeing the live transfer of an event. Consistent with a phonological concept of writing, files are located on the meridian between spoken and written language. They are discovered and praised for operating in quasi-oral fashion, for writing up while writing *along.* They not only fix a result but also shed light on their own development, on that which precedes grand acts of writing such as the clean copy or the legal institutes and institutions. That is, they allow access to that which came before the law, the legally binding verdict, the issued deed. Within the imagined chain of replacements for the spoken language, *supplements,*[12] files are closest to the presence of speech. Hence they attract all researchers who are interested in origins and who leaf through written documents in search of the words that once were spoken.

The historian Leopold von Ranke was full of praise for this close proximity of files to events. Archived records revealed to him the totality of a present past, and with it the possibility of venturing behind state history to retrieve the life that had been deposited in files. According to this idea, files store an unadjusted history of becoming. Their comments, annotations, and marginal notes contain the traces of past struggles over political decisions and other such matters. Ever since Ranke, this diplomatic rough state has been the focus of historiographic attention: "Just consider for a moment how little we would know, say, of nineteenth-century political history, if we were only in possession of the 'public records' rather than the giant mass of files. If we only knew of the officially published 'Ems Dispatch' but not of the telegram sent by Abeken that Bismarck edited; if we were only familiar with the finalized Reich Constitution of 1871 and not with the drafts and outlines dating back to June 1866; if we were only in possession of the wording of the final declaration of the Congress of Vienna but not of the files stored in archives and state chancelleries."[13] Historians suspect that files contain the entire drama of political action condensed into writing, so they search for the struggles that preceded decisions and succeeded the processes of decision making.

An official file note is an instruction for historians to call up the state from its archived material. If "files . . . are the deposit of all its actions in given matter,"[14] they contain the possibility of reviving the actions on record. But the "aggregated information contained in a written file note"[15] is not only a challenge for historians to translate it into a temporal sequence, but it also stimulates the research of twentieth-century sociologists. The "processual analysis" of organization theory, likewise, is concerned with the reconstruction of official decision-making processes from files.[16] Likewise, linguists have surmised that files record not results but processes, hence the object of research is located exactly on the line running from literacy to orality, or in more legal terms, from law to execution. By virtue of their intermediary position, "files are mediators between the laws and specific oral utterances (in court, in offices etc.)."[17] They compensate for the transitoriness of speech but without abandoning presence. Files preserve something of the conditions under which things came about—conditions that inevitably are thrust aside by result-oriented forms of writing. Thus files offer material for an analysis of speech acts as they appear in the aggregate state of files. "The analysis of files . . . is not primarily focused on the results of institutional acts but on the process of institutionalization and on the part played by the pragmatics of speech in the bringing about these results."[18]

The belief that files are capable of capturing the immediacy of speech acts and other acts is not only due to the self-protocol performed by con-

trol signs, it is also an effect of specific technologies of presence and simultaneity. The very term *Akten* emphasizes the quality of action (*Han-
dlung*). *Akten* derives from Latin *agere*, to act. The Old and Middle High
German *händel* or *hendel* for *Akten* also contains *handeln* (to act). The
term suggests that files should be examined for preconstitutional, procedural, or action-based forms of recording. For instance, if documents
pertaining to a *procedure* are collected as a file, and if this loose collection
of papers remains open for *updating*, then we are dealing with a protocol
operation to which we can attribute the qualities of spoken language. The
unlimited capacity for addition and circulation turns files into a medium
of presence. It endows them with the same characteristics as speech, with
the result that they appear to be up-to-date, live, ever-changing, acting,
and inexhaustible. Files take on ontological qualities.

From this phonocentric perspective, files capture everything that other
forms of writing no longer contain—all the life, the struggles and speeches
that surround decisions. "It's all in the files themselves."[19] Bruno Latour's
admiration for the thoroughness of Prussian files is right on target. Files
are comprehensive recording devices that register everything in the medium of writing, even that which is not writing. They register events,
voices, gestures, and appearances. It is not until the twentieth century,
when competition arises in the shape of the analog recording of events by
technological media, that the inaccuracy of written files becomes apparent. From then on, these new technologies set the standard for recording
accuracy and promote the linguistic analysis of the loss that accompanies
the conversion of speech into files. "It is not until linguistic pragmatics provides the appropriate framework that the replacement of speech
by writing . . . is understood and problematized as a replacement."[20] In
much the same way, sociological "records analysis" doubts the high fidel-
ity of files when it comes to recording social reality, as soon as technological recordings are available instead of manual records. No longer do files
contain "everything"; they merely report on "sectors of reality and determine possible processing steps."[21] Compared to the standard of analog
recording technologies, files occupy a subordinate position in the universe
of storage media. The selective written deposit of communicative acts sets
the boundaries, so to speak, of "its own reality."[22]

Of course, historians such as Ranke had praised the fullness of presence
in records rather than warned of their lack of recording accuracy. But
there is no difference between enthusiastic nineteenth-century historians

and skeptical twentieth-century scholars insofar as they all treat files as replacements for communicative acts, as a special supplement that despite all differences is still very close to speech. According to this point of view, files are presentist without the fleetingness of spoken words, and eternal without the selectivity of written records. Linguists, sociologists, and historians appreciate files for their self-documenting qualities, that is, for the fact that they contain their own origin and record the genesis of political and legal results that, if communicated in purely oral fashion, would have been irretrievably lost.

These disciplines, then, exhibit a reflection on files. Only the law, which provides the bulk of the material for this study, has nothing similar to say about files. Legal studies lack any reflection on their tools. Of course, lawyers consult files to recapitulate past events. But they are of no interest in themselves, and they certainly do not turn into objects of scientific investigation. Files are the basis for legal work. Their validity resides in their truth value and their everyday operations. "Administration uses its files [*Akten*] as deposited acts [*Akte*]."[23] It is only when records are removed from the self-referential, administrative context—for instance, when they are introduced as evidence before courts or parliamentary inquiries—that their own status becomes an object of scrutiny. How a file came about determines the degree to which it can be used as evidence. Beyond the immediate context for which they were compiled, the question arises whether their truth claim is justified, whether and in what way they are capable of reliably reproducing past events. While historiography develops auxiliary disciplines that specialize in the critical assessment of sources, the law evolves procedural means for determining their probative force. In criminal proceedings, past events recorded in writing will become part of a *hearing* once they are translated back into an oral format. But beyond these legal procedures, there is no reason for the law to analyze and evaluate the files it produces on a daily basis.

Files remain below the perception threshold of the law. Writing from a historical distance, a legal historian has attempted to explain this blind spot of jurisprudence: "To the modern jurist the commerce with files is so natural that he will hardly consider what it means that modern administration and jurisdiction apparatus produces these bundles of papers."[24] From the perspective of the law, files are annoying instruments, incessantly breeding beasts that must be caged and tamed. They are therefore hardly suited to becoming an object of reflection. When subjected to legal criteria, files are nothing. They are a noninstitution, a nondocument, nonlaw, nonproperty, legally nonbinding; they have neither author nor originator and count as "writs without addressee"[25] without any claim to validity, and they are of no duration. These nonqualities become the focus of other disciplines adjacent to the law, such as history or sociology.

The rule that files only become an object of discourse when they encounter their opposite is confirmed whenever files are scrutinized by other disciplines. Thus the appearance of imperial constitutions in Roman law encouraged medieval historians to ponder records and to attempt to explain what had taken the place of these imperial constitutions prior to their introduction (see chapter 2). Accordingly, the emergence of charters in the early Middle Ages prompted researchers of documents to pay more attention to files. Diplomatics assigned to files the status of a noncharter and, proceeding from that distinction, started to analyze them (chapter 3). Finally, the nineteenth century's abstract constitutional setting of the law fueled scholarly interest in the phase that preceded the law. Historians discovered archived records as the other side of the law, as that which stores the concrete aspects of life that are expunged from abstractions of the law (chaper 4). In the twentieth century, the guiding difference between public and secret incites an interest in files. Secret files were and are perceived to be the opposite of democracy. The political demands for access to records turned them into objects of political, legal, and sociological discourse and into an indicator for the transparency of politics and administration (chapter 5). And finally, when the possibilities of electronic data processing evoke the ubiquitous promise of the paperless office, files encounter their opposite in the shape of computer hard- and software. This is a wake-up call for artists, among others, to take possession of this somewhat anachronistic object called the file in order to estheticize it (chapter 6); and it also evokes in a more general sense an investigation of the law as an epoch of files.

Any inquiry into files and filing techniques depends on how the topic has been broached by other disciplines. For what could be said about the filing systems of antiquity without the research undertaken by positivist historiography around 1900? What would we know about the chanceries of the Middle Ages without the contributions of diplomatics? What would be the value of a description of Prussian archives if it were not linked to the governmental discourse on these archives? And finally, what could we reveal about the power of the twentieth century's secret files without their critique, that is, without any reference to the concerns that fuel demands for an opening of the archives? Even if records *exist*, even if they are always already existent and filed someplace, it is only by virtue of these debates that they turn into an object of investigation. This indebtedness also applies to an inquiry that aims to penetrate the discussion of files to reach the topic itself and make concrete statements about the filing and registries of centuries long past. It has to respect the conditions that make these statements possible, yet at the same time it has to filter out the hopes and fears, the phantasms that have been invested in the discourse of files. It therefore does not directly draw from the archive, it has no pure source; rather it will move in roundabout ways, much like its object of investigation. That is to say, it aims to translate files as they appear over time into a genealogy of the law.

This genealogy is not written by the law itself, for the law remains silent about its records. It works with them and creates itself from them. In other words, it operates in a mode of difference that separates it from the varying formats of files. Files are constitutive of the law precisely in terms of what they are not; this is how they found institutions like property and authorship. They lay the groundwork for the validity of the law, they work toward the law, they establish an order that they themselves do not keep. Files are, or more precisely, make what, historically speaking, stands *before the law*.

Kafka's Chanceries[26]

Before the Law stands a doorkeeper. To this doorkeeper there comes a man from the country who begs for admittance to the Law. But the doorkeeper says that he cannot admit the man at this moment. The man, on reflection, asks if he will be allowed, then, to enter later. "It is possible," answers the doorkeeper, "but not at this moment." Since the door leading in to the Law stands open as usual and the doorkeeper steps to one side, the man bends down to peer through the entrance. When the doorkeeper sees that, he laughs and says: "If you are so strongly tempted, try to get in without my permission. But note that I am powerful. And I am only the lowest doorkeeper. From hall to hall, keepers stand at every door, one more powerful than the other. And the sight of the third man is already more than even I can stand." These are difficulties which the man from the country has not expected to meet; the Law, he thinks, should be accessible to every man and at all times, but when he looks more closely at the doorkeeper in his furred robe, with his huge pointed nose and long thin Tartar beard, he decides that he had better wait until he gets permission to enter. The doorkeeper gives him a stool and lets him sit down at the side of the door. There he sits waiting for days and years. He makes many attempts to be allowed in and wearies the doorkeeper with his importunity. The doorkeeper often engages him in brief conversation, asking him about his home and about other matters, but the questions are put quite impersonally, as great men put questions, and always conclude with the statement that the man cannot be allowed to enter yet. The man, who has equipped himself with many things for his journey, parts with all he has, however valuable, in the hope of bribing the doorkeeper. The doorkeeper accepts it all, saying, however, as he takes each gift: "I take this only to keep you from feeling that you have left something undone." During all these long years the man watches the doorkeeper almost incessantly. He forgets about the other doorkeepers, and this one seems to him the only barrier between himself and the Law. In the first years he curses his evil fate aloud; later, as he grows old, he only mutters to himself. He grows childish, and since in his prolonged study of the doorkeeper he has learned to know even the fleas in his fur collar, he begs the very fleas to help him and to persuade the doorkeeper to change his mind. Finally his eyes grow dim and he does not know whether the world is really darkening around him or whether his eyes are deceiving him. But in the darkness he can now perceive a radiance that streams inextinguishably from the door of the Law. Now his life is drawing to a close. Before he dies, all that he has experienced during the whole time of his sojourn condenses in his mind into one question, which he has never yet put to the doorkeeper. He beckons the doorkeeper, since he can no longer raise his stiffening body. The doorkeeper has to bend far down to hear him, for the difference in size between them has increased very much to the man's disadvantage. "What do you want to know now?" asks the doorkeeper, "you are insatiable." "Everyone strives to attain the Law," answers the man, "how does it come about, then, that in all these years no one has come seeking admittance but me?" The doorkeeper perceives that the man is nearing his end and his hearing is failing, so he bellows in his ear: "No one but you could gain admittance through this door, since the door was intended for you. I am now going to shut it."[27]

BARRIERS

Lured by a law that is unreadable, delayed by a judgment that fails to appear—that is how the entry to the law appears. A gate, in front of it a gatekeeper, and a man from the country who desires admission to the law but is detained by the gatekeeper—those are the coordinates of Franz

Kafka's story "Before the Law." The story about the futile request to gain access to the law and the story's inaccessibility determine each other. By nesting form and content, the story shuts itself off from all attempts at interpretation and advances its own truth: the truth of how the law becomes an instance of truth. The story is about this instantiation; it offers an access to the world of files, to the world before institutionalizations, to the world before the law.

The first point of access to the history of the law before the passing of laws is the story's *gate*. In Roman antiquity a plough was dragged around the yet-to-be-built city to mark the spot where the gate was to be. The portal, whose name derives from the movement of the drawn plough (*portare*), paves the way into the future city. It opens up the space behind and frames the unbounded fields. The gate creates the *ager Romanus*, the urban area of Rome. With the city the law comes into being. City and law are coextensive. Derrida bluntly speaks of the "city's law."[28] It discloses itself by gate and door. But what exactly is disclosed? "A door, my God, opens onto fields [*sur les champs*]."[29] Jacques Lacan, the classically versed psychoanalyst, impatiently alludes to the connection between plough, gate, and open field, briskly adding: "In its nature, the door belongs to the symbolic order, and it opens up either on to the real, or the imaginary, we don't know quite which, but it is either one or the other."[30] In Kafka's story, the gate allows the man from the country to see just enough to trigger the question of what lies beyond. But it not only stimulates the man's curiosity as to what is beyond the opening, it also binds him with its secret, which consists solely in the framed opening with its constricted expanse. The gate constitutes the whole difference between a simple emptiness and a binding secret.

The story makes clear that the door is always open. According to Derrida, it "lets the inside (*das Innere*) come into view—not the law itself, perhaps, but interior spaces that appear empty."[31] Empty spaces, *les champs*, loom behind the door. The framing of the door turns the manifest emptiness into a secret, something that remains inaccessible. Since the gate limits access to the city and thus to the law, questions of law are reduced to questions of access. In a fragment by Kafka entitled "The Problem of Our Laws," "our laws" are nothing but the secret of a "small group of nobles."[32] This brings to mind the patrician families of Rome, whose power indeed rested on arcane politics of exclusion. Consuls, augurs, or pontifices, all political offices were reserved for the nobility alone. Kafka has one of the excluded speculate: "We are convinced that these ancient laws are scrupulously administered; nevertheless it is an extremely painful thing to be ruled by laws that one does not know." *Tradition* alone, that is, the fact that they have been handed down over centuries, provides some reassurance. "Of course, there is wisdom in that—who doubts the wisdom of the ancient laws?—but also hardship for us; probably that is unavoidable. The very existence of these laws, however, is at most a matter of presumption. There is a tradition that they exist and that they are a mystery confided to the nobility, but it is not and cannot be more than a mere tradition sanctioned by the age, for the essence of a secret code is that it should remain a mystery . . . —everything becomes uncertain, and our work seems only an intellectual game, for perhaps these laws that we are trying to unravel do not exist at all."[33] Though there is no certainty regarding the existence of the laws, there certainly is a will. That is why the mechanisms of doors and legislations, of secrecy and validity remain in power no matter how doubtful the existence of the laws may be.

Gilles Deleuze and Félix Guattari highlight the empty ground of authority: *"Where one believed there was the law, there is in fact desire and desire alone."*[34] It is the desire to enter, the phantasm that there is something behind the bounded entry, that creates the law. Thus the response to Lacan's question would be that the imaginary resides behind the door. In Lacan's trinitarian order, the gate itself belongs to the realm of the symbolic. In Kafka's story, the gate to the law refers to a law that resides behind it. Behind the first gate there is a further gate and then another one. Those who try to pass through the first gate to penetrate the second are guided on and on. The symbolic order is made up of gates that refer to gates. Ultimately, "we vaguely feel . . . a structure of referentiality."[35] The legal order consists of nothing other than this chain of references. It is "rien d'autre que l'état de la Référence, plus exactement du rapport à la Référence [nothing other than the state of Reference, more exactly the relationship to Reference]."[36] Pierre Legendre, the legal historian and psychoanalyst indebted to Lacan, emphasizes above all the juridical structure of referentiality and amasses all the formations of the law in *La Référence*. Kafka's "Before the Law" serves as one of his many examples that the law is arranged according to, and draws its authority from, an absolute reference devoid of any content.[37]

But doors and gates are not only parables of the referential structure of the law. Kafka's novel *The Trial*—which frames the story "Before the

Law"—teems with gates and doors that distinguish themselves not only by being inaccessible or because they lead us out into the imaginary. The whole architecture of entries and barriers testifies above all to the *technologies* of reference adopted by the law. Kafka's novel first alludes to this by way of a very specific sign that does not simply act as a decoy by falsely promising access, but that announces an ascent to the place where laws are actually made and applied. "Law Court Offices upstairs," is written on "a small card . . . in childish, unpracticed handwriting"[38] pinned next to a stairway. This note, however, will send Josef K. through virtually endless bureaucratic channels and enmesh him in a network of referrals that lead directly and literally to *chanceries*. From a synchronic point of view, the chancery is the place before the law. This is where laws are issued. But it is also before the law in a diachronic sense, for this is where the rule of law is processed. In the words of a historian: "The appearance of the word *cancellaria* indicated a very specific moment in the development of the most important Western states."[39] It is the "moment" in which power is exercised through laws—that is, the emergence of public law.

The novel's chancery corresponds to the story's gate of the law. Chanceries and gates are barriers: they create and limit an arcane space, they exclude and establish connections. In fact, chanceries derive etymologically and functionally from barriers. Their name stems from the so-called *cancelli*, the "latticed and hence transparent bars" of Roman antiquity.[40] Wherever they were installed, their function was to limit access and mark a space that could not be entered by everyone. The Romans used *cancelli* to refer to "a latticed door equipped with crossing bars that closed off the space of a political or official assemblage, especially that of a court of law."[41]

Barriers need to be operated. Just like gates, they require gatekeepers. Since the fourth century, the term *cancellari* refers to those who control public access:

> *Cancellarius* originally refers to a door steward. . . . The official title is derived from *cancelli*, that is, the latticed and hence transparent bars that closed off the space of the law court to the public. The C. was originally positioned at that door, where he had to grant access to those seeking an audience with the judge as well as receive writs and documents and pass them on to him; in short, he had to mediate between the judge and the outside world. To the task of presenting documents for signature was later added the authority to make them public. Initially, however, they were really nothing more than door stew-

ards; subsequently their rank—even of those who served the emperor—was
so low that it featured last in the *Notitia dignitatum* which listed all the imperial *Officia*. Nonetheless their power was considerable, given that against their
will, nobody could gain access to the higher officials. As a result petitioners
frequently had to pay considerable sums. And since the C. was the only subaltern who could freely be appointed by his superior, the position was normally
given to those who had gained their trust; as a consequence they were given
many duties that far exceeded the initially very limited scope of their office.
In due course these occasional extracurricular activities became a regular part
of their service, which increasingly broadened their competency. As a result
in the sixth century the C. was regarded as the most noble in the *Officium* to
whom all the others owed obedience. . . . The dignity of the C. increased with
his responsibilities. In the sixth century the C. of the prefects owned a senatorial rank and were regarded as *vir clarissimus*.[42]

Kafka's story reproduces this impressive rise from subaltern usher to highest official by reference to a hierarchy of doorkeepers. The very first already claims: "I am powerful. And I am only the lowest doorkeeper." His
words refer to a pyramid of gatekeepers whose apex is inconceivable. The
same seems to apply to the judiciary system of *The Trial*: "The ranks of officials in this judiciary system," it says, "mounted endlessly."[43] The novel's
many gatekeepers, the judges, high-ranking officials, lawyers, ushers, messengers, and young girls, add up to a whole system of bars and barriers, a
scaled order of thresholds, steps, and stations. What the story still alludes
to as a linear progression—"from hall to hall, keepers stand at every door,
one more powerful than the other"—the novel turns into a thoroughly
confusing administrative structure: "An organization which not only em-
ploys corrupt warders, oafish Inspectors, and Examining Magistrates of
whom the best that can be said is that they recognize their own limita-
tions, but also has at its disposal a judicial hierarchy of high, indeed of the
highest rank, with an indispensable retinue of servants, clerks, police, and
other assistants, perhaps even hangmen."[44]

The utterly confusing nature of this legal entourage has a certain logic
to it. There is no place from which the entire architecture of barriers can
be grasped, none that renders comprehensible the master plan that appears
to control everything. The *cancellari* are positioned at specific barriers and
may only deal with that particular part "which was prescribed for them by
the Law."[45] The individual segments are entangled into a complex system
of local, personal, and institutional barriers, a lattice of entries, corridors,

officials, messengers, and chains of command. "K. himself, or one of the women, or some other messenger must overrun the officials day after day and force them to sit down at their desks and study K.'s papers instead of gaping out into the lobby through the wooden rails."[46] These idle officials are quite literally chancery officials. Not only do they gaze through the very *cancelli* through which papers were handed into medieval chanceries, but they are themselves barriers or impediments the messengers have to "overrun."

Anybody working in a chancery is able to either refuse receipt, block the progress and thus terminate a procedure, or advance matters, that is, "grant access to those seeking an audience with the judge as well as receive writs and documents and pass them on to him; in short, to regulate the commerce with the outside world."[47] The gatekeepers can be "interrupters as well as messengers."[48] Blockage or handoff—with this binary option in place at every barrier—the system is neither continuously flowing nor at a complete standstill, with the result that "this great organization remained, so to speak, in a state of delicate balance."[49] The chancery resembles the intermittent motions of a machine. Deleuze and Guattari described Kafka's mega-machines in terms of segments and blocks. Setting them in motion, they freed his topographic indications from all spatial stasis. Thus Kafka's spaces arise from strings, series, concatenations. Their basic layout is a flowchart. Chanceries are, from this perspective, nothing but the spatialized mechanism of opening and closing gates—that is, the relays of the law.

The small lore of gates hidden in Kafka's novel allows us to write a history of the law centering on gates. More precisely, a history that has as its point of departure the ways in which gates facilitate or deny access, establish or interrupt contact, attract and exclude, mediate, regulate, allow entry, subdivide, transform, block, seduce, bar, ensure transfer, or the ways in which the gates themselves are overrun and torn down. Deconstruction, too, begins at the gates in order to arrive at the established laws and their rightful institutions: "This right imposes or supposes a bundle of barriers which have a history, a deconstructable history. . . . This deconstruction in progress concerns, as always, the institutions *declared* to be insurmountable, whether they involve family law or state law, the relations between the secret and the non-secret, or, and this is not the same thing, between the private and the public, whether they involve property or access rights, publication or reproduction rights, whether they involve classification and putting *into order*."[50] In all cases, barriers deny insight into the processes of institutionalization, though it is questionable whether the deconstruction of physical or textual barriers can lead to a "law in the making." To be sure, destroying barriers is insufficient; the act of destruction still obeys the logic of the barrier, which triggers a desire for the closed-off space. It only leads to the discovery that the reference is a structure, not a substance. Deconstructing barriers hardly results in a genealogy of the law, for it is a deconstructive impossibility to observe the erection of those barriers that enable the law in the first place. The latter remains the privilege of literature, more specifically, of Kafka's *Trial*.

The chapter "In the Cathedral," which contains the story "Before the Law," is about barriers that are being set up. Not coincidentally, the story is told in a cathedral, where the legal and sacred are not yet differentiated. Sacred and profane spaces within the cathedral, in turn, are separated by barriers. "The cancelli at Rome are equivalent . . . to the 'altar rails' that divide off the sanctuary."[51] The altar rails, also known as ambo, mark an elevated space for reading scripture that is only accessible by stairs. The place of the preacher, who also belongs to the species of mediators and gatekeepers, was initially "close to the cancels,"[52] until in the thirteenth century a further isolation of the altar gave rise to the *cancellus*, or pulpit. From then on, sermons were held from the pulpit, which—as long as the legal sphere exploited the mediatory powers of the sacred—also served for the public announcements of secular laws.

The story of the doorkeeper is proclaimed from the pulpit. The "vaulting of [its] stone canopy . . . began very low and curved forward and upward . . . in such a way that a medium-sized man could not stand upright beneath it."[53] The pulpit's oppressive proportions resemble those of the chanceries in the attic. The architectural similarities establish a connection between pulpit (*Kanzel*) and chancery (*Kanzlei*), which is enforced by the murky light and the many arches (reminiscent of a vault) that because of their gate-shaped form (*arcus*) may have provided the archive with its name. The vault above the pulpit cover has an acoustic function. Pronounced from the pulpit, Joseph K.'s name is "inescapable."[54]

According to ecclesiological concepts, the cleric calling out K.'s name is charged with administering a mystery; he is, in short, a minister. He is expected to mediate the word of God from the pulpit. But he "had not preached a sermon, he had only given K. some information."[55] Was it an official notice, such as those issued by governmental ministers? The

events in the cathedral—do they follow some unknown code of procedure, or is it a liturgy? The barriers are ambivalent. Here, they turn out
to be traps. A minor displacement, an imperceptible change, and "the
proceedings . . . merge into a verdict."[56] *Cancelli* dissimulate into *carcer.*
For K., the meaning of chancery as a "closed, caged space"[57] is literally
realized. The barriers where he hears his story will be his prison. He ends
behind bars, the "ideal place for writing."[58] The priest turns out to be a
prison chaplain.

The power of barriers resides in their ambivalence—an equivocation
of the law that Walter Benjamin criticized.[59] The law erects barriers to
create an area of execution that is barred from view. Based on secret laws,
Benjamin writes, "the prehistoric world exerts its rule all the more ruth-
lessly."[60] This prehistoric legal world operates in a twilight zone. Barriers
are porous as well as inaccessible; they emerge and disappear. They pro-
voke indictments without acts, offenses without intent, verdicts without
law. They enforce a permanent trial over one's own self.

PREAMBLES

The gates and barriers of *The Trial* create an ambivalent legal topography oscillating between chancery and incarceration, priests and prison
guards, doorkeepers and executioners. This ambivalence is mirrored by
the speech of the minister or judge-priest that begins with the words: "In
the writings which preface the Law. . . . "[61] In legal discourse, a law's pref-
atory writings are called preambles. These include prologue, prooimium,
praefatio. From a technical point of view, they are nothing but a textual
barrier. They are to the order of the text what a plough is to the future
city: they have an annunciatory function. Just as the barriers organize the
physical access to legal sites, preambles pave the hermeneutical access to
legal texts. They introduce a law and guide its application. They do not
possess any legal force because, just like courtroom ushers or prison chap-
lains, they belong to and mediate the law but they are themselves not the
law. Preambles intone the law that itself has no voice. Laws are founded
on the legal force of writing (*ratio scripta*), but they are made public by a
preface, spoken by the *persona ficta* of the legislator, and rhetorically composed as a prosopopoeia.

Preambles contain the concerns, the legislator's motives, and the historical context of a given law. They are supposed to narrate, and thus

remind us of, the conditions under which a law came about. Diocletian is said to have been the first Roman emperor to decorate his laws with extensive prologues; the preamble to his Edict on Prices in AD 301, which summarizes and reminds those concerned of the hardships that preceded the new piece of legislation, "appears as an attempt to convince the audience of the necessity, the efficiency, and the legitimacy of the law which followed."[62] Preambles confer upon the law a legitimizing legend. They tell a story that the law does not and cannot contain, because the notion of a generally valid law does not allow for stories: "To be invested with its categorical authority, the law must be without history, genesis, or any possible derivation."[63] The law therefore does away with persons and stories, it banishes all the diplomatic entanglements, political struggles, passions, and intentions to the introductory narratives. Effaced from the law, all these impure stories reappear in the preambles in stylized fashion: "INSTILLED WITH THE DESIRE . . . ; IN THE ENDEAVOR TO . . . ; IN VIEW OF . . . ; GUIDED BY. . . . " Treaty prefaces are replete with phrases like this, which tend to be written in block letters—a typographic differentiation designed to preclude any intermixing of history and law.

Eager to avoid any contamination with history, the law reduces the latter to a literally domesticated story that is assigned a place before the law. Derrida has described the preamble as the parasite of law: "Though the authority of the law seems to exclude all historicity and empirical narrativity, and this at the moment when its rationality seems alien to all fiction and imagination . . . , it still seems *a priori* to shelter these parasites."[64] Law and preamble are said to be subject to the law of hospitality, according to which the host depends on the guest. Stories are the a priori of formal law, which, without them, would remain inaccessible. In other words, narratives guide the process of understanding, applying, and interpreting laws, for that which cannot contain any stories has to be mediated by them. In technical terms, preambles occupy the domain of narration, the space of literature, which is why it makes sense to leave their composition to authors like Christa Wolf, who in 1990 wrote the preamble for the draft of a constitution of the "Round Table" involving civil rights groups and the tottering bureaucracy of the old East German regime.

The story "Before the Law" is a preamble. It was written by an author or, more precisely, a jurist, who spent the night composing a tale rather than a piece of official writing. The tale produces the paradox of a preamble without a law, which is especially evident in its publication as a

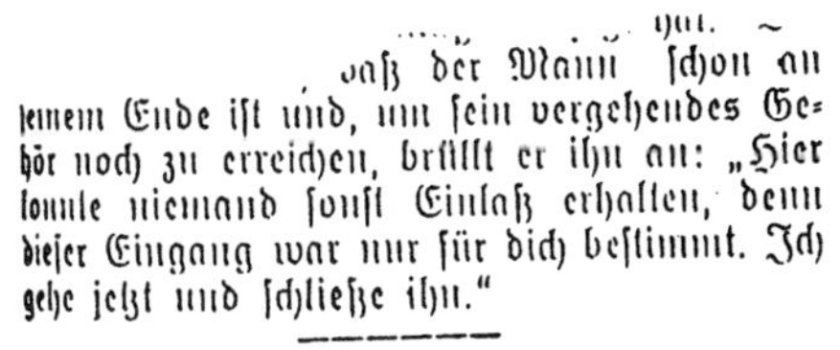

> ..... ˙ ˙ ˙ ˙ ˙ ᵌᵘᵗ. ~
> ˏ ᴡᴀᵬ ᵬᵉᵣ ᴹᴀᶰᶰ ˙ ᵬᶜᶰᵒᶰ ᴀᶰ
> ᶰᵉᶤᶰᵉᶰ ᵌᶰᵬᵉ ᶤᶴᵗ ᵘᶰᵬ, ᵘᵐ ᶴᵉᶤᶰ ᵛᵉᵣᵍᵉᶜᵉᶰᵬᵉᶴ ᵌᵉᵌ
> ᵬᵒᵣ ᶰᵒᶜᵈ ᶾᵘ ᵉᵣᵣᵉᶤᶜᵈᵉᶰ, ᵬᵣᵘᵘᵗ ᵉᵣ ᶤᵈᶰ ᴀᶰ: „ᵬᶤᵉᵣ
> ᶤᵒᵘᵘᵗᵉ ᶰᶤᵉᵐᵃᶰᵬ ᶴᵒᶰᶴᵗ ᵌᶤᶰᶰᵃᵬ ᵉᵣᵬᵃᵘᵉᶰ, ᵬᵉᶰᶰ
> ᵬᶤᵉᶴᵉᵣ ᵌᶤᶰᵍᵃᶰᵍ ᵗᵛᵃᵣ ᶰᵘᵣ ᶴᵘᵣ ᵬᶤᶜ ᵬᵉᶴᵗᶤᵐᵐᵗ. ᴵᶜᵈ
> ᵍᵉᵈᵉ ᶤᵉᵗᶾᵗ ᵘᶰᵬ ᶴᶜᵈᵘᶤᵉᶴᵉ ᶤᵈᶰ.“
> —————

FIGURE 1. Facsimile of the first print of "Before the Law" in *Selbstwehr* (September 7, 1915). Malcom Pasley (ed), Franz Kafka. Der Proceß, *Marbacher Magazin* 52 (1990), 32.

separate text entitled "Before the Law" that is not embedded in the novel's "Cathedral" chapter. It is well known that Kafka wanted the entire novel destroyed with the exception of this story. It was first published in 1915 in the Prague weekly *Selbstwehr* (Self-defense), where it was followed neither by a law (as one would except after a preamble) nor by the name of the author (as is customary for literary publications). It ends "without author or ending,"[65] with nothing but a dashed line.

In an essay on Kafka, Jean-François Lyotard writes of another dotted line —the lines drawn by the apparatus in Kafka's "In the Penal Colony": "In late Latin these lines are referred to as praescripta, predrawn lines, a bit like sketches: lines that determine the execution."[66] A dotted line turns the preceding text into a pre-script (*Vor-Schrift*). It sketches the law that is to follow. The law, in turn, is the execution of the order in the pre-script. Regardless of why the initial publication of "Before the Law" ended with a dashed line, it confirms the story's prescriptive status as well as its preambular content. The story is about a prescript (*Vorschrift*), though it remains an announcement—an announcement that announces another and yet another, and so on. The preamble-barrier before the law does not allow the story to get beyond itself; it keeps deferring the law it introduces. The announced law "is this deferral itself."[67] No law can follow a preamble published under the title "Before the Law" if it is indeed to remain true to that title. What the title announces is a story about the situation before the law, and this positioning of the story before the law, in the space of preambles, is what the story is about. The prescript prescribes that it is a prescript, which makes the story a law, metalaw, or parable of the law: the law of the prescript.

Read as a law, the story demands an interpretation—which is in part accomplished if it is read as a preamble. It contains the announcement that, as a law, the story is about the inaccessible world that came before the law. But if questions of access are spatialized questions of interpretation, the story contains its own inaccessibility. The attempt to interpret that which remains outside the interpretative prescript produces a hermeneutical paradox, or interpretations without end.

Josef K. promptly reacts to the interpretative imperative of the preamble-story. To his ears, the tale recounted in the cathedral sounds like a key to unlock the law that governs his trial. It could contain a guideline for interpreting his own strange story, which has summoned him before the law. The priest's tale promises insight into his own situation by announcing: "Your are deluding yourself about the Court. . . . In the writings which preface the Law that particular delusion is described thus: . . . "[68] Listening to these words, K. cannot but anticipate some insight into his own delusions, and to make certain that his delusions have been removed by the story, he questions the priest, who provides "instructions for reading legal preambles."[69] After all, as a mediator of the arcane, he is authorized to conduct such exegeses. His response to K. is an exemplary interpretation. As if quoting from legal commentaries, he provides official pronouncements and dissenting opinions, which in turn trigger new interpretations on the part of K. None, however, is able to enter the circular structure of the preambular story that only refers to itself. Its perfect recursivity defies all interpretations that would exceed the text of the preamble and hence would not be covered by its literality. Subsequently, the priest wards off K.'s interpretative attempts by referring to the "unalterable" status of the scriptures in the face of "various opinions."[70] Opinions can only deceive, even if they are not consciously deceptive. They cannot overcome the inalterability of scripture. There is no "message of salvation"[71] for K. His interpretations are put forward "with finality, but it was not his final judgment."[72]

Were it not for Joseph K.'s weariness of fathoming the intentions of the law, this chain of interpretation and rejection could go on forever. After the story "Before the Law," distorted by countless interpretations, has "lost its clear outline" because it is buried under so many analyses, simple exhaustion terminates the interpretative process. K. "was too tired to survey all the conclusions arising from the story."[73] Fatigue instead of decision, exhaustion instead of a final verdict. Within the story, solving the question of access is also a matter of time; it comes about because the doorkeeper, anticipating the imminent death of the man from the court, closes the door to the law.

CANCELS

The "unalterable" status of scripture invoked by the priest and other professional interpreters of the law contains the barriers' third dimension, which, following the spatial-institutional and the textual modus described above, may be termed the graphic or paleographic. As indicated by the handwritten notes in *The Trial*, its origin is the chancery. From a technical point of view, the writing that stands before the law is a draft or prescript. Chanceries are responsible for producing written exemplars, and here too *cancelli* are at work. It is they who change a draft (*scheda*) into a clear copy (*mundum*). By the mid-fifteenth century, ushers and messengers had turned into full-fledged scribes. Initially responsible for regulating the access to council meetings, they had also been assigned some paperwork on the side; and this marginal activity had now become their principal vocation. Their colleagues in Roman antiquity were known as *tabelliones* or *tabularii*, that is, "concessionary private scribes" who did not work in chanceries. "People sought out these literate, legally trained representatives of the public" in the proximity of the archives where they had their office.[74] In 1905, the Prague legal historian Ivo Pfaff, whose lectures Kafka attended around the turn of the last century, published one of the most extensive treatises in existence on the *tabelliones*. It starts with a reflection on the various interpretations of these legal intermediaries:

Various opinions have been put forward regarding the position held by the Roman *tabellio*. . . . Essentially there are two: The one is to view the *tabelliones* as private individuals engaged in composing documents and the like, the other is to regard them as notaries in the modern sense of the word, or at least as precursors of the modern notary. Among those who hold the former view, many characterize the *tabellio* as a "composer of legal texts," "author of certificates." . . . The other view, according to which the *tabellio* is a modern notary, or at least a precursor thereof, is held by Savigny, Heffter, Rein, Glück, Lauck, Bopp. . . . In reality, however, it was only in exceedingly rare cases that *tabelliones* were deemed to be very credible.[75]

The diction of the priest in *The Trial* seems to parody this passage. Without a doubt the figure of the *tabellio* molds the features of the doorkeeper in "Before the Law." As in the case of the latter, the reputation of the *tabellio* grows with the ranking of the barrier he operates; subsequently, his credibility suffers in the same way as that of the doorkeeper, of whom it is said in the story that he is corrupt—just like his historical role model, and just like all who guard a threshold.

But there is another, far more literal link between barriers and *tabelliones*. In the most literal way possible, the latter determine the letter of the law when they use lines and strokes to cross out a draft that has been copied. Because of the "latticed" appearance of the deletions, this act is referred to as "canceling." Derived from Latin *cancelli* grating or lattice, from which are also derived 'chancel' and 'chancellor'—the word means "to cross out, from crossed lattice lines drawn across a legal document, to annul it, hence destroy or delete it."[76] Annulling drafts is indispensable for the operation of a chancery. After they have been copied, drafts must be crossed out so that the clean copy can become the unmistakable original. The act of copying, then, is followed by the act of canceling. Latticed lines or bars exclude the draft from further copying. The lattice covering the writing literally bars textual production, it puts an end to the chancery's babble of voices arising from dictation and public reading, and releases the clean copy, the written law, into a "zone of silence."[77]

Just as consigning a manuscript to oblivion serves to validate the final version of a book, the law is authenticated by the latticed prescript. "La cancellation, autre usage du treillis et de la grille, est le pôle inverse et complémentaire de sa fonction de validation [Canceling, another use of lattice and bars, is the polar opposite and complement of its validation function]."[78] Canceling endows a writ with authority and force of law. The chancery, the site of this particular activity, derives its names from this act. Crossing out, it seems, is more elementary than the more productive act of writing down. Deleting rather than writing establishes the symbolic order of the law. The canceled signs are *signifiants barrés*. There can be no more literal proof of Lacan's claim that the entry into the domain of the symbolic starts with deleted letters behind bars. The chancery reveals the pragmatic aspect of this analytical principle. With the creation of the clean copy, the draft forfeits its prescriptive function, which is why it prescribes its own cancellation. It is "the obliteration that, paradoxi-

FIGURE 2.   "Scripsi" enlarged. Adriano Capelli, *Lexicon Abbreviaturarum: Dizionario di Abbreviature Latine et Italiane* (Milan, 1994), 411.

cally, constitutes the originary legibility of the very thing it erases."[79] The phantasm of the *ur*-writing, then, has its medial reality in the shape of canceled writing. In technical terms, the chancery temporalizes the *archi-écriture*'s metaleptic operation in two connected steps. The act of copying is followed by the act of canceling. The latter, in turn, establishes an unreadable *ur*-text.

In cultural memory, however, these technologies of effacement have themselves been effaced. The inaccessible law before the law, the unreadable writing before writing, turned into a metaphor once mid-thirteenth-century chanceries had condensed the performative act of cancellation into a sign. Replacing the crossed-out draft was a cancel ideogram that indicated the completion of the clean copy.

Here, however, another paradox awaits. Cancels, to employ the technical term, are a paradox insofar as they annul their own existence. To quote a printed study of cancels, it is "rash to describe as blank a leaf which one has never seen."[80] The author, Robert Chapman, distinguishes between *cancellandum* and *cancellatum*, that is, the text before and after its cancellation. The cancel in a printed text normally consists of a leaf that has been pasted over a faulty page. The new leaf may be printed or blank. Statements on *what* was canceled can only be made as long as the page has not been replaced: "If a 'canceled' leave survives, it survives because it escaped cancellation." Following an effective cancellation, every canceled leaf is inevitably an "imaginary sheet."[81]

The more thorough the cancellation, the less visible the traces left behind by the deletions. But sometimes "slips"—irregularities, displacements, mistakes—remain. Once the "agency of the letter in the uncon-

scious" (Lacan) leaves its traces on the margins, any typographic treatise
on *Cancels* inevitably becomes a psychoanalytic undertaking. Chapman
provides instructions for an analysis of the suppressed in the world of
letters: "Keep an eye on the inner margin as you turn the leaves, and a
'stub,' or a trace of pasting, will pretty easily be spotted." According to
the analysis in *Cancels*, it is not easy "to give any rational account of the
pleasure which the survival of blanks undoubtedly gives."[82] It is as if in
an unprotected moment the law had been caught red-handed, fabricating
its secret in the real. It is as if there were an access to the law that neither
reconstructs in the imaginary how the law erects its barriers nor decon-
structs the barriers to reveal the imaginary that lies behind.

"Cancellation," as Chapman's grammatology of *Cancels* succinctly
notes, "involves destruction";[83] it is an act of violence. The barrier of writing operates in the real. The door Lacan spoke of therefore also opens
on to a real that resides behind the threshold. At one point Joseph K.
opens a closed door that leads into a storeroom, where he comes across
the tools of cancellation, the leftovers from the writing orgy of arcane
powers: "Bundles of useless old papers and empty earthenware ink bottles
lay in a tumbled heap behind the threshold."[84] The utensils of the powers
of literacy, the realia of the law, have been banned to a back room, and
there we find that which endows the law with its aura.

In the storeroom of the law, whose low ceiling, reminiscent of the attic
and the pulpit, indicates that it belongs to Kafka's chancery architecture,
Joseph K. witnesses a sadistic whipping scene: a torturer with rod in hand
and dressed "in a sort of dark leather garment which left his throat and
a good deal of his chest and the whole of his arms bare,"[85] is performing
his duties. He belongs to the ambivalent zone of the law, just like the ushers, ministers, and civil servants, who according to the jurist Paul Johann
Anselm von Feuerbach are nothing but "a dubious cross between judge
and myrmidon."[86] The function of the whipper in Kafka's novel is to perform the "most inhuman office": to carry out the law in a place that defies
representation, the chamber of the real. K. is its only witness. As if acting
under a repetition compulsion—the novel speaks of "habit"[87]—he opens
the door to the torture chamber the next day. Noting that nothing has
changed, "he ran almost weeping to the clerks, who were quietly working
at the copying-presses," and asked them to "finally" clear the storeroom.[88]
As if one could remove violence from the law! Here at the barriers, the

law produces the ambivalence of its own enforcement between interpretation and execution, between judges and hangmen, and also between whippers and clerks.

In this legal twilight zone, where torture chambers and chanceries, executions and pardons, punishments and verdicts, interpretation and decision merge beyond distinction, even the whipping scene is ambiguous. It reads like a distorted echo of a scene from the Last Judgment, which reputedly will pass sentence on each and every one on the basis of a book that has recorded works and deeds. The kabbalah has frequently envisioned this scene. The apocryphal Gospel of Abraham comes closest to Kafka's torture scene. It speaks of "a book lying on the table (of judgment), six cubits thick and ten cubits in breadth. To the right and to the left were two angels holding a leaf of paper, ink and a pen. . . . And the judge said unto one of his servant angels: 'Open the book and search out the sins of this soul.' And opening the book he saw that the sins and the good deeds hung in balance, and he did not hand them over to the torturers or to the saved, but placed them in the middle."[89] Two serving angels, two whipping servants—in perfect symmetry to the storeroom scene depicted in Kafka's novel. All the places before the law are endowed with double significance. Both writing tools and rods are among the instruments of the law. In other words, the chancery is a site of legal violence. It is the place before the law, the site at which the law encounters writing and decides about the distinctions that are performed in the symbolic.

Bartleby, Consumer of Files

While Kafka's novel depicts the powerful influence of the chancery on Western law, the gradual decline of this institution and its replacement by the *office* are part of another famous chancery tale. Herman Melville's story marks the other end of the arc that describes the genealogy of law. It points toward the media-technological assessment of files that unfold their power in the writing workshops of the law.

Because of the decline of the mediatory function of chanceries around the 1850s, the term and the office of *cancellari* started to vanish as well. The unemployed scribes are now free to serve as literary models. As the introduction to "Bartleby, the Scrivener" notes, a number of stories about "law-copyists or scriveners"[90] began to appear. "Bartleby" itself was written by a scribe who was employed as one of the last of his kind at the New York State Bank. A few months prior to its composition a similar story about one the "last copyists" had appeared in the *New Yorker*: "'The Lawyer's Story' by a Member of the Bar." The Bar, the American association of lawyers, posits a part for the whole: its name derives from *bar* or *barrier*. In his story, the anonymous author, who poses as a member of the bar, recounts the experiences of a jurist with his assistant. The author presumably is a New York lawyer and thus a colleague of Melville's brother. The latter's own scribe story, which is written after this tale "by a member of the bar,"[91] transfers the signifier *bar* from the title into the name *Bar*tleby.

With Bartleby, the "bar-tender"[92]—that is, in the most literal sense the guardian and the operator of the bar—the epoch of the chancery comes to an end. The copyist is standing at the threshold of a new age, without handwriting, that is associated with Remington, manufacturer of the first typewriter to be ready for office usage and mass production and which from 1880 on is used first in courtrooms and then in offices and law firms. In its wake, handwriting becomes an anachronism, or at best a literary activity. Accordingly, twentieth-century writers recognize Melville's hero as one of their own. "Comrade Bartleby,"[93] who is introduced at the outset as belonging to a "somewhat singular set of men,"[94] is as replaceable as any copyist; hence he becomes a favored object of identification for all those for whom writing has become a form of life.

Like his kinsman Joseph K., Bartleby turns a long historical development on its head. As one who sleeps where he works, he arrives at that point in the history of the law when living spaces and offices were still indistinguishable. Before the establishment of chanceries, cultural practices such as writing and dictating were intertwined with other quotidian activities. It was only with the differentiation of these functions—roughly since the early modern age—that scriveners no longer slept where they worked. The chancery became a space of its own, thus satisfying Max Weber's bureaucratic criteria: "In principle, the modern organization of the civil service separates the bureau from the private domicile of the official."[95] Bartleby's individual regression, however, parodies the progress of modernity, in the course of which writing had been assigned an exclusive space. He lives in a law office on New York's Wall Street, leaving his abode rarely, and finally not at all. He can't leave the office because he is incessantly writing. His ability to mechanically copy all legal and other documents handed to him—pale, intent, regardless of day- or nighttime, by "sun-light and by candle-light"[96]—makes him a pure "recording entity."[97] He turns into something that lawyers of 1853 (the year in which the story was written) can only dream of: a recording machine that without any sign of fatigue copies whatever it is presented with. Bartleby's inexhaustible copying capabilities anticipate the typewriter and thus the removal of his species. Linked to "typewriting women" mechanical typewriters "replaced 'men copyists.'"[98] The fact that Bartleby's employer suspects him of being blind may allude to the fact that the first typewriters were developed for the blind.[99]

Bartleby's story is a chancery story about *bars*. It is crossed by walls and barriers. The original subtitle was to have been "A Story of *Wall* Street." Bartleby's affinity to walls is so strong that he envisions himself as walled in. Walls of stone, glass, and cloth explain the story's spatially limited environment. "Within three feet of the panes was a wall, and the light came down from far above, between two lofty buildings, as from a very small opening in the dome."[100] As in Kafka's *Trial*, the architectural structuring unfolds from a dome with limited incidental light. The description of the office building suggests a comparison with a gigantic stone file. In fact, American skyscrapers are frequently presented as such: "Each office within the skyscraper is a segment of the enormous file."[101] An architecture of files and barriers rules the interior of Bartleby's chancery. Cancels in the shape of "ground glass folding-doors" separate the lawyer's workspace from the rest of the premises. They are transparent enough to leave the lawyer undisturbed yet not completely cut off from his surroundings. Opening the doors allows him a commanding vision of his busy employees; and there, between the master employer and his subordinates, Ginger, Turkey, and Nipper, is Bartleby the mediator, shielded by a "high green folding screen" of which it is said that it can be "folded up like a huge folio."[102] The fact that this particular object is called a *screen* indicates that it is related to the chancels that subdivide churches, chanceries, and law courts. According to the *Encyclopaedia Britannica*, chancels are the "cancelli or lattice work screens of a 'basilica' or law court, which separated the judge and counsel from the audience."[103] Just as later television screens will facilitate the democratic public's participation in, as well as exclusion from, power, the lawyer is concerned with the effects of a permeable separation "which might entirely isolate Bartleby from sight, though not remove him my voice."[104] Outside the range of vision, the master's voice dictates. It is only when the latter is drowned out by the rattle of typewriters that "His Master's Voice"—perhaps not coincidentally listened to by a dog called Nipper—turns into a well-known EMI record label.

Before it is partly mechanized by the typewriter, copying is a "very dull, wearisome and lethargic" activity. This, however, does not diminish the productive use of one of the last human recording devices. But though Bartleby's output is so enormous that it should be immensely gratifying to his employer, the latter, a good humanist, is plunged into deep melancholy. If Bartleby were paid "at the usual rate of four cents a folio (one hundred words),"[105] he would be immensely wealthy. But he is not interested in making money. He consumes texts. Avoiding all detours that involve the transformation into money or food, he lives directly off the copying and rumination of words. "As if long famishing for something to copy, he seemed to gorge himself on my documents."[106] Bartleby devours written words. Even more insatiable than his colleague Ginger (himself hooked on Ginger Nuts) or the other scribes, Turkey and Nippers (also named after edibles), he consumes files. But unlike them, Bartleby works without fuss or foible; he doesn't spill ink, he makes no noise, and he is no glutton. He lives for his one passion: letters.

Bartleby is hired because his employer, having been appointed a "Master in Chancery," is expecting a sizable amount of additional work to come his way. The existence of this particular office, which originated in Elizabethan England and was still in existence in the United States after the Declaration of Independence, is tied to the bilateral makeup of the Anglo-American court system, comprised of a court of common law and a court of equity, also called chancery. In the sixteenth century, chancery courts were defined with their powers of cancellation in mind: "Chancellor and chancerie court, from Latin *cancellarius*—and that from *cancello* signifying to make Lettises, Grates, Crosse-bares, to enclose anything withall; and metaphorically, to bound and containe anything within certain barres and limits. Refers well to his two functions—to cancel, deface, make void a Record because this vacat thereof is done and likewise in his court of Equitie he doth so cancell and shut up the rigor of generall law."[107] Within the sphere of legislation, these acts of annulling or crossing are designed to counterbalance the strictness of common law. While common law courts were charged with the rigid application of the law with no possible exception, chancery courts were able to compensate for the unjust consequences of such a mechanical sentencing—that is, they were able to practice "equity." *Equity* derives from *epieikeia*, the Greek word for discretion and equitableness; it also contains the idea of mercy. The equity court is endowed with a scope of discretion aimed at compensating for the rigor of the strictly applied law. The crucial point is that the discretionary power is not to be left to some court machinery; it has to be enacted in person: "Equity acts *in personam* because conscience does."[108] According to common law, the conscience of the king was embodied by none other than the chancellor, whose very title derives from his power to cancel, that is, to absolve from all legal obligations. As a *iustitiae filius et minister*, he is responsible for just equity. "The chancellor was supposed to hold jurisdiction basically for rectification, or setting aside, or cancellation of deeds or other written instruments; the specific performance of contracts and, furthermore, he was asked when laws were unknown to common law or when the machinery of the courts did not produce enough evidence."[109]

The bicameral legal system, comprising common law and equity, scarcely fits into nineteenth-century American legal architecture, which had done away with the twin peaks of king and chancellor. In a democratic society, the existence of a court of equity is tantamount to admitting that the judiciary produces injustice that has to be compensated. Hence the states start abolishing the chancery courts around the middle of the nineteenth century. In New York its power is transferred to the supreme state court—at the very time, incidentally, when Melville marries the daughter of a supreme court justice. Melville's story takes place that very year. The narrator-lawyer defends the "good old office, now extinct in the state of New York, of a Master of Chancery," against this "sudden and violent abrogation." The demise of this particular institution, after all, is costing him his "life-lease of the profits."[110] In his humanist eyes, however, the financial forfeit is negligible in comparison to the loss humanity is suffering. "Equity was a human system,"[111] a human institution that does not cite and deal with plaintiffs *at the bar* but positions them *in equity*—that is, within justice.

Bartleby epitomizes the transition to clerical work devoid of any human factor, that is to say, no *chance*ry in the face of a mechanized bureau.

With the dissolution of the chancery courts, an "extra-copyist," who was to be responsible for the extra work of the Master of Chancery, turns into a machine whose "incessant industry" is unstoppable despite the fact that there is no work. The recording machine is running idle; catching sight of it, the lawyer sighs: "Ah Bartleby! Ah humanity!" Those are his last words, as well as those of the story itself. For the narrator, the two exclamations are synonymous. Without the abrogation of the "good old" chancery office, Bartleby would not have turned into a machine, and without Bartleby, humanity would still reside in chancery. The fate of the extra-copyist is so inextricably linked to that of the chancery that he cannot survive the demise of the institution: He is found "asleep" among his own, "with kings and counselors."[112] A deputy from a distant world of royalty and chancellors, he bears witness to a past, more human law. This is not only the view of a mid-nineteenth-century New York lawyer. At the end of the twentieth century, jurists are still invoking Bartleby to lament the decline of the law: "Law without spirit, institution without justice, body without soul, life without emotion." The last human typewriter is turned into the victim of a long tradition "that has denounced soulless law as . . . dead letters."[113] Copyists and subaltern scriveners, however, do not operate in the pneumatic mode of the living spirit. They reside exclusively in the world of chancellors and are subject to the order of dead letters or *gramme*, which includes both signs and laws.[114] Whenever they cross out what they have copied, they perforce produce dead letters. For all his writing skills, Bartleby, a former employee of the "Dead Letter Office at Washington,"[115] is first and foremost a dead letter expert. His "crimpy hand"[116] establishes the link between handwritten (alphabetic) letters and undeliverable (postal) letters: unreadable letters in postal addresses condemn letters to the dead letter office.

Upon his death, Bartleby leaves behind a lawyer's office that has been turned into a dead letter office. The transmission of letters is blocked not because of his incessant writing but because he ceases to perform related duties. His boycott disrupts the everyday routine: "It is, of course, an indispensable part of a scrivener's business to verify the accuracy of his copy, word by word. Where there are two or more scriveners in an office, they assist each other in the examination, one reading from the copy, the other holding the original."[117] Bartleby's employer describes with great precision clerical work based on word-per-word units. His office, however, falls short of that ideal. His assistant—or rather, one particular sentence from the mouth of the latter—wreaks havoc with the smooth procedure. Asked to ensure the accuracy of a minor copy, Bartleby for the first time utters the awkward sentence or sentence fragment: "I would prefer not to." This utterance becomes so embedded in the office that in due course parts of it are used by the other copyists, as well as by the lawyer himself. At first hearing, it appears to be an innocuous sequence of words, but it comes equipped with the qualities of a virus: it is both unidentifiable and contagious. "The formula bourgeons and proliferates."[118] The virus affects the digestive tracts of all the copyists: soon the office is rife with dyspepsia, anorexia, and consumption. Bartleby's coworkers reproduce in the shape of bodily symptoms the digestive troubles and congestions of the paperwork caused by his formula. Clean copies can no longer circulate, manuscripts are piling up, copies are not filed, letters are not posted because the redemptory act of cancellation that confirms the word-for-word accuracy of copies is not being performed.

Deleuze says of the blocking sentence that it is "grammatically correct, syntactically correct, but its abrupt termination, NOT TO, which leaves what it rejects undetermined, confers upon it . . . a kind of limit-function."[119] It is a syntactic barrier. "With [Bartleby] something . . . comes into play, . . . much like the zero in algebra. It neither adds nor subtracts, but—as the case may be—it can raise to, annul or lead into inapprehensible dimensions."[120] The elliptic form of the sentence pushes for a completion, one way or another; hence the fragment enters into every possible relation with the sentences uttered in its vicinity. Responding to the request "to examine a small paper,"[121] the formula "I would prefer not to" automatically adds the preceding imperative, thus resulting in the unspoken "I would prefer not to examine a small paper." The formula's indeterminate but literal negation evokes a determinate semantic utterance. The echo of the preambular sentence turns the cryptic formula into a complete sentence. Its meaning—or rather, its effect—is rooted in the refusal of the preceding order. Thus the formula could be defined as the performative speech act of nonperformance. It causes an order not to be carried out. In this respect, it resembles the chancery's annulment of a legally binding verdict. The formula consumes whatever enters its semantic orbit; it is the linguistic form of a cancellation. The self-canceling speech act evades all juridical mechanisms of imputation. Although the copyist utters the statement, he cannot be held responsible for its annulling effects. It requires an imputation, an unprovable assumption, to claim that it was the subaltern called Bartleby who refused to carry out this or that task. He has done nothing; from a legal point of view, he is not guilty of any nonfeasance. He simply repeated a certain statement—a statement that like all performative utterances takes on an uncontrollable life of its own. From the lawyer's point of view, the passive resistance of his employee does not amount to a reason for dismissal. He would not be "justified in immediately dismissing Bartleby,"[122] although he does consider all the legal possibilities.

It is striking how frequently in the course of his legal consideration Melville's lawyer uses the expression *to assume*, as in: "I *assumed* the ground that depart he must."[123] It appears eleven times in different contexts, showing that Bartleby's juridically trained employer is familiar with the fifteenth-century "doctrine of assumptions."[124] The "principle of *assumpsit*, a chancery writ issued in the case of nonfeasance (nonperformance),"[125] became a statute of Anglo-Saxon law pertaining to cases of reproachable acts of negligence. "There had to be something more than nonfeasance: it might be misfeasance, it might be deceit, or it might be injurious reliance."[126] By adding something to a simple nonaction, the *assumpsit* principle turns it into objectionable nonfeasance. This assumed "something more" turns nonfeasance into an act for which somebody may be held accountable. With regard to firing Bartleby, however, the lawyer concedes that his assumptions will meet with little success: "The great point was not, whether I had assumed that he would quit me, but whether he would prefer to do so."[127] By "assuming" that Bartleby would "prefer" not to work for him, the lawyer sets the stage for a legal-rhetorical battle between the verbs *assume* and *prefer*—more precisely, between the doctrine of assumptions and Bartleby's formula. For the act of *preferring* derives from the realm of the chancery: it designates a legal act "apposite to the situation of equity pleading as opposed to common law pleading."[128] When *prefer* collides with *assume*, assumptions succumb to preference. The force of preference is superior to that of assumption; hence all assumptions bounce off Bartleby's crippling insistence of preference. "It means only what it says, literally."[129] Literalness, a word-for-word exactitude that defies all hermeneutics, is the modus operandi of those working in chanceries. Anything that transgresses the boundaries of the literal is subject to assumptions and is therefore rejected. The lawyer is forced to concede that he has lost: Bartleby is "more a man of preferences than assumptions."[130]

The piles of noncopied, nonposted, and nonfiled papers visibly testify to the ultimate victory of the chancery principle of preference over the advocate's principle of *assumpsit*: the basic transmission blockage results in ubiquitous *waste paper*. The more the office becomes a form of life, the more its functions are suspended. The copyist renounces copying, quits posting the mail, and refuses to perform even the most marginal tasks, such as holding "his finger . . . on the incipient tie of a big red tape."[131] One by one, the office duties fall by the wayside, until nothing remains other than an inactive, close-lipped ex-copyist. Bartleby, the supremely accurate recording device, no longer copies letters; rather, he mimics the wastepaper environment he has created. He himself turns into a "wasted Bartleby."[132] As a dead letter figure, he succumbs to their deadly fate. The chancery clerk regresses to the status of a *cancellus*; he becomes a barrier and spends his days sitting on a banister. The speech act of cancellation is now turned against him. The sentence devours its speaker. Bartleby himself is canceled; he becomes a consumer of files, a victim of his absorbing passion. He lives "without dining," possibly afflicted by consumption.[133] In line with his professional life, he ends, just like Joseph K., behind bars, "the ideal place for writing."[134] Bartleby's biography progresses from chancery to jail, from high-rise domes to "The Tombs," as the New York jail was unofficially called. The latter amounts to a literal confirmation of Buckminster Fuller's theory of geodetic domes (with its reference to the ur-syllable *OM*): "The D was interchanged with T in designation of the dome as mortuary shrine."[135] A dome is destined to be a tomb, a shrine for the dead, a repository for dead letters, as well for *dead-letter-men*. Indeed, the New York prison resembles a shrine: "The yard was entirely quiet. It was not accessible to the common prisoners. The surrounding walls, of amazing thickness, kept off all sounds behind them."[136] Chanceries, which were removed from sight, become prisons, whose architecture is one of sensory deprivation. In his soundproof cell, Bartleby dreams his "deadwall reveries."[137]

And ever since, his successors—writers and poets—dream of Bartleby. For instance, when observing America's administration edifice, the Empire State Building, as caught on screen by Andy Warhol, who filmed it from eight in the evening to sunrise, with only one of its 6,400 windows illuminated in the deserted darkness: "Inside: nobody . . . unless it were Melville's scrivener Bartleby, hidden on every floor in his loneliest, emptiest night; the office copyist who wants nothing but to stay in the building, even at night, in order to continue copying 'the files,' invisible behind his screen."[138]

§ 2   From Translating to Legislating

In the early sixteenth century, the Parisian humanist Guillaume Budé undertook several trips to Italy. He belonged to those Renaissance travelers who, much like pilgrims, ventured abroad without any specific assignment. They were compelled to travel not by colonial curiosity but by a love for writing, and they returned bearing not marvelous or exotic gifts but the most classical item the Occident has to offer: handwritten texts. These, however, were neither read nor copied; rather, the travelers treated them as valuable finds from distant lands and proceeded to examine their external characteristics: the material on which they were written, the size of the letters, the composition of the ink, the appearance of seals and stamps, the history of their transmission through time and space—in short, everything that is of interest to present-day media studies. In time, the inspection of old texts inaugurated new disciplines, such as paleography, codicology, and diplomatics. Around 1900 these media-related disciplines, which came into being literally *avant la lettre*, were pushed aside by the historiographical focus on *content* and reduced to the status of mere ancillary sciences. From that point on, media-technological *textual* analyses were made to assist historiographical *factual* analyses. In what follows, however, we will reverse this relationship: teasing out the mediality of texts, we will attempt to ground the law in files and records.

Budé's philological pilgrimage led him to Pisa, where he planned to scrutinize one very special manuscript among the many rediscovered by the epigraphic travelers of the Renaissance. His eyes were set on the occidental law of all laws: the Pandects, or, as the legal codex compiled at the behest of the late Roman emperor Justinian is also called, the Digest. It was treasured and guarded "like a holy relic and only very rarely shown in the light of torches and candlesticks."[1] On those occasions, the display of the precious item is reminiscent of *ur*-scenes like "Before the Law": "The legal scholars were barred [quite literally in the case of Budé, who saw the manuscript only through a grate] by guardians of the precious Codex who allowed visitors only fleeting glimpses of the relic."[2] The stolen law, according to legend a piece of Florentine "scholarly booty"[3] stemming from the 1406 war against Pisa, was behind bars and guarded by gatekeepers. It consisted of two parchment volumes totaling nine hundred pages dating from the sixth century, which puts it fairly close to the original produced in AD 533. About four hundred years after its abduction, the manuscript surfaced in Pisa; it was later called "(littera) Florentina" in honor of its looters. Another four centuries later, typography rendered the unique manuscript so precious that it turned into an object of philological desire. Florence, the print metropolis, paved the way to the partly forgotten, partly caged Roman law. The first, manuscript-based printed edition of the Digest in 1529 was the work of Polizian, an acquaintance of Budé's. Twenty years later Lelio Torelli composed a new edition, letter by letter.

But Budé was not interested in the glimpses of the abstract Roman law offered by the manuscript. Instead he was engrossed in the concrete residues of its materiality: "He was attracted to Roman law . . . as a battered relic."[4] The occluded view through the gate kindled a burning desire for the text—philology, the effect of barred manuscripts. The inaccessibility of the *ur*-text and the fragility of its transmission stimulated the quest for the text behind all texts. According to Budé, members of those faculties participating in the genesis and transmission of Roman law were entitled to inspect the matrix of occidental law: jurists, theologians, poets, and chroniclers. They were called upon to reconstruct the lost past of the law and uncover its buried origins. Nineteenth-century historians would continue this fixation on origins so prevalent among Renaissance humanists and jurists. Since the Pandects only contain abridged and garbled extracts of the original quotes, it became their declared editorial goal to reconstruct the original legal texts in full. The Roman law historian Theodor Mommsen, for example, praises the Florentina as the "mother of all other manuscripts."[5]

The phantasm of a not yet canceled origin governs the research focusing on the interpolations of Roman law—that is, on textual differences resulting from "retroactive, intentional and hence unmarked changes."[6]

Guided by an array of archaeological and archival techniques, it works its way through the vulgates back to the putative origin. In due course, this obsession with discovering an undisguised *ur*-text produces, as a side product, a media-technological knowledge of the fragile, at times ruptured ways in which Roman law was transmitted. "Rome" becomes an absolute reference for the law—one which by way of rejection and resumption, forgetting and rewriting (all the while still pursuing the notion of an undisguised, uncanceled text) resembles what Budé was able to briefly catch sight of in Pisa. The reconstructive work is fueled by "fleeting glimpses of the relic." The gaze through the grate shapes Roman law into a closed, orderly system. Whether (to allude to Lacan) this gaze opens into the real or the imaginary remains undecidable. Both are involved when Roman law emerges from the reconstruction of its transmission. But it is possible to decide upon, specify, and elaborate the media-technological conditions of its transmission.

Rome did not have to wait for the confluence of war, print, and philology in sixteenth-century Italy to become relic and relict, matrix and cipher of occidental law; the latter merely strengthened the chances of a transmission that was already the goal of the recording technologies of late Roman antiquity. These chances rapidly increased once diverse and heterogeneous texts were turned into a unified, closed codex. Prior to that, texts existed as scrolls or *rotuli* that came about by "gluing together the individual reports written by scribes in the strategist's office." Researchers therefore refer to these scrolls as "files."[7] But codices, the medium that succeeds scrolls, also meet this criterion, for wax-covered wooden tablets hinged together are equally capable of being brought up to date. Like scrolls, they are "notebooks,"[8] and in appearance they resemble today's files more than they do scrolls. "A whole cluster of tablets was called a *caudex* or *codex*. . . . Except for its bulkiness, the codex could be compared to a file consisting of paper documents held together by a metal fastener."[9]

Referring to *rotuli* and *codices* as files emphasizes their function as recording devices that can constantly be updated, but it glosses over the degree to which they belong to very different realms of law and writing. The gradual transition from scrolls to codices, which began around the second century AD, splits Rome into two parts, each equipped with its own guiding medium. In what follows we will therefore have to differentiate be-

FIGURE 3.   Wax notebook, used in Greece and Rome since about 500 BC.
Louis Leitz Firma (ed.), *Schriftgut und seine Aufbewahrung: Aktuell seit 5000
Jahren*, Stuttgart 1980, 5.

tween scroll-files and codex-files, and we will use this difference to retrace
the media-technologically induced shift from translation to legislation.

The advantages offered by the codices are, quite literally, there for everyone to see. The new reading posture offers readers an escape from the
defenseless position of having both hands attached to the text. The emperor Domitian, for one, was unable to ward off his murderers because
he was reading a scroll. Reading a codex requires one hand only—or a fist
(*pugnus,* hence *pugillares,* or "fist-size," is another term for codices). The
ability to quickly leaf through a text in both directions in search of a specific item is another obvious advantage of the codex. Scrolls, on the other
hand, only permit serial text searches; retrieving a specific item requires
continuous re-reading with no jumps. Scrolls, no doubt, make bad reference works because frequent uncoiling damages their upper layer.[10] The
possibility of adding further layers to any part of the loose leaves prior
to their binding frees codices from the purely diachronic recording logic

of scrolls. The sequence in which the leaves are tied together does not have to be identical with the temporal sequence of the actual recording. By virtue of these optimized usage features—random access, up-to-date writing, ease of binding, storage, and rearranging—codices gradually replaced scrolls as "functional texts."[11] These comprise Rome's official and administrative writings.

The switch from scrolls to codices was linked to a change of writing material. For their codices, the second-century imperial Roman administrators increasingly used parchment instead of papyrus, which made them independent of the unreliable Egyptian papyrus monopoly. The switch of material entailed further changes, such as the adoption of a different writing instrument—the *stilus* replaced the tube called *calamus*—and the new technique of continuous rapid writing in minuscule, which is possible on whitewashed parchment but not on fibrous papyrus. The most significant material advantage of parchment was its greater durability. In contrast, papyrus decays after a comparatively short period of about one hundred years. Harold Innis established a link between the change of writing material and Rome's transition from territorial unit to eternal empire: "The Byzantine Empire developed on the basis of a compromise between organizations reflecting the bias of different media: that of papyrus in the development of an imperial bureaucracy in relation to a vast area, and that of parchment in the development of an ecclesiastical hierarchy in relation to time."[12] On the basis of their material, the media technologies scroll and codex determine differing concepts of time and law. Papyrus scrolls are linked to the purely actual, coextensive law of an imperial administration. In contrast, the organization of files as loose-leaf collections in connection with their independence from the act of writing predestines codices for the retroactive compilation of legal texts. This underlies the double meaning of *codex*, which refers both to the files of the imperial Roman administration and to its normative legal texts. Among the first such legal texts in the fourth century were compilations containing constitutions or imperial laws, for instance, the Codex Gregorianus and the Codex Hermogenianus. The title of the law combines the designation of the medium with the name of the compilation's initiator.

The legal collection glimpsed by Budé was also in codex format. The medium and the technologies that turn a codex into a *codification* shaped the notion of a stratified, circumcised law. Unlike papyrus, which is produced by kneading and rolling, the manufacture of parchment is associated with cutting and gathering. Parchment is the product of detached and processed animal skin with fine hair on one side and flesh on the other. A knife is used to cut it to size. Papyrus, the stuff of scrolls, is made in a completely different way, using a biotechnological procedure that was in existence in Rome since 330 BC and which included the uncoiling of sheets composed of Nile water, fungal cultures, and Cyprus papyrus plants. It is wholly consistent that the knife becomes the symbol of the law codified on parchment. Not only is it used for cutting the membrane, but by scraping off the surface it also ensured that it can be used again. The knife, then, is part of the technologies of cancellation that enable the law to cross the threshold into the symbolic and attain legal force. It is a weapon, just like the *stilus* used for writing on parchment. In addition, the very laws that are based on the work of these instruments are considered weapons. The introduction to one of Justinian's judicial textbooks, the *Institutiones* of AD 533, states: "It is expedient that the Imperial Majesty not only be distinguished by arms [*armis*], but also be armed [*armatum*] by laws."

That venerable legal compendium, the Pandects or Digest, is the product of a double cancellation. Not only is the view of the *Florentina* obstructed by a grate, but the codification itself is the result of a series of deletions. The writings of various jurists are included only in abridged fashion. Unlike the transcription of scrolls, this procedure, commonly referred to as compilation, is not primarily or exclusively interested in conservation. "On the contrary, compilation itself was to become the murderer of the entire mother literature that generated it."[13] The murder metaphor used by the legal historian Franz Wieacker brings to mind liquidation and extinction rather than preservation. From this point of view, a codification, or retranscription from scroll to codex, may be defined as a premeditated deletion of transmitted legal texts, that is, as the murder of a living law that incessantly updates itself. Ever since the textual criticism of the Renaissance, reading codified Roman law appears to be tantamount to murdering texts. The certain knowledge that what did *not* become part of a codex, which was "*not* transcribed, . . . has perished for good," underscores not what a compilation preserves but what is irretrievably lost. It focuses attention on the loss, on the garbled and illegible behind the legible, codified text. Compiling, no doubt, irreversibly interrupted the stream of tradition; it marked a caesura. Legal codices were barriers erected against irregular, nonauctorial, and nonauthorized currents of transmission. The Digest codex is not only a Pisanian booty; on the textual level, too, it is loot or, in Latin, a compilation. After all, the compilation "constitutes . . . an archetype that as a rule blocks all other recourse to surviving scrolls."[14] In paleographic discourse, an "archetype" is the oldest extant or deducible text,[15] the *pater familias* of legal texts. Codifications, in other words, put an end to the fatherless age of law.

In the sixth century AD, Emperor Justinian commissioned the compilation of Roman law, which resulted in the production of three books: the Digest, the *Codex Justinianus*, and the *Institutiones*. Following the printing of the collected edition of 1583, Dionysius Gothofredus combined all three as the *Corpus Iuris Civilis*. The fact that this body of law is no more than a *corps morcelé* did not escape the attention of observers like François Hotman, Budé's French critic. He did not devoutly linger in front of the caged icon of Roman justice, instead he proceeded to desecrate it in surgico-philological fashion. For Hotman, the body of the law was not the "Corpus Juris Civilis" but a different, whole body that the codification had dismembered as if with a knife.[16] Franz Wieacker, in turn, calls this intact body prior to codification the "mother literature."[17] He projects a maternal body that gave birth to the codified law of the *Corpus Iuris*. The legal matrix leads to a maternal expanse of undefiled and unlimited textual regions before the law, to noncodified files in the shape of infinitely extendable scrolls or codices that can be expanded at will. Hotman justified his criticism of the codified and hence dismembered body of the law in his famous "Anti-Tribonian," directed at the chief codifier Tribonian. He doubted the legitimacy of *Justinian's* paternity, thereby confirming the *principle* of paternity as a legal instance. There is no law that is not the law of the father. Every search for the incipient law inevitably becomes a "search for paternity."[18]

In his search for the father of *all* laws, Sigmund Freud's investigative analysis of the distortions of the original Mosaic tables had revealed them to be dissimulations of a real patricide. Patricide, force of law, homicide, and distortion form a unit. They are the bedrock of the force of law. Before the law comes the transgression; before the legible commandments written down by Moses there was the canceled *ur*-version—as reported in the biblical account of the smashing of the tables of the law. The research focusing on interpolations, which since the sixteenth century aims to descry a law before the law, operates according to the same analytical model. Based on the legal principle of paternity, the goal is to search for the undistorted legal texts that preceded codified law. The distortion—that is, the murder of the mother literature—is ascribed to the emperor Justinian, who occupied the position of the father. To provide evidence of his textual murder, researchers track down and expose his codificatory interventions, but rather than deconstructing the patriarchal order of the law, the evidence gathered serves to support it. The constitutive effect of this particular research reveals what is underneath all the talk about the great loss of material caused by the process of codification: It is a discourse of self-justification intoned by the law.

The philological quest to uncover the murder of texts turns into a hunt to expose the deletions reputedly carried out by Tribonian, the jurist charged with editing the Pandects. Significantly, this "chasse aux tribonianismes,"[19] the search for the not yet canceled legal texts, was launched in the Renaissance, that is, at a time when the use value of manuscripts had sunk below their historical value and the advent of typography retired manuscripts and exposed their uniqueness. No longer in use, they turned into relics, cult-like objects on display:

> This is how I imagine things took place. Nowadays we prefer more recently printed books to older editions because we assume that they have been corrected, and this was also the case with manuscripts prior to the invention of the printing press. (The Medici Library is a striking example; it showed a marked preference for recent manuscripts written by educated Greek refugees because they were thought to be superior, while old manuscripts considered less valuable were sold off without any second thoughts to the Palatina Library in Germany.) If you were in need of parchment, you simply reused old manuscripts whose content either had no value or had been transferred to more recent manuscripts. If booksellers were forced to cut up old manuscripts to have them copied more rapidly by a set of scribes, they preferred old manuscripts over newer ones because it mattered less if they were torn apart and gradually used up. To pitch it to customers as a "new, revised edition," it was essential for the manufacturers to have a competent reviser familiar with the latest scholarship correct the new transcriptions using an allegedly superior original. Thus I consider it very likely that the scribes responsible for the Florentinian manuscript based their copy on the torn-up pieces of an older manuscript, while the *ordinarii correctores*, working under the influence of the Byzantine legal school, revised it using supposedly improved copies, not without now and then arbitrarily inserting corrections based on their own learning.[20]

These nineteenth-century philological deliberations on the origin of the Florentinian manuscript establish a remarkable correspondence between the use of handwritten and printed texts: The very same pressures that require the ongoing manufacture of updated editions are also at work in the realm of manuscripts. These, too, are constantly brought up to date. The users' interest is noticeably at odds with the historico-philological desire to secure traces by obtaining the oldest possible extant version. From a historiographical perspective, all the revisions and corrections linked to administrative processing amount to an ongoing mutilation. Administrations are bent on the latest version, while historical research is fixated on the oldest. Thus two ways of ranking textual stages are diametrically opposed: usage versus history, administrative technologies of updating and innovating versus the principle of ancientness. Our attempt to construct a media-historical history of the law from files takes into account the pragmatics of administrative updating, but it does not condemn it as an ongoing practice of mutilation. It is not a matter of joining the chorus of humanists, philologists, and legal historians, who lament the loss of an illegible, mythical corpus of texts, but rather of reconstructing the latter's media-technological conditions.

Imperium Romanum: Time of Files

From the times of the early Republic up to the reign of Justinian, Rome teems with files, notebooks, official minutes, diaries, municipal records, protocols. The forms are as diverse as their agents. All Roman officials—magistrates, praetors in particular, provincial governors, senators, consuls, emperors—compile records, containing whatever is to be carried forward and transmitted: "Decrees, senate consultations, magisterial edicts, the instructions and correspondence of other offices, . . . decrees of the collegium."[21] This disparate bundle of legal and administrative material, devoid of all ceremonious décor (but destined to rise above its original private status and find its way into archived collections), is known by several names: *commentarii, codices, tabulae, gestae* or *regestae, libri, cottidiana, adversaria*, and sometimes simply *acta*, in Greek: *hypomnémata* or *hypomnematismoí*. The late Roman *notitia dignitatum*, a kind of administrative handbook that endeavored to bring order to the baffling confusion of the administration of Rome and all its provinces, conveys first and foremost an impression of the complexities involved. The activities as well as the designation of the offices involved derived their names from the type of texts they handled: *a commentariis, a cura epistularum* or *ab actis*, among others. Apparently there was no administrative office in Rome that did not deal with files in one way or other.

It was usually the *exceptores* (*notarii*), who for the sake of memory recorded everything on wax or papyrus, from official acts of the magistrates at public banquets to disputes on the marketplace. They took notes whenever it appeared necessary. There were no regulations concerning form and amount. "It appears that as a rule the magistrates' record-keeping was confined to an official journal (*commentarii, gesta*), the size of which depended on circumstances as well as on the whim of the magistrate responsible. Its main goal, however, was to record their decrees."[22] These records were aide-mémoires. As Hans-Georg Gadamer says of *hypomnémata*, it is their "external appearance . . . as writing"[23] that serves as reminder. The Greek term for files was derived from the verb *hypomnematízesthai*, which means precisely what Gadamer expressed in philosophical terms: "to write down as a reminder" or "to put on file." By virtue of being arranged in columns and lines that indicate where particular items of information were to be added, the official diaries already followed a rudimentary logic of place value. The Greek term for the act of noting something in a file, *katachorizein*, literally translates as "putting something in its place."

These barely formalized magisterial notebook files were the result of disorderly updating. "What was new was added without deleting the old; or the latter was deleted at one point and kept at another, and so on."[24] Partial rewriting kept the files, predominantly in scroll format, up to date. The continuous usage was interrupted solely by the one-year rhythm that governed all terms of office in the administration of the Roman Republic. At the conclusion of the year, a new official journal was begun. The praetorian edicts, which were kept in an *album*, were subject to this annual rhythm since AD 67; for one year the praetors were bound to the decrees contained in the *album*, after which the edicts of the preceding year could reappear as precedents (*exempla*). If still deemed relevant to current decisions, they were consulted, copied, revised, and modified, thus connecting one term of office to the next. A chain of transmissions was established, an empire of files in the rhythm of the successive terms of office. A similar principle applied even to the files of deceased emperors: "Upon the death of an emperor, his successor had the right to use, or dispose of his predecessor's files as he saw fit."[25]

Acta was the most basic term for all administrative and recording acts carried out by the Roman administration. One can observe a shift in meaning from oral acts to written records that mirrors the basic legal differentiation between orders and laws. The early Roman Republic expanded with the reach and density of its command structure. *Imperium* denotes, after all, order or command. As yet, the empire had no boundaries, just as *acta* were not closed units. Comprising all official acts, the latter were "essentially without a boundary."[26] Initially, they were enacted orally for the most part; writing accumulated only gradually, until it came to predominate and *acta* existed formally only in and as files. In today's linguistic usage, the acts connoted by files (*Akten*) have been completely displaced by the acts of writing and recording. "The word *files* is no longer understood to refer to acts; it has come to designate no more than a combination of written texts."[27] This significant shift from act (*Akt*) to file (*Akte*) corresponds to the evolution of an administration that increasingly linked the official character of its acts to their recording: in German, "the plural of act (*Akt*) is *Akten*, or files, hence an act is an administrative act as soon as it has taken place, issued, officially recorded, and put *ad acta*."[28]

The basis for Roman transition from oral utterance to written file was the *imperium*, that is, the authority of the magistrates that had emerged from a military command structure. A command is normally issued orally, and its orality is maintained even if the order is also present in writing, in the shape of a decree or an edict. Even the law, *lex*, derived from *legere*, maintains an etymological connection to reading out loud and selecting (counting). The written commands are modeled on an oral imperative that derived "from an originally Indo-European form of oral message."[29] A letter, then, is nothing but a transmittable order. "Normally the couriers were handed messages in the form of a letter, but the latter were introduced and written in such a way that by reading them aloud they could be communicated to the addressees. As can be deduced from the format of the letter, the act of reading it out loud, as opposed to simply delivering it, was performed by the messengers, as is clearly indicated by the format of the letters."[30] Hence formulaic letters are prescribed commands. Reading them aloud guarantees their literal transmission. The courier is left with virtually no leeway. In other words, messenger and message coincide. Subsequently, the former is named after the materiality of the medium, *tabula*; and *tabula* in turn give rise to the *tabularius*—he who conveys files and letters.

The magistrate carried out their duties orally, by way of spoken commands. Written texts were used only to enable commands to bridge time or space. They were the medium of delayed transfer. Transmitted by messengers, the orders passed through various stages; they were tied to a chain of command in which orality and literacy were not opposites but differing aggregate states of one and the same command. To be more precise, they themselves contained a consecutive chain of command. The address on a letter was at the same time a command that it be delivered. The delivery command was fulfilled the moment the delivery had been completed; if a letter was to be retained after its delivery, this required a separate order. The efficacy of a command is independent of the domain of the law; it is linked neither to any form of public reading nor to any other form of publication or preservation. Unlike laws, commands do not come into effect. Whether or not a law is in place is hence not dependent on the power to erect barriers; it is a matter of updating transmissions. It was the magistrates' rather contingent recording practice that decided what was valid at the moment. Taking note of official acts, "be it . . . by order or initiative, creates a new state of law."[31] Everything that was recorded in files could therefore become *lex*.

Imperium and *acta*, the command and its mode of transmission, correspond with and determine each other. The transmissions relied on courier systems that in turn were linked to communication routes. The fact that the Roman Republic lacked a fully developed and centralized bureaucracy did not impede the effectiveness of the transmitted commands. Rather, the imperial transmission system appears to confirm Max Weber's thesis that the size of an empire is not necessarily tied to an evolved bureaucratic structure.[32] In the case of the Roman Empire, it depended on a structure of transmission. The presence of over a hundred languages—among them, Latin, Oscian, Umbrian, Etruscan, Gallic, Greek, Aramaic, Hebrew, Punic, and Syrian—and almost as many writing systems required that every command be accompanied by a translation. Acting as interpreters, imperial agents transmitted commands to the expanding empire and in turn enlarged the empire with words until Rome was wherever Latin was heard. The administrative-linguistic fusion of messengers and interpreters turned the Roman borough into an exportable entity.

An imperial surplus emerged from the practical necessity of having to translate all commands traveling to and from Rome. Ritualized interpreting underscored for all to see who had the authority to issue such orders.

It endowed Rome with a voice that could also be heard outside the city. The *imperium*, the Roman command authority, arose from acts of public proclamation. To read letters out loud, to literally recite them, follows the rhetorical procedure of prosopopoeia, or investing a voice. It transmitted "Rome's commanding voice"[33] in all directions. Wherever Latin could be heard in combination with a foreign language, interpreters provided an idea of the reach of Rome. Speaking—in particular, speaking in front of a court or issuing a command—depended on translating. What is frequently praised as Rome's liberal language politics is in fact an effective imperial strategy. It appears that the empire deliberately employed a language mix, a willful, premeditated Babel, in which all official utterances had to pass through the bottleneck of that initially inconsequential Italian dialect called *lingua Latina*. The result was an infiltration of Latin transmitted along the principal Roman roads. Their major junctions formed the subcenters of the Roman *lingua franca*. Here, at the communication hubs, translations ensured that everything and everybody became compliant and compatible with Rome.

Where transmission was, there tradition shall be. With the senate's rise in power, the magistrate's transmission practice shifted into the domain of the written word. The double meaning of *acta*, always oscillating between acts and files, clearly gravitated toward the realm of writing contained in files. The act of recording acquires independence once it is not the transmission itself but the control of the transmission that is emphasized. *Acta* are no longer the relays in an unending race; it is no longer their sole purpose to transmit orders and order transmissions. In the wake of the senate's political ascendancy, *acta* were also used to limit their further use. The senate would adopt magisterial practices and also refer to its own collection of files as *acta*; a *senatus consultum*, however, was a recommendation to the magistrates that came about by a numerical majority. "Resolutions passed by the senate do not contain any word of command."[34] While retaining the file format, the mode of action shifts from an administrative form of discourse to an authoritarian one. At that point of the senate's rise to power, the media-theoretical distinction between storage and transmission affects the files themselves. *Acta* are differentiated into commands concerning transmission on the one hand, and evidence of the execution of the command on the other.[35] The stored evidence constitutes reports on matters of the past and thus constitutes a Roman past. The magistrates may already have compiled files on past acts (*actus*), but these files did not lay claim to any truth.

The truth claim emerged when files were no longer personal notebooks to refresh one's memory but documents kept in public places, such as municipal depots. Now it was possible to make copies to prove a legal claim, provided one was lucky enough to find the record in question, which could take years, since the documents were not equipped with any retrieval function. By virtue of their public safe-keeping, files became an absolute means of storage no longer tied to any one person. This emancipation of files from those who compile them heralded the switch from information to account, and hence prepared a change in the dispositive of power from transmission to tradition, from command to report and along with it from administration to law. This shift was tied to the senate's rise to power and the corresponding decline of the magisterial authority. From the very beginning, senate resolutions were located in the domain of the law, *auctoritas*. When the *senatus consulta* gained quasi-legal status in the second century AD, they came equipped with features that attested to their validity: signatures, the fact that they constituted the notes of a deliberation, and their being deposited in an archive (*delatio ad aerarium*). In due course, senate resolutions were not only to be delivered to the main archive, they were also to be deposited in the Temple of Ceres, administered by two plebeian aediles. According to Livy, this was done to prevent the decrees from becoming "subject to suppression or alteration at the whim of the consuls."[36] Notes were a further preventive measure against falsification, since they attest to the orderly procedure of the *senatus consulta*.

The senate's emphasis on producing evidence replaced the magistrates' focus on transmitting news. The imperative, prescriptive form of discourse turned into an evidentiary, descriptive one. And this is an effect of the prescript itself. It requires an alignment with its execution. Here the regime of literalness arises with the question of truth: is what was written down an accurate recording of what was said? Does what is stored correspond to what took place? Is it complete? It becomes necessary to establish criteria for the reliability of written records and to furnish means to authenticate them. On the other hand, a command, as Jean-François Lyotard reminds us, will or will not be obeyed, but it cannot be validated.[37] It is either carried out or not.

The evidentiary function is linked to *taking protocols*, a media technology that is integral to files. Whereas the magistrate issued commands, the senate took notes. "Jurists conceive of protocols as legal documents as opposed to letters (*epistula*)."[38] Unlike letters, protocols do not transmit a command; nobody has to abide by them. Instead they profess to seize and preserve an act; in short, they claim to be true. The fact that they are capable of providing proof turns protocols or records into legal documents or *instruments*—in Latin, *instrumenta publica*. Certifying records took their name from *protokollon*, the papyrus sheet bearing the insignia of the imperial Egyptian papyrus manufacturer, which for purposes of authentication was glued to the beginning of the roll. Only those contracts featuring this material preamble were valid. A scriptural barrier protects against forgery. It is described in one of the most exact treatises on protocols: "The writing surface . . . is surrounded as if by a wall [!], the upper page is completely covered by a long crossbeam, each letter is connected to the next, and the lower parts of the first line are virtually glued to the upper parts of the next; . . . [they are] locked as if with a bolt."[39]

The *protokollon*, formerly a material sign indicating the authenticity of escrows, served to guarantee accurate recordings of senate transactions. Its function was to bear witness to the completed *acta* of the past. Normally, senate deliberations were recorded by the magistrate responsible in *hypomnémata* fashion—that is, by using keywords only. Sometimes individual members of the senate recorded the debates and their outcome from memory. During Caesar's consulate in 59 BC it became obligatory for the senate to record its transactions and publish the minutes in the *acta urbis*. When, following his consulate, senate meetings ceased to be public, there was no longer any demand for publication, though the senate remained obliged to keep minutes. In 29 BC Augustus appointed record-keepers bound by his own instructions (*curatores actorum senatus*, also known as *ab actis senatus*) to keep a tight rein on the senate's records. The dominance of the protocol enabled the senate to procure the power of control in the political domain. As a result, Mommsen was later able to decipher the body of rules and regulations that grew up around senate protocols in the late Roman Republic as a struggle for power between magistrates and senate.

Unlike the power of the written law, which draws its authority from the act of canceling, the authority of protocols derives from the fact that they came into being at the same time as the transactions they record. This simultaneity enables protocols to enter the sphere of officially recognized and communicated truth. The oral act guarantees the truth of the written; in turn, the written record enables the oral act to meet the demands of truth—a relationship between guarantee and transcription that resides in the space between the oral and the written and profits from the double meaning of *acta* as act and record. Both are combined into a third meaning, *acta facere*, the Latin term for "keeping the minutes." Similarly, the Greek verb *hypomnematízesthai*, which, as Gadamer reminds us, encompasses both "remember" and "add to the record," also refers to protocols.[40] In practical terms, the connection between "compiling a record" and "taking a protocol," which is hardly present in modern English or German, is obvious: an act is recorded in the shape of a protocol, the protocols are compiled in files. In terms of its arrangement, a file is nothing but its own protocol. It contains itself as a transaction; it is its own record. Once a protocol has been added to a file, the act itself is terminated, but it can still be addressed as an act; reading the file means that the act it refers to is actualized. *Acta facere*, therefore, belongs to the basic operation of a written, positive law that is never present but in terms of application and execution is always oriented toward presence. The senate minutes were aiming for this presentist effect. They appear to be in search of the aura of the authentic. Beyond noting mere results—who voted for what employing which arguments?—they re-create in writing the entire deliberation, down to the last acclamation.

To provide detailed records requires a protocol *technique* that can keep up with the spoken word. Its origins reputedly lie with Cicero, who had ordered four senators with fast and proficient handwriting to record the questioning of the Catilinian conspirators. Legend has it that when the consul opened with his famous question, "*Quousque tandem abutere, Catilina, patientia nostra?*" the initials *q-p-n* of the impatient inquiry became the first signs ever to be rendered in speedwriting. One of Cicero's private secretaries, the freed slave Marcus Tullius Tiro, developed a system of speedwriting—that is, a tachygraphic synchronization of speech and writing—that was named after him: Tironic notes. It worked by reducing words to single letters, an abbreviation of speech that not only allowed takers of minutes to keep up with the speed of senatorial speech but also equaled the transmission speed of the empire as a whole: according to one chronicler of stenography, speed writing arose with the empire, and when the latter declined, it too passed away.[41]

To synchronize speech and writing, Tiro's system called for a surface that does not impede the flow of writing. Avoiding unruly materials like papyrus, stone, or wood, the speedwriters or *exceptores* responsible for files and protocols drew their letters in wax, which, in Quintilian's words, puts up as little resistance to inscribing as it does to erasing, and hence "is the only way of ensuring real, deep-seated progress," as opposed to slow writing, which "delays thought."[42] The stenograms etched in wax were erased using the blunt, rounded edge of a stylus that sometimes was shaped like a spatula, thus enabling a new round of writing. The two ends embody the complementary acts of producing and canceling letters (*stilum vertere*). "[A] pointed stilus scratches the surface, the depressions upon which constitute 'the writing,'"[43] but according to the rhetoric specialist Quintilian, "It is as active as it ever is when it scratches something out."[44] With one sharp and one blunt end, the stylus unites writing and erasing, those two fundamental chancery operations, in *one* instrument. Herein lies an analogy to the workings of memory: just as the Greek verb *hypomnematizesthai* equates filing and remembering, its opposite, *exaleíphein,* combines a practical act and a function of memory by referring both to forgetting and wiping off.

The *metroon*, the building that housed the state archive of ancient Athens, was the site at which a democracy founded on amnesia enacted its regulated forgetting.[45] The connection between obliteration and oblivion is immediately evident when *stelai* are destroyed, engraved legal texts are chiseled out, or limestone walls whitewashed and thus removed from memory.[46] The traces of this erasure are a reminder of what a memory- or, rather, archive-centered culture is prone to forget: that it rests on all manners of cancellation. Ever since Plato, philosophy has used the wax tablet to illustrate the way forgetting enables memory. The unlimited storage capacity of the *tabuli* corresponds to the storage capacity of human memory; the erasure on the planar, destructible wax surface is equated with forgetting. Finally, Freud's reference to wax tablets as models of the subconscious, which serves to illustrate that the obliterating psychic act is merely superficial because memory traces are engraved in the deeper realms of memory, also has its equivalent in the real medium: in the traces that remain on the *tabuli*, on the wood or the lower wax layers, which, if held under light, may still be deciphered.[47]

What psychoanalysis and deconstructionist philosophy "inscribe" into the model of the trace is, when observed in light of changing filing technologies, the distinction between two mutually constitutive forms of writing: an erasable writing on wax tablets and its transcription into a durable inscription.[48] The latter can attain validation and truth functions because it is preceded by a canceled ur-writing that has been rendered illegible. The doubling of writing into draft and clean copy puts an end to the time of the magistrates, with its emphasis on pure transmission without duplicates. Based on the technique of *acta facere*, writing inscribes itself into the sphere of the force of law. With the taking of minutes, the law designs its own truth of reality. What Paul de Man, from a linguistic point of view, termed a "fact of language"[49] could from a media-theoretical perspective be applied to the act of taking notes: it is a performative, fact-producing act. From a media-technological point of view, the synonymous use of "acts" and "*taking note [prendre acte]* of the fact,*"*[50] as performed by Derrida in "Acts," his reading of Paul de Man, is perfectly admissible.

The performative, reality-producing operation of putting things on file brings to mind the saying *Quod non est in actis non est in mundo*. There is no evidence that it was already current in Rome; the choice of words appears to indicate a medieval origin. In any case, the proverb crops up in various literary and judicial texts referring to the written legal foundation for Roman court proceedings. It is only in the fourth century, however, that the latter becomes the leitmotif of bureaucratic rule. The free-floating sentence resembles a rumor. It is known, but nobody can say how it got there. The double negation—*not* in the world and *not* on file—succinctly summarizes the performative operation of the law in constructing reality. Phrased positively, reality is what is found in files. Any attempt to weaken the file-world, therefore, is obliged to show that files and world do *not* coincide. As indicated by the double negation, files reverse the burden of proof and thus resemble the effects of Bartleby's famous formula. It is up to the world to prove that something which is not on file indeed exists. However, it is impossible to prove the nonexistence of something. Which reality is strong enough to contradict files, if files alone pave the legally acceptable way to reality? As protocols of reality, they consume everything outside the law. The law operates not *in mundo* but in the medium of literality; it believes only what is written—more precisely, what it has itself written down. This is the simple yet highly effective mechanism of public belief (*publica fides*) in minutes. With the compilation of a file, a truth attains a common status; it becomes generally valid. Conversely, only within the sphere of the law can it be proven that a file is incorrect. There has to be something wrong with the formal prerequisites that authenticate a protocol. In terms of speech act theory, there have to be grounds that block a successful speech act—for instance, insufficient competence to produce a valid protocol. The world, or *mundus*, does not have a dissenting voice; it has to bow to file performances.

But if only what is on file is in the world, then destroying said files will suffice to erase any unwanted reality. In the final years of senate rule preceding the empire, entire consulates were wiped from history by destroying all their records. One such case of *damnatio memoriae* concerned the *acta principis* of Julius Caesar. Their destruction was designed to complete the assassination, that is, to go beyond the mere physical extinction by attempting to remove all the political effects of Caesar's rule not only from history but also from memory. This power to undo an entire consulate was also used by Emperor Hadrian. Pursuant to an amnesty he had granted, he ordered the public burning of all the tax records from the previous administration.

Scrinia: File Spaces

With the dominance of written acts introduced by the senate's handling of records, record-keeping became an issue. And here one can observe how simple storage turned gradually into storage with a retrieval function, how the archive gave rise to the office.

The material base of the Roman administration gradually took shape in the *Aerarium*, the principal archive located in the vicinity of the Capitoline Hill. It was the resting counterpole of the circulating documents. Ever since the early days of the Republic, it had housed precious metals, reserve funds for soldiers' pay, insignia, valuable medicinal concoctions, senate resolutions, and scrolls in special file racks—in short, everything that was counted among the riches of the empire. The *Aerarium*, the state treasury, was a holy site, part of a temple dedicated to the god Saturn, to whom the invention of writing and of external order were ascribed. The precious texts, however, were not deposited in the treasury to be retrieved; there were no access facilities. The *Aerarium* was a repository that guarded a potential referent. It existed in order to assure the empire that it could take stock of its own treasures. This imperial stockpiling obeyed an economy of deferral. A politics of reserve turned the Temple of Saturn into the Fort Knox of the Roman Empire, whose steady stream of orders was increasingly also covered by file reserves in the currency of letters.

Once files are removed from circulation and brought to a specially designated repository, their function fundamentally changes. With their transfer to the capitoline main archive, notebooks turned into *monumenta publica*. They became public mementos—in Greek, *archeon*—which acted as a reminder that Rome had a past; and the more the empire sought to legitimize itself through recourse to its history, the more important files became. Livy, who was instrumental in providing Rome with a genealogy, observed that following the Punic Wars more files found their way into the archives than before. The archival work in the aftermath of destruction was a state-sponsored politics with the past, an official instruction to forget and remember. "For the archive is . . . the retroactive control of the contingent."[51] It interrupts the flow of command and renders files out of date, thus creating a body of texts that can be addressed as a *monument* of the past. To put a stop to continuous recording is to start the process of securing the inventory of the law and usher in a new phase in which files are monumentalized. It is no longer the prerogative of the magistrates to compile files, to prepare and store copies, and to refer to them or not. The law is no longer a chance product resulting from a mixture of opportunity and extant or retrieved records. According to the ideal of the archive, the law is the sum of all files on record. They are the capital of the law.

To hoard the precious raw material of records like a treasure, officials had to be dispossessed. The archive could only become a functional state agency once files were deemed government property and private collections were transferred to public repositories. As long as there were no regulations in place, it seemed quite natural that files belonged to those who compiled them. Every magistrate kept his own record, which subsequently became part of his possessions and was at his disposal. It was customary for an official to retain ownership of his files even after his term in office was over, and to use them at home "to instruct his sons and grandsons."[52] The decisive change occurred in 78–79 BC, when the *Tabularium* on the Capitoline Hill became the first official archive building. From now on, office holders were required to turn in their records at the conclusion of their tenure, and a quaestor would incorporate them into the archives according to when they were submitted. Given that files were arranged by term of office, the temporal intervals turned into spatial, archeo-archival strata. This "stratified law"[53] consisted of layers of archived files that, in effect, spatialized administration. Henceforward, archival matters recorded the expansive movements of the empire. The "official directories, lists, tables and charts stored in the imperial archive . . . [become] increasingly diverse, [because] the territorial changes of the empire . . . entail revisions and renovations."[54] More profoundly, the territorialization of the empire was an effect of archiving, that is, of immobilizing files. The streams of records flowing into the capitoline archive served to align the ramified net of transmissions that traversed Rome during the rule of the magistrate toward its center: "The capitol, the most important sacred site, is the center of Rome; the Forum Romanum with the government and administrative offices are spread out in the center of the city; there, in the Temple of Saturn, is the state treasury, the *aerarium*; there, too, Augustus erected the *milliarium aureum*, the Golden Milestone, which indicated the distances between Rome and the other principal cities of the empire."[55] The image of the great charioteer vividly captures how the monopoly of files brought about this centering on Rome: the messengers and letters sent out from Rome inevitably produced "in those who held in their hands the many threads that reached into the empire the need to develop means to oversee their many reins. Since only one had the power to do so, the records necessary for the various branches of government were united as imperial files in one archive or office."[56]

Archive or office: one merges into the other, for in both cases the simple fact of storage generates work with and on that which has been stored. The file stacks in the Tabularium turned into a structure with access facilities; the symbolic or virtual reference to a treasure of old texts was replaced by the real access to numbered files enabling specific, target-oriented searches that no longer were subject to chance. Public records facilitated a file-based administration—in other words, a bureaucracy. Max Weber has formulated in principle what the large-scale expropriation files in 77–78 BC enacted in practice: the emergence of genuinely modern forms of administration "goes hand in hand with the concentration of the material means of management."[57] Put the other way, this means that expropriated, socialized files deposited in archives shaped governmental administration in the modern sense of the word. No office without an archive, no imperial chancery without a Tabularium. Once the contours of the former emerged, the legal and administrative historians who had never gotten a firm grasp on what the magistrates were doing finally en-

countered familiar concepts that enabled them to analyze Roman administration. Recognizing modern bureaucratic forms shapes the research
into ancient times; and the following remarks, too, depend on this to
approximate imperial administration.

On the whole, the archival principle of keeping files in one place had a
territorializing effect on the administration of the empire. While the official duties of the magistrates and the deliberations of the senate were conducted in changing buildings and on outdoor stages, the administration
of the principate was restricted to functionally defined, closed spaces that
were supposed to be permanently accessible by means of "letterboxes."[58]
An administration that, with its ceremonial readings and translation ritu-
als, conveyed an image of imperial grandeur in earlier days was transformed into a survey facility. The new, firmly situated chanceries provided
a vectorial alignment to the expansive movements of the empire. The *imperium* (that is, the word of command) was disseminated "by the central
organs of administration . . . throughout the entire Roman Empire by
way of innumerable channels."[59] The reins gathered in the hands of the
charioteer are centralized transmission channels. To be sure, until the age
of Diocletian, imperial commands were issued in the shape of letters, just
as in the days of the magistrates, but now these letters were also filed in
the archives, which, as Jack Goody has pointed out, required the quint-
essentially bureaucrat act of "making a copy."[60] Since drafts are hardly
suited for storage, a copy was made and handed over to the archive, where
the individual items were glued together.

There is only one difference between the dispatched letters and the
stored document: "A tablet or a papyrus with an imperial decree that ends
with a final salutation indicates that the text derives from a communication that was received by an addressee; a tablet or a papyrus ending with
a *rescripsi* (*scripsi*) is taken from the imperial chancery in Rome."[61] Salutation instead of notation: this minimal difference between transmitted and
stored version structured the work of the capitol's chancery. Circulating
and depositing, dispatching and hoarding, copying and pasting turned
into complementary, correlated operations whose institutional equiva-
lents were the chancery and the archive. Letters corresponded "to imperial
commands put down in files."[62] To guarantee that dispatched commands
and deposited files were identical, letters were closed, folded, and then
sown through or wrapped with a thread whose end was sealed. It is easy
to see how "such letters soon turned into state secrets."[63] The sealing of

letters severed the link between the act and the object of transmission: messenger and message, envoy and missive go their separate ways. Letters were no longer automatically communicated by public reading; delivering, reading out loud, and translating no longer necessarily followed each other. Sealed letters were meant for silent reading. Reading them out loud was an additional operation, not—as in former days—just another stage of one and the same transaction. The prefect to whom a letter was addressed transformed the content rather than its exact wording into a command to his audience.

Codex: File Out of Files

JUSTINIAN'S CODIFICATION

The primacy of legislation over translation that gradually emerged during Diocletian's reign entails a concept of the law not as a response to queries but as something constituted and—literally and metaphorically—laid down. The legal notion of *leges generales* is associated with Galla Placida (daughter of Theodosius I, wife of Constantius III, and last regent of Rome on behalf of her son Valentinian), whose colorful biography straddling the eastern and western portions of the empire mirrored the complications arising from the move of the imperial capitol from Rome to Constantinople. After the dominance of imperial legislation had put an end to the expansive Roman politics of transmission, the policy of Emperor Constantine had been dedicated to regaining lost territories by reestablishing and renewing imperial conditions of existence. The move east in 324 that relocated Rome to the geographically more advantageous, Greek-speaking community of *Byzantion* created the difference necessary to revive the stagnant transmissions. On its own, however, this move away from a pagan Rome did not result in a *translatio imperii*. The mere relocation of a Latin chancery into territory where Greek is spoken did not in itself amount to a new translation agency. It was to take centuries before a legal renovation managed to subject reconquered territories, including those in North Africa, to Roman law.

In the sixth century, Emperor Justinian's politics of translation reenacted Constantine's geopolitical transfer on a textual terrain. It was by virtue of relatinizing the East, a kind of belated linguistic transfer, that Roman law, spreading in tandem with the Latin language, was able to assert itself. Around 535, Justinian ordered the East Roman chanceries (which effectively had already switched to Greek) to employ Latin as their official second language. Once again, interlinguality was a necessary ingredient of the legal transmission structure. Furthermore, by pursuing a gigantic compilation project that encompassed the entire legal repository of the old empire, Justinian sought to code and codify Byzantium according to its Western heritage. The empire's Byzantine future, in short, was to be found in its Roman past. Like so many rulers after him, the emperor was chasing the "old jurist's dream"[64] of the *unus liber comprehensus*. It is the dream of a closure of the law that puts an end to the volatile proliferation of files, the vision of the completion of the law in a single codex that once and for all regulates what is to be regulated and provides a complete overview over all the movements of files. In the words of the panoptician Jeremy Bentham, it is the desire for a *General View of a Complete Code of Laws*.[65]

From his seat in the eastern half of the Roman Empire, Justinian issued the instruction to codify the legacy of the Western half. The goal was not to immediately put to use these codifications; they were, after all, primarily written in Latin and hence of little value to a Byzantine chancery operating in Greek. Rather, Justinian's reconstruction project benefited from a virtual reference to Rome as an absolute referent that legitimized power. Once more, the switch between languages moved an act of translation into the center of legal transmission. The material from which the new code of law for the old empire was to be constructed was as heterogeneous as the empire itself. The politics of reconstruction drew on legal statements, comments, and opinions, on textbooks and primers that had been handed down by scribbling students, as well as on the data pool of the imperial chanceries in Rome—that is, on all the records that had survived the mayhem of tribal migrations and the destruction of the main Roman archive because they had been transcribed over the course of two or three centuries. But instead of adding yet another layer of copies for the purpose of preservation, the Justinian codification aimed at a radical reordering of the transmitted material. Its goal was nothing less than an entirely new arrangement of old legal texts. An ongoing story was to be refashioned by means of a switch from scrolls to codex—and that, after all, is the meaning of codification. A loose chain of tradition that boasted no fixed reference, that had neither beginning nor end, was to be terminated. This file made out of files obliterated the very principle of files and installed a basis for the force of law that was removed from, and immune to, the changing constellations of power. The codification inaugurated a new economy of texts. It was no longer a matter of unruly records constantly eroding and invalidating each other; rather, their prescribed reduction created a stable legal foundation.

Justinian entrusted the selection and arrangement of the transmitted material to the jurist Tribonian who, as the *quaestor sacri palatii*, the official in charge of the main archive, happened to be the empire's supreme supervisor of records. The first result of Tribonian's imperial inventory was the *Codex Justinianus*. To the satisfaction of the emperor, this official compilation of laws—a file made out of files—managed to bring "into perfect harmony the Imperial Constitutions hitherto involved in confusion."[66] Two years later, at the instigation of the chief codifier, the harmonizing enterprise was expanded. Tribonian supervised the edition of the Digest, which, as already indicated by its name, aimed to order things by abbreviating and arranging the bewildering confusion of countless legal texts, opinions (*sententiae*), and briefs responding to real or fictitious queries (*responsae*), as well as judicial teaching matter authored by various legal experts into a closed opus. The command to do so appears in the preface of the book: "You shall divide the entire law into fifty books, and into a certain number of titles following, as far as may be convenient for you, the arrangement of Our Code, as well as that of the Perpetual Edict [*Edictum perpetuum*], so that nothing may be omitted from the above mentioned collection; and that all the ancient law which has been in a confused condition for almost fourteen hundred years shall be embraced in the said fifty books, and this ancient law, purified by Us [*a nobis purgatum*] shall be, so to speak, surrounded by a wall, and shall have nothing beyond it."[67] The intial command conjures up the phantasm of a pure law that increasingly has been defiled by the incessant growth of legal texts. Codifiers act as purifiers, as the champions of a monotheistically structured law that allows no other laws save those which it has codified itself. This notion of contamination guides the textbook for law students that bears the name *Institutes*. The law has been cleansed of old stories, *ab antiquis fabulis*, to ensure that henceforward students "may absorb nothing that is useless or incorrect, but whatever is in accordance with reason in all things," be it principles that have always been in use or "those which, after having been obscured by disuse, have been illuminated once more by Imperial restoration."[68] Against old stories and rivers of files that never run dry, against whole oceans of texts, a dam is erected by industrious codifiers. It interrupts the transmissions made up of references and deletions, usage and oblivion, updating and destroying.

The image of the wall employed by Justinian must have made immediate sense to anybody residing in Constantinople around 530 AD. More
than one wall was being erected; the whole city resembled a construction
site. At the same time as the textual debris of old scripts was being used
like a "quarry for the creation of a new code of law,"[69] the ruins of the
Theodosian church destroyed in the Nika revolt were recycled for the construction of the Hagia Sophia. Both works turned out to be archetypes:
the Hagia Sophia would become the blueprint for all Christian cupola
churches, the Digest the basic model of all occidental codes of law. The
latter, a book made up of quotes, adopted the most effective technique
of codification to turn into the work of reference par excellence. The final reference to the abundance of transmitted law consisted in specifying
which legal text or briefs the excerpted reference is from. After that, however, the quote devours the quoted, which is precisely what researchers
interested in tracing interpolations are trying to undo. But all nonquoted
convolutes inevitably fade into oblivion once their material carriers decompose. After that, there is only the Digest left to quote from.

The wall designed to surround the symbolic order of the law once the
codification is complete turns everything outside into rubbish and file
trash. What has been excreted from the procedure of incorporation or
digestion can only be registered numerically, not according to its content.
When explaining how the compilation of the Digest processed such huge
numbers of texts, Friedrich Bluhme, a student of the great nineteenth-
century jurist Friedrich Carl von Savigny, regarded the records handled by
Tribonian's committee as a mere *mass* that was divided into three separate
submasses, which in turn were handed over to three separate subcom-
mittees. Of the two thousand books analyzed and evaluated by the well-
organized committee over the course of three years, one-twentieth—that
is, 150,000 lines—made it into the Digest. A meager yield, it would seem,
but by no means insignificant. The compilation survived the test of time.
A booty of war and reading, it will cast its spell not only on humanist
pilgrims but also on succeeding generations of jurists.

Following their codification, the files return to the domain of the real.
The masses of texts could only be understood as long as they were used.
The practical knowledge of the chanceries, that is, the tacit knowledge of
how to use files (which had already been fading in the Byzantine chancery), fell into complete disuse because the sequential mode of transmission from file to file was interrupted. Files became unintelligible, incom-

prehensible, inexpressive. Their details were rendered absurd, and their curtness was nothing less than baffling, as anybody knows who has ever tried to read a file that records events he was not privy to. Integrated reading operators now perform what was once the function of usage- and time-specific insider codes. The legal text is now a whole. Dividing the Digest into fifty numbered books allowed the reader to access any desired passage without having to draw on the old tacit knowledge of how to use the texts. By arranging the books according to their titles and chapters, the Digest was transformed into a reference work decoupled from its material, scriptographic basis. Even before the advent of further, typographic standardizations, such as standardized font and numbered copies, this identical arrangement of all the copies allowed for cross-references between the copies. Facilitating access to any passage in any copy (and not just to those at the beginning of a scroll) was the goal of codification.

THE LAW OF TRANSLATION

Emperor Justinian's order to edit the materials that went into the Digest specified that they were to be published as if from their very first appearance they had been transmitted unaltered: *quasi ab initio scriptum.*[70] For Tribonian, the chief redactor, and his sixteen collaborators, this meant they had to treat the many diverse texts of Roman law in exactly the same way, regardless of how they were being used and when they had come about. The principles governing the arrangement of the codex turned the many heterogeneous archeo-archival layers of the law into a comprehensive repository of the old empire, in which everything that had ever been regulated or examined existed simultaneously on one level without contradicting or annulling anything else. The fiction of a holistic legal reservoir, however, the denial of the way new files pushed aside old ones, coupled with the desire to synchronically read the obsolete, forgotten, and unused texts, created a new problem that had not existed in the earlier time of files: the empire's multiplicity of signs. If forgotten texts are to be invested with force of law, redundancies and contradictions become inevitable. Put in modern terms, the law is plagued by problems of compatibility. Praetorian edicts and imperial rescripts were replete with *perversiones* and *confusio*, they were brimming with distortions and perplexities that had to be excised to establish a homogenous text. Hence the Tribonian committee was given comprehensive authority to purge and edit texts—that is, it was authorized to interpolate: the unnecessary was to be weeded out, repetitions were to be avoided, and contradictions to be smoothed over. The same applied to the preparation of the Codex as textbook; the goal was to "supply an unbroken and consistent apology of a canonic text."[71] Techniques of interpolation prepare heterogeneous legal texts for eternity by transforming them into a universal reference system for the law. "In a kind of montage, fragments [were rewritten] into a continuous text"[72] made up of chains and catena. An empire that operates on the basis of discontinuous files is homogenized into a closed legal text; its diachronic structure is translated into the synchronicity of a single text.

Whereas the public reading of an order produced unanimity, the written law allowed for differing interpretations. The codex put an end to the imperial practice of ongoing commentary, renewal, and replacement, thereby turning translation exercises into problems of interpretation. Once Rome's *fabulae antiquae* were translated into law, the act of interpreting attained a stature that is not far from the importance it enjoys today. Every translation of a fixed immutable legal text is also an interpretation, but to maintain a distinction between interlingual and interpretive translations, antiquity already mobilized the notion of the immutability of scripture later used by Kafka's priest to invalidate K.'s interpretive attempts. Writing turns into a barrier that separates it from mere opinion. It separates law from translation, just as it draws a line between the legal text and its commentary. From a purely media-technological point of view a codex is just a file composed of files, but from a legal perspective, it is a code of law which demands that we acknowledge the immutability of writing. This respect for the letter of the law implies that interpreting is no longer tantamount to rewriting, and that commentaries must be relegated to a different page. But evidently these security precautions were deemed insufficient. Nothing, it appears, scared codifiers more than the prospect of invasive opinions disfiguring their beautiful rulebooks. Among their greatest fears was that exposing contradictions would undermine their authority, and that commentaries might even be abused for spreading heresies. Justinian and, in his wake, later codifiers and legislators acted like thieves bent on protecting their loot from other thieves: they deprived the legal experts of all power over the compilation by regularizing, and if need be even prohibiting, interpretations. And should explanations nonetheless be permitted, in most cases only *one* authentic interpretation would be acknowledged.

In bi- or multilingual texts, the problem of maintaining control over commentaries becomes more pronounced because translations imperceptibly merge into interpretations. Given that the Latin version of the Digest was in part translated into Greek, further barriers became necessary to separate law from commentary. Comparisons revealed that every translation ran the risk of deviating from, distorting, or falsifying the Latin version that had been installed as the original text. Whereas translation and translatability had been indispensable for the Roman Empire, they turned into a precarious venture for Byzantium. To lessen the risk, the translations themselves became objects of legislation. In its bilingual introductory section, the Digest defines the rules that govern permissible forms of translation. Both the Greek and Latin versions state that a translation may contain neither more nor less than the original, which is why it must follow the order and sequence of the Latin words: "*Nisi tantum si velit eas in Graecam vocem transformare sub eodem oridine eaque consequentia, sub qua et voces Romanae positae sunt (hoc quod Graeci katà póda dicunt)*" (Unless someone may wish to translate them into the Greek, [then] it must be done in the same order and the same sequence in which the Roman words appear [what the Greeks call *katà póda*] or "according to the foot").[73] This directive not only inscribes the primacy of Latin, but its emphasis on literality also implies the postulate that there is indeed such a thing as a correct translation. Its main criterion is the adherence to the chancery's base unit "word for word" or, to provide a different translation for *katà póda*, "one foot after the other" or "step for step."

Katà póda was the sequence of steps prescribed by Justinian to his translators. The obligation to remain faithful to the word demanded the same attitude that Benjamin expected from translators. Rather than search for syntagmas or analogical constructions, they are to follow the *ordo* and *consequentia* of a sentence: "This may be achieved, above all, by a literal rendering of the syntax which proves words rather than sentences to be the primary element of the translator."[74] The sentences that are to be rendered into another language are treated by the translator as if they had already been translated. The individual syntactic elements, then, can be literally translated back into the first language. According to Benjamin's theory, the law that governs Justinian's translation into Greek may be understood as the result of a translation, as the product of a subdivision of texts into smaller units and their recombination into a codex. But while Benjamin ponders the inscrutability of the act of translating, the Justinian decree simply states that it has been carried out successfully. The official translation is from a legal point of view the correct one. Nowhere is Justinian's emphasis on literal translation more obvious than in the Latin introduction to the translation, which leaves the crucial Greek instruction untranslated: "Hoc quod Graeci *katà póda* dicunt [what the Greeks call *katà póda*]." Here, the rule itself is, as it were, its first application: the most literal translation is an omitted one. Just as the Latin introduction leaves the Greek word in the original, many Greek interpretations by Eastern Roman legal specialists leave certain Latin terms untranslated, thus attesting that a number of Roman legal institutions have no Greek counterpart. But what is untranslatable is all the more capable of asserting itself as law. Nontranslated words convey the attached legal institutes as immediately and literally as possible.

Apart from the *katà póda* rule, the constitution introducing the Digest contains two further translation rules. Translators are allowed to make use of the *paratitla*, a collection of parallel passages, and the indices—that is, verbatim summaries of the compilation's content. Both act as additional barriers to further proliferation of legal texts by providing discrete bodies of text that facilitate legal references. According to the German legal historian Franz Wieacker, "In the hand of the compilators the index . . . controls inventory and edition."[75] In addition, there is a ban on adding to the text by way of commentaries as well as on shortening it by an "obscure method of abbreviation"[76] that could contain subversive messages. Rulers have never approved of cryptographic alphabets that they themselves did not authorize. These translation rules have to be followed; those violating them will be punished for falsifying imperial laws. Finally, those who deviate from the prescribed paths of translation so as to spread heresies (such as Judaism) risk corporeal and even capital punishment.

One of Justinian's amendments to the Digest, Novella 146—which, according to Pierre Legendre, protects the Christian principle of reason from the uncontrollable movements of the disseminating Jewish signifiers[77]—is a further law that guards against mere analogous translation and uncontrolled interpretation. It is concerned not with the law but with the language of cult and religion. It initially refers to the Septuagint, which for reasons of faith had to be considered a successful word-for-word translation. Proof of this is the well-known linguistic miracle according to which seventy translations made independently of each other were all identical. Novella 146 turns this miracle into a law. It allows for the possibility of correct translations by letting the Greek and Latin versions stand next to the Hebrew Old Testament, and it outlaws those that could covertly spread heresies.

NOVELLAS

Novella 146 represents a new type of law: the amendment. Novellas complement Justinian's codification project. Whereas the codification bears witness (*testimonium*) to the past, amendments make reference to the present, which allows for a reconciliation between the two antagonistic functions of the law, preservation and updating. Codifications governed by the *katà póda* rule had a conserving effect. The very same strict translation rules that protected the body of work later united into the *Corpus Iuris* from all nonliteral translations and nonrational commentaries also gradually rendered the *Corpus* obsolete. Interpretation techniques that would enable an updated adaptation of the codified material were lacking in Byzantium; hence it became necessary to follow the creation of the Roman legal repository with its Byzantine amendment. Justinian had already, during the preparation of the codex, anticipated the necessity to adapt to changed circumstances and cautioned in the Digest: "But for the reason that only divine things are perfect, and that it is a characteristic of human jurisprudence to be always indefinitely extending, and that there is nothing in it which can endure forever . . . [w]e expect that certain matters may subsequently arise which, up to this time, have not been included in the restraints of the law."[78] Thus from the very beginning the codification is subject to the caveat that everything that has been codified may have to be temporalized. In tandem with the immortalization of the law, legal amendments will effect the permanent renovation of the empire. Amendments do not create a law (*legem ponere*), they clothe it in contemporary garments, which is why they refer to the "old" codification. This reference to Rome provides amendments with a noncontingent origin, while simultaneously allowing them to act in innovative ways without being subject to the charge of eroding the state. By adopting the Roman dating system in Latin letters, the amendments of the eastern empire literally inscribe themselves into the codified western empire. Rome becomes a datum for Byzantium.

Novellas contain fewer innovations than their name suggests. They frequently merely repeat in Greek the constitutions of late Roman emperors. The novelty does not reside in what the amendments regulate but in their framework. They form a contrast to the codification, but that is how they create the immortal body of the law. They are not written in Latin, and they are not compiled in legal codices; instead they are to be found in files that can be updated indefinitely "un accroisement indefini [an unlimited accumulation],"[79] which, much like a loose-leaf collection, can be rearranged according to usage. Their validity is not tied to any closed codex; they are isolated and thus in principle already approximate abstract law. Appeals to "the vicissitudes of life"[80] and other such formulas replace the reference to concrete issues; specific addresses yield to general procla-mations "*ad populum urbis Constantinopolitane et ad omnes provinciales*,"[81] or, even more unspecific, to "all the subjects, as many as there may be in the East, as many be shone upon by the setting sun, and as many as may reside in both directions."[82]

Once an address no longer entails a direct command to communicate a letter, the worry whether or not a missive has been delivered to an indi-vidual address turns into the question whether or not it will meet with the acceptance of the general public. To achieve the latter, laws directed at all subjects "are not written in our language but in commonly used Greek, so that it will be known, and easily understandable, to all."[83] It is this pop-ularization that makes the novellas innovative. Unlike commands, laws addressed *ad populum* have to tell stories to communicate their mean-ing. These preambles, called *prooimia*, precede the amendments. In or-nate—and later stereotypical—fashion they praise the legislator's motives; no doubt the ease with which parchment can be inscribed encourages such stylistic prolixity. The official responsible for the stylization is the quaestor; he is not only in charge of the archives but, as the "depart-ment head linking the scrinia to the emperor,"[84] he also acts as a media-tor between the chancery and the highest authority. Whatever legal ex-perts "passed on to him, he translated into a language with public appeal, which, as long as it correctly reproduced the content, was neither obliged nor even allowed to pay any consideration to legal terminology, since the latter was not deemed capable of improving the ways in which subjects regarded the authorities."[85] It is at this intersection that commands issued by the chancery turn into tales: law becomes literature. During the age of Boccaccio, legal *novellae* turn into literary novellas, which serves to prove that in law as well as literature, novellas are news, news that give notice of the eternal.

§ 3   From Documents to Records

From the sixth century on, Europe witnessed a widespread "decline of public record-taking":[1] Roman chanceries, though retained by the Ostrogoths under Odoacer, disappeared from Gaul, Spain, and Africa. Following the conquest of Alexandria, imperial papyrus imports ground to a halt, literacy decreased, and especially in the Visigothic empire, familiarity with Roman law started to fade away. It was only on papyrus and parchment that a certain legal expertise managed to survive, combined with a knowledge of how chanceries operated. Its transmission was in no small measure due to the former senator and imperial minister Cassiodor (app. 485–580). His policies regarding Germanic tribal migrations may have met with little success, yet as a highly effective *praefectus praetorius* of the Ostrogoth chancery, he developed his own network for the transcription of Roman law and Christian literature. But though many texts were passed on, they did not contain the chanceries' tacit knowledge. Most of what was known about the latter was handed down as part of the *gesta municipalia*. The form for imperial rescripts, with which the late Roman chancery had operated, was also part of the continuing tradition. It programmed successive generations on how to apply the law. Its transmission helped Roman law survive the fall of the Roman Empire, but it slowly turned into a different type of legal text: the document.[2]

The practice of ruling with documents, inaugurated by the Visigoths and continued by the Franks, displaced the old record-based regimen inherited from Rome, with the shift from "the age of records to that of documents"[3] concluding in the twelfth century. Documents follow a different logic than do records. What they proclaim counts for all ages—*ad perpetuam rei memoriam,* to quote a customary formula on diplomas. Their function was to preserve, not to transmit. They were not stored in any central repository, for they stored themselves. Documents follow a distributive mode; they are kept by the recipient. A mobile staff of messenger-scribes (*referendarii*), as deployed in the Merovingian empire, distributed the directive documents. Similarly, Carolingian capitularies were "flying leaflets"[4] that were not tied to a stationary point of dissemination; they circulated by means of ambulant *missi*. And since none of these texts was centrally registered, nobody—as Charlemagne complained—was able to keep track of the missives and directives that had been issued. No surprise, then, that from the ninth century on, attempts were made to compile the flying leaflets.

Documents or certificates differ conspicuously from records by their representative use of writing. They are not designed for any particular administrative use; rather, they are made to impress. Their letters are signs of power; their very appearance represents the authority of the issuer. The layout of a document is a "gesture of power."[5] Disregarding all aesthetic concerns related to typeface, page format, and placement of letters, it is the prestigiousness of the signs alone that determines the size and arrangement of the letters on a document. The more mysterious the signs, the more imposing the gesture. Hence legibility is of little concern to such "heraldically staged texts."[6] Diplomas are first and foremost trinkets, made by hand out of precious materials. They are produced in specialized writing shops that had little in common with the legal *and* scriptographic agencies of the chancery. Thus the disappearance of the chancery was a certain indication of the looming epoch of documents. Ornamental writing also served to certify the document. Once there were no longer any chanceries that could authenticate issued writs, the latter had to compensate for this absence by means of an elaborate semiotics. The certificates vouched for themselves; they guaranteed their own correctness by means of a semiotic code designed to enforce validity. In other words, writs and documents relocate chancery functions inside a text.

As a result, formats—developed by the chanceries—turned into formalities endowed with legal force. Seal and signature, writing surface, and letter shape—all of which had been administrative practicalities during the Roman Empire—now vouched for the authenticity of a piece of writing. Forms designed by the Roman administration for economic reasons turned into a formal requirement. The seal, too, changed its function: it was no longer a sealant but a sign of certification. Unlike letters, certificates no longer closed with an administrative note but rather with the name of the issuer or scribe placed underneath the concluding salutation. In due course, this addition of the name turned into the most important item; handwritten signatures may be found on almost all medieval certificates. The signature emerges as one of the most important operators attesting to the binding force of documented law, making it the equivalent of the modern signature.

To the degree that their unchanging parts are endowed with authenticating force, documents emancipate themselves from the issuer. "Royal writs . . . attain . . . their own value independent of legal and administrative procedures."[7] But it is a problematic independence. Once the document is no longer coupled to the agency that produced it, forgeries are more likely to occur, for as long as certain formalities are observed, writs and certificates can be manufactured anywhere. The papal chancery was the first to react to mistakes and imitations, introducing fixed formats and laying down guidelines detailing how such documents were to be produced. Hence preventive measures rather than economic considerations initiated administrative formalization. Because the formal specifications were part of the chancery's secret knowledge, it was very difficult to adhere to them when producing nonauthorized reproduction: The mistakes of the copyist convict the forger. Given the vagueness of the instructions, however, the falsifying power of formal requirements did not amount to much. The effects of the falsifications, which derived from the autonomous validity of documents, were stronger. The numerous writs lacking issuer or origin certified rights and possessions by invoking customs, conventions, or practice. In a court of law, these documents had probative force. Whole centuries created ownership and law by means of allegedly age-old titles. Diplomatics speaks of "determining forgeries."[8] The fact that it is impossible to distinguish between forged and legitimate documents, as long as they authenticate themselves without any recourse to external criteria, forces historians to simply accept the validity of such documents. For Ernst H. Kantorowicz, the historian of juridical medieval fictions, it was therefore a given "that misunderstandings—just like forgeries—can be historical facts of the first order, which in themselves make history."[9]

To compile a history of these fact-creating *malentendus* and *malfaçons* on writs and charters is one thing; it is yet another thing to put history on trial for these forgeries. In 1681 Jean Mabillon published his *De re diplomatica*, which aimed to put an end to document-based fictions and to introduce clear, unambiguous distinctions into the hitherto more or less accepted smooth transition from "factifying" to falsifying and forging. The critique of documents gave rise to diplomatics, a new discipline whose only goal is to provide infallible and legally accepted criteria for determining whether or not documents have been forged. Toward the end of the nineteenth century, diplomatics was turned into a veritable science. Its exclusive object of research is documents, including those that did not originate in the early medieval heyday of document creation. Observers are struck by the fact, however, that there is no corresponding science that dedicates itself to systematically analyzing records, either from the seventeenth or the nineteenth century. Despite their sheer numbers and their influential role in European state politics, files lead a shadowy existence. In his standard account, Johannes Papritz—who as director of the Prussian Archives was acutely aware of the quantity of archived files and, as the official in charge of the Reich index that registered all Jews living under National Socialism, was bound to know something about their lethal power—expressed his astonishment over the discrepancy between extensively researched documents and mostly ignored files: "The question arises how it . . . came about that documents . . . , which in comparison to the millions of files resting in German archives constitute no more than a small minority, were granted the privileged status of a special archival genre."[10] The answer appears obvious: diplomatics subjects documents to the binary code of true or false, *veri ac falsi*, thereby establishing a scientific basis for its research. Files, by contrast, are subject neither to formal instructions nor to criteria of authenticity. They proliferate and decay, but they do not conform to a binary scheme.

Any research that dedicates itself to establishing the authenticity of a text, as well as any historiographical inquiry focusing on certified dates and datable events, will by necessity only deal with writs, certificates, charters, and diplomas—that is, with texts that establish legal structures. It is blind to texts that are neither designed for perpetuity nor carry any probative force, which neither lay claim to any legal effects nor are charged with safeguarding tradition. Hence the fact that files were underestimated by archival and historical research and remained unstudied for so long is not simply due to the negligence or misinterpretations of the researchers; it is an effect of the dominance of the paradigm of diplomatics. The latter focuses attention on the transmitted law, not on the transmission itself. As a result, the erratic side of the law—the administrative operations, the transmission medium itself—remains a blind spot of legal history. When the emphasis is on results, certifications, validity, and storage capacities, files, as mere transmission media, have no epistemological place.

It is not until the beginning of the twentieth century that files turned into an object of historiography. The new research program was first spelled out in 1908 by Harry Breslau, Michael Tangl, and Karl Brandi in the preface to the first volume of the *Archiv für Urkundenforschung* (Archive for document research): "Traditional diplomatics . . . is exclusively concerned with charters and acts. But by shifting our focus of interest onto the conditions under which they came about, we are narrowing the gap that has separated issued documents from the drafts and outlines, the letters, files and books located in the same offices and scriptoria. This means that for the first time a hitherto widely neglected source of archival documents is subjected to methodological scrutiny, providing our science with the means to go beyond its original field of research, the early Middle Ages, and to include antiquity as well the latest developments in the realm of documents and files."[11]

To be sure, the epistemological shift announced in the *Archiv für Urkundenforschung* implies that files had been promoted to the rank of objects of scientific investigation, yet still under the auspices of diplomatics. The archival *lore* developed in the 1950s, especially by Heinrich Otto Meisner, was still part and parcel of a systematic scrutiny of documents. But because files are not charters, acts, or deeds, because they do not satisfy any of the criteria that were developed in the context of the latter, they were simply treated as the other of diplomas, as nondocuments: "Files as such are nothing independent, they need to be complemented. . . . Documents may be isolated without the risk of being completely separated from a context that files, on the other hand, can only establish together with others. It is no coincidence that the former are stored individually, partly because of their external appearance (parchment, format, hanging seal), while files are always part of basted, bundled, or bunched collection."[12] Statements along the lines that allegedly context-dependent "files . . . are only valid if included in an administrative registry . . . while documents are independent of it"[13] have allowed historians ever since to make archival files speak, rather than treating them, as Michel Foucault, for instance, demanded, as monuments.

It is no coincidence that Meisner's influential research was conducted in the context of fifteenth- and sixteenth-century files, for it was at that point in time that files became an object in the order of discourse. Up until then, they had been nothing but the protean product of their particular usage, but around 1500 chanceries started to issue guidelines concerning the production, appearance, and compilation of files. Meisner neglected these historical conditions in favor of a typological distinction between documents and files. In so doing, he also missed out on the intermediary formats, especially on the simple chancery technique that brings about the decisive "transition from the ceremonial issue of individual charters and acts to the ongoing processing of files"[14]—creating registries. Registries that note the expedition of all official writs pave the way into the "age of files."[15] They process an administrative apparatus that will culminate in a file machine called *government.* With this in mind, it was highly consistent that in 1908 the *Archiv für Urkundenforschung* dedicated its first investigation of the materiality and mediality of files to registers of Frederick II.

Registrum Friderici II: Continuum of Files

Following his defeat at the hands of the English in the Battle of Fréteval on July 3, 1194, Philip II of France was robbed of the very centerpiece of his power: "Captus est etiam Regis Franciae thesaurus magnus et capella regia et cartae universorum hominum."[16] Richard the Lionheart had seized possession of the great treasury of France, which contained the royal chapel—that is, the repository of documents relating to spiritual matters as well as all the papers of the kingdom. With one stroke, the administrative foundation of the entire realm had been extinguished. Deprived of all legal documents governing power and possessions, France would have been forced to start over had it not been for the young Gautier of Nemour, who for six years traveled throughout the country reconstructing the purloined letters, lists, writs, and mandates. By complementing these notes with particulars concerning the ongoing administration, he inaugurated a new governmental media technology. His notebook was "the first royal French registry. Its main function was to replace the archive, which from then on could be left at home, given that the registry volume contained all or the most important items of the archive."[17]

According to this legend, a stolen treasure marked the beginning of the post-Roman filing system that had been interrupted by the drawn-out age of documents. It is the reason why stationary archives turned into portable shrines, or *arcae*. An abduction, a cancellation sui generis, established the administrative technique of compiling a registry, thus securing both the mobility and the continuity of political power. The rule of kings around 1200 was the rule of registries. It was a state(ly) technology that was soon adopted throughout Europe, and our childhood hero, the valiant Lionheart, had a hand in it. He may have won the battle, but he soon lost his booty, the *thesaurus magnus*, to the new chancery technique. A paper thesaurus canceled his victory; a registry replaced the pilfered treasure.

The origin of the registry in the thesaurus is still present today, as for instance in the definition of DIN 1463 (German Industry Standard): "With regard to documentation and information, a thesaurus is an ordered listing of terms and their (primarily common-language use) meanings used for indexing, storing, and retrieving items in a specific context."[18] According to this modern textual concept, registries are (cross-)reference systems for databases (thesauri). They are the addresses that link spatially separated textual items (archived and transmitted) to the symbolic order. This indexing principle was already used by thirteenth-century communal and papal registers. Here, registries referred to *issued* writs. It was only later, when specifically registered concepts rather than mere excerpts of the transmitted texts found their way into the registry, that a distinction was made between files and registries. Files represent a material thesaurus, a repository that can be accessed in the real using registries operating in the symbolic. But as long as files and registries, or *acta registrata*, were not yet separated, they acted as a storage as well as a retrieval system. They recorded their own operations and thus resembled both a chronology and a chronicle. They were literally *res gestae*—that is, regesta or daily entries noting events and actions, minutes recording official acts. They built up the registry's treasure by creating an "inventory of preserved *res gestae* . . . , of regesta or 'registered things,' that is to say, records."[19] Records are the thesaurus of a particular entity that is taking shape while recording its own actions: the government.

Once dispatched texts—and this applies particularly to flying leaflets— were linked to a registry, documents lost their innate verifying force. Central registration pulled the carpet out from under a flourishing forgery industry that specialized in old documents. Registering issued writs put an end to a rather contingent system of documents and "medieval mass certification of documents"[20] ascertaining more or less fictitious rights and privileges. Documents issued in the interest of the beneficiary were replaced by closed letters retained by the issuer, indicating that in file-based systems of power the emphasis had shifted from the addressee to the addressor of documents. Registries provided invulnerability: lost letters or stolen writs no longer entailed the collapse of a kingdom. In other words, registries ensured the sovereignty of power. In due course, the complex task of keeping a registry could no longer be performed by a single *cancellarius*; he was replaced by an agency, the *cancellaria*. In all likelihood, its first preserved official mention is in a decree by the Staufer emperor Frederick II from 1240 that contains the phrase "*ante domum cancellariae*."[21] Frederick's Sicilian chancery was both a site and an institution; it was a locatable and thus literally retrievable topos. Due to a virtuoso import of various elements from Arab, Egyptian, canonical Roman, and Byzantian administrations, the Sicilian chancery turned into one of the most progressive in Europe. It is the focus of the following examination of files and registries around 1200.

From an archival point of view, all that can be said about the registry of Frederick's Grand Court is based on a small excerpt from the Staufer administration—to be precise, on one single registry volume of 116 pages containing entries related to mandates issued by the Grand Court between October 1239 and May 1240. They refer to financial expenditures for musicians, new building projects, and royal hunts, among other things. Until 1943, historians were able to examine the precious original. In the nineteenth century, the "registry fragment" was inspected by the "royal archival secretary of the Royal Prussian State Archives, Dr. F. Philippi," during his epigraphic pilgrimage, and praised as an "especially valuable treasure."[22] In the twentieth century, Wilhelm E. Heupel, a collaborator of the Munich-based *Monumenta Germaniae Historica*, which must have equipped him with a historian's professional habituation to loss, undertook a closer examination of the precious debris of the thesaurus. He had an entire empire of files arise from the preserved fragment: "Of all the records that were once kept in the archives of the imperial Grand Court of Sicily, of all the chancery's intake and output registers, cadastres, tax lists, and court records, today only this fragment of one annual volume of the chancery register for court matters survives."[23] This homage to a single file sets the stage for Heupel's study of the Sicilian administration. He was to be its last eyewitness. The original registry was destroyed by German soldiers in 1943, which amounted to an erasure of the very part of history that had inspired German imperial dreams since the Second Reich. And while these aspirations found a misunderstood echo in Ernst H. Kantorowicz's life of Frederick II, the very same author had shown in his great study *The King's Two Bodies* how the pragmatics and the ideology of Frederick's rule already contained features of the modern state.

REGISTRIES

Just as the Roman Empire can be separated into papyrus and parchment, the shift from documents to the rule of files in the Staufer protostate came about with the switch from parchment to paper. Within the European administrative bustle, the new writing material was first put to use in Frederick II's Sicilian chancery, where it was employed for the manufacture of registers. Like those used by Italian municipalities, they consisted of cotton-based paper sheets measuring nineteen by twenty-six centimeters. Four sheets were folded to make eight leaves that were bound to so-called *quaterni*. Thanks to good connections to Arab suppliers, there was no need to be stingy with paper. And quite apart from the fact that paper was less forgeable than parchment, it was also less costly. Though paper decays at a more rapid rate than parchment, a fact that in papal eyes made it inferior, it was precisely this ephemeral quality that made it so important for those kingdoms that were competing with papal universality. While the pontifical power was striving for eternity, Frederick's kingdom gained its might from its ability to be permanently updated. Registers do not serve to provide evidence for all times; rather, they operate in a comparatively limited temporal range. References to past events in a register do not date back beyond two years. Whatever the chancery issued earlier may fall into oblivion since it has already been adjusted to current conditions.

Registers inaugurated a new economy of writing that has become in-dispensable for the administering of texts. Paper is cheaper and easier to write on than parchment, hence it is no longer necessary to make max-imum use of it. Because one is no longer obliged to cover both sides with writing, paper enables a layout that topographically reproduces the administrative process of compiling a register. Allowing themselves the luxury of partly blank pages, the Sicilian registers had every month begin with a new page. The schematic arrangement rationalized the texts of the individual entries, which provided keyword summaries of the content. There was no plan for further storage of the issued writs—for instance, by producing a complete copy. Registers are, electronically speaking, a form of working memory. The spatial positioning of the entries makes use of a place value system's implicit transmission of information: their arrangement already indicates certain illocutionary circumstances without having to spell them out. In short, waste of space saves writing time. On every page the header indicates the month (*calendas*) and sometimes the place, making it unnecessary to repeat this information at the start of each entry. For quick viewing purposes, the date—that is, the day of issue, e.g., *Kalendis Ianuarii apud sanctum Minianum / Primo Ianuarii*—and the name of the addressee are located in the left margin. Other instances of the new writing economy include the avoidance of repetitions and use of the abbreviation *eodem* to indicate identical dates, and of *similes* when identical writs were issued to several addresses. Registries dispense with salutations and greetings. They do not repeat anything that is already contained in the coded margins, instead concentrating on *information*. Information, we may conclude, is that which is entered by hand on the preformatted leaf, while the margins provide a frame for the expected constant and repetitive entries.

The fixed and unchangeable format of the registries goes together with a new economy of reading. It provides a system for the registration and retrieval of unknown quantities of official acts and decrees. The margins, consisting of a header indicating location and month and the daily dat-ing of the vertical column, already endowed the registry with the retrieval functions that are central to today's filing systems. There is no sequential procedure for retrieving an entry; rather, the procedure is determined by the coordinates of the registry's grid. The dates entered on the margins indicate that the entries are to be read not only from left to right but also from top to bottom. This also determines the position of an entry at the intersection of column and row, which makes it easier to find the desired passage. It is easier to retrieve information that is contained in a vertically arranged list than it is to find something in flowing text without special typographic marking. An address system utilizing marginal data that structure the text replaces tedious rereading. At the same time that theology turned to registries, it recognized the rationalizing process of systematizations. Replacing the "copying of major works," they now serve "as a substitute for time-consuming and painstaking studies."[24] Systematizations like those already put to use in the compilation of the Digest save reading and searching time; they facilitate focused access to Aristotelian, patristic, or legal texts. Systems, in short, are virtual registries or "mental filing systems."[25]

The dates in the margins decompose time into discrete, countable units, thus creating retrievable elements equipped with their own addresses. The address—that is, the unit to be retrieved—is the date. With this specific form of writing, which combines a content-based entry with a date in the margin, registers link acts and time: *actum et datum*. The coincidence of the two produces an event. To observe how such an event comes into being in writing, one has to take both terms literally: *actum* is the moment when the act is performed and *datum* is the time when it is handed over. Both concepts have a temporal index: once you date the registration of an act, that act can be addressed as an event in time. This already indicates what the Sicilian registers were aiming at: they were for the main part administering time. Other conceivable ways of structuring information, such as may be found in the curial chancery or at other European courts, were ruled out. Generally speaking, this registering technology removed power from the realm of eternity and subjected it to time. By vertically linking together the many diverse and disparate *acta* in the margins, the register made visible the continuous flow of time. The calendar is the principle of progression and continuity that leads from individual entries to the entire volume, from the particular moment or event to the series. With this temporal aspect in mind, registers anticipated chronologically arranged file sequences. The chronological ordering principle grants power in and over time. Hence registries were more than nifty administrative techniques designed to economize on reading and writing; they were nothing less than the media technology for a state as a permanent entity.

Kantorowicz was not only able to demonstrate the connections between this continuous passage of time and the keeping of registries; he also linked it to Thomas Aquinas's conceptualization of time.[26] Aquinas gave a theological twist to the registries kept by his father, Count Landulf of Aquino, in the chancery of Frederick II between 1220 and 1229, by positing a temporal continuum located between *aeternitas* and *tempus*, between divine and human time, which was referred to as *aevum*. Roughly translated as "alwaysness," the aevum comprises a time in which past and future exist simultaneously. "The aevum is there all at once (*totem simul*); yet it is not eternity, because before and after are compatible with it."[27] But that is precisely the definition of a registry. The chronological technique of the Sicilian registry makes that which came before and after its acts *totem simul* visible. The aevum, in other words, is a total registry; it is the steady basis of the state.

Unlike the sequential and exhaustive recording principle of the Sicilian registers, papal registers restricted themselves to the most important matters, and of these they only contained selections. For the pontifical administration, however, the decision which items were the most important frequently depended as much on factual considerations as on the fees that were introduced for the registration of documents in the thirteenth century. By contrast, the Sicilian registers were interested in inclusiveness rather than profit, but since Frederick II's administration was in every respect designed to surpass the papal chancery, it too made use of general registers (*quaterniones grande, quaterni generales*) that only recorded select major events. They were compiled for posterity as well as for the outside world, to make official copies and also to write history, thus realizing the potential of the *res gestae* to turn into a *chronicle*. In addition, the principle of a *chronology* was manifest in the register's daily specialized entries. They were not intended for an audience but designed "exclusively for the internal official communication of certain agencies."[28] On the basis of this comprehensive chronological register, the state, as institutionalized during the reign of Frederick II, became an apparatus of repetitions, a file machine.

Registers not only homogenize time, they also standardize spatially and functionally diverse official acts. They are "universal exchangers,"[29] processors that link diversities by establishing correspondences on paper and between papers, as a synopsis and reconciliation of debit and credit. The accounting terminology must be taken literally, for registers evolved from this very technology. Format and layout of the Sicilian registers resembled the twelfth-century accounting ledgers used in Italian municipalities. They were the first visible instance of the generating principle that fueled registers and files in general. This principle consisted in the obligation to give accounts. The Fourth Lateran Council (1215) had decreed that all Christians must confess their sins once a year; lists, the most primitive of all forms of registering, were used to keep account of who was, or was not, fulfilling their duty. The introduction of registers, then, promoted a thinking in balances far beyond the fiscal domain. The metaphorical use of double-entry bookkeeping is closely aligned to its literal use in the chanceries. Regardless of whether we are dealing with profane and sacred spheres, merchants or private individuals, it is always a matter of opposing and settling two items: *deve dare* on the debit side and *hoc dato* or *abbiamo avuto* on the credit side. Registering an unpaid debt facilitates deferment or, in the language of financial transactions, credit. Registers enable us to compensate for our lack of cash with promissory notes, to obtain loans, and to settle fines and bans against debt. A whole arithmetic of punishments on earth and in heaven follows from this. After all, registers are completely neutral regarding their content; they can be used for any purpose, from the administrative to the hagiographical. Registering saints is as easy as registering taxpayers. As a universal exchanger, a writing-based register operates within the empire with no regard to spatial, temporal, or any other distinctions.

Registers became especially important to the Sicilian chancery once it gave up its traditional seat in Palermo. Dissolving a center of administration requires ubiquitous forms of power—that is, mobile technologies or some form of remote control. When the administration becomes itinerant, the center is located wherever the registries are kept. For work that has to be done on the road, it becomes regular practice to assign scribes, *notarii actorum*, to the *officiali* (legal experts with executive and judicative competence) and the *baiuli* (officials responsible for executing orders). Their presence embodied the chancery. Registers as well as the officials responsible turned into a public display through which the rule of the Staufer emperor asserted itself in the Sicilian kingdom. In later centuries, files were to disappear into the anonymous gray monotony of chanceries, but at this point they were part of the spectacular procession of the Grand Court, the government of the Sicilian king. When the government was on the road to Lodi, Pisa, Foggia, Lucera, Celano, or one of the other administrative castles, it reputedly was accompanied by dancing Saracen girls and animals unknown in Italy: "elephants, dromedaries, camels, panthers, lions, leopards, white falcons" and "other things," such as carriers bearing the crown jewels and packhorses loaded with paper treasure, the *scrinia*.[30] The latter was the name for mostly leather-covered woven chests, cases, and coffers containing files. They housed the transportable thesaurus of the state: original documents, honorary titles, service obligations, testaments, marriage certificates, contracts, and other diplomatic documents, but in particular registers. Journeying through the country, the packhorses of Frederick's menagerie put on display the state's entire store of data.

The parade of Frederick's *scrinia* represents a brief historical moment in which there was no contradiction between a bureaucratic device—registers as an early form of files—and the sphere of representation. Processions and processors of the state followed one and the same logic. Without any further mediation, files represented the rule of the Staufer emperor; it was their very visibility that impressed and dazzled, not the intimidating invisibility that would become their hallmark in subsequent centuries. At the same time, the papal power remained unaware of the demonstrative evidence of the administrative; it strictly differentiated between administrative interior and the spectacular ceremony of exterior representation. There could be no greater difference between the publicly exhibited "files" of the Staufer *magna curia* and the papal registers, which for reasons of secrecy remained under wraps in the back rooms of the Vatican. Nonetheless, Frederick's parade of administrative armaments was clearly superior to the clandestine politics of the papal chancery. Not that the imperial registers were any less secret, but their secrets were, in an almost dialectical fashion reminiscent of Poe's purloined letter, contained in the greatest most possible public display of the itinerant chancery. The exposed files guarded their mysteries well. At no other European court was the system of registers more attuned to administrative demands; at no other court were the certification procedures more complex and surrounded with more precautions than in the Sicilian chancery under Petrus de Vinea. A politics of visibility and effective tactics of secrecy were two sides of one and the same strategy of power.

The paradoxical visibility of the Staufer administrative apparatus was not confined to the processions of the Grand Court. In the fully allegorized state of Frederick II, there existed no administrative detail, however humble, that did not mirror the entire order of the state. An *ordo cancellarius* regulated governmental procedures and relationships such that they reflected their divine counterpart. The *ordo* from the year 1240 has survived; it is clearly directed against ad hoc practices and venality, that is, against the papal chancery. Around the same time, the latter had published a *liber cancellariae*, which, however, was not a set of guidelines for future use but a concluding look back, a summary of—rather than a program for—administrative practices. The frequently improvised administrative procedures of the papal court were not regulated until after the pontificate of Innocent IV. By contrast, the *cancellaria* of Frederick II, with their regularities, discrete units, serial files, and rotating filling of positions, operated within the aevum, the temporal order of the state. Indeed, the chancery itself was subject to fixed time management. According to instructions, petitions were to be received not whenever required but twice a day.[31] Responses were to be issued three to five days later. Without these regulations, the delivery of a petition would have been a matter of chance, subject to the arbitrary whim of inscrutable chancery officials.

The regulated chancery hours corresponded to the compulsory attendance demanded of notaries, five of which had to be present in the chancery at any given time. Bound by instructions, they no longer worked as independent entrepreneurs: whatever the task performed by the officials of the Sicilian chancery, it was legitimized by the power of the emperor. Documents issued by the chancery attained force of law only after having been read publicly. In practical terms, the reading performed in the presence of the penitent made it possible to immediately incorporate their objections: *audientia litterarum contradictarum*.[32] Ideally, the reading served to establish by acoustic means the presence of the absent emperor. His voice could be heard everywhere; the *cursus*—a specific type of intonation

and one of the chancery's tightly guarded secrets—made it recognizable.
The responses issued by the Sicilian chancery came equipped with breath-
ing and stress marks. This "decomposition into dynamical speech units"[33]
in turn produced discrete units—a liturgy of the *aevum*.

The degree of harmony achieved under Frederick II between the philosophy of the state and its media technologies can be glimpsed in a letter
from the Sicilian council of notaries. Following Frederick's death, governmental order had increasingly fallen into disarray. Lamenting the great
disorder of things, the notaries turned to Nicola de Rocca, a teacher of
rhetoric who had been in the service of Frederick II. They implored him
to return and restore order to the chancery, and thus to the government as
a whole. Their letter, composed sometime between 1252 and 1258, paints
a picture of an ideal chancery that amounts to an exact description of the
political program of the Staufer emperor for basing his power on a fusion
of scholastic concepts with media technology:

> Discreto viro magistro Nicolao de Rocca cetus notariorum regie curie salutem
> et celerem reditum ad ovile. Ad instar facta celestis pretorii secularis in ter-
> ris curia tunc debite dispositionis regimine gubernatur, cum a sui exemplaris
> ymagine non exorbitat nec recedit. Nam sicut sunt ibi quedam subtiles intel-
> ligentie et animalia oculata ad divini nutus intimam contemplationem affixa
> et quidam administratorii spiritus vel activi, qui, quod a superiorum domi-
> nationum intellectu de divina voluntate recipiunt, per quamdam influentiam
> in creaturis inferioribus exequuntur, et sunt utrique tam apud superos quam
> apud inferos ratione situs et ministerii in excellenti gloria et honore, sic est
> et eodem modo dispositus in seculari curia supremorum officialium duplex
> ordo: alter videlicet, quos locum et officium illarum celestium potestatum
> tenentes ab effectu consiliarios appellemus, et alter, qui quod ab illis recipiunt
> de terrene maiestatis consilio, per scripture stilum mandant ad inferos per
> eos ducendum effectui, quos a notando notarios sive scribas vocamus, quibus
> omnibus ratione misterii et etiam ministerii generalis reverentia cum honore
> debetur.[34]

To the wise teacher Nicola de Rocca. The royal chancery's community of
scribes extends its salutations and wishes for his speedy return to their circle.
Just like the acts of the heavenly throne, the earthly chancery is guided by
purposeful instructions, provided that the latter follows the example of the
former and does not deviate. For there we find celestial beings and intel-
ligences mindful of divine indications, as well as some administering, active

angels who execute what they have learned from higher powers about the divine will by exerting a certain influence on inferior beings. Both types of angels, the superior and the inferior, enjoy by virtue of their assignment and their service extraordinary fame and respect. The worldly chancery, as well, is subject to such a double order: the first encompasses those whom according to their duties we call councilors or jurists, because they occupy the place and the office of the heavenly powers, and the second order encompasses those who, by using the stylus to put into writing what has been imparted to them concerning the designs of the earthly power, instruct inferiors to carry out their appointed tasks. According to their duties, the latter are called writer-notaries. As ministers and administrators of mysteries, all deserve great honor and acclaim.

Ministry—mystery: the letter concludes with a programmatic pun. It encodes secular offices using divine forms. Together, the earthly-administrative and divine-mystical spheres result in a double order, *duplex ordo*, from which the Sicilian chancery derived its sovereign power. Ever since Frederick II had broken with the curia following the death of Pope Honorius III in 1227, he made use of the unguarded semiotic inventory hitherto confined to papal use and proceeded to apply heavenly labels to each and every aspect of his chancery. The "insignia apparatus"[35] of papal power was provided with a media-technological update and deployed in the Sicilian *curia magna*. This explains why the letter penned by the council of notaries makes note of all administrative details, up to and including the stylus, when referring to the desired ordering power of the chancery. Within this highly intricate double order, *consiliari* or jurists are the earthly equivalent of heavenly angels. In accordance with the subtle gradations that distinguished composing and copying angels, *notarii* assumed the post of active angels. On earth as in heaven, they took care of daily chores by maintaining registries and compiling files.

State officials are angelic beings, be they pure or active. According to Thomistic lore, angels inhabit the intermediary realm of the *aevum*. "In the very being of an angel considered absolutely, there is no difference of past and future."[36] They assume all shapes of time and adapt to all orders of being. Time passes through them. Angels are not composed of a substance, rather they are co-extensive with the structure of order they create in writing: "Un esprit pur, un ange, par exemple, réalise d'un seul coup la perfection d'essence et existence que son être comporte [A pure spirit, an angel, for example, accomplishes all at once the perfection of essence and existence that its being implies]."[37] Angels remain in a me-dial position; they mediate between transience and eternity. And because they shuttle to and fro between God and mortals, they are messengers: "For angels, Greek angeloi, are . . . etymologically employed in the service of the *angareion*, the Persian postal system."[38] Given this relay function, there is nothing anthropomorphic about them. They are switchpoints, hollow molds, or functions. And that is what they share with jurists, their earthly counterparts: "The de-individualized fictitious persons of the law-yers, therefore, necessarily resembled the angels, and the jurists themselves recognized that there was some similarity between their abstractions and the angelic beings."[39]

Maximilian I, the White King: Disenchantment of Files

The papal chancery that moved through the streets around 1500 tended to invite mockery rather than overwhelm competing powers with its dis-play of files. The papal parade was summarized in numbers: "One legate who in 1496 was sent to meet Emperor Maximilian I was accompanied by seven trainees, one dator, thirteen abbreviators, fifteen scribes, one magis-ter, one consultant, sixteen scribes for the *Registrum supplicationum*, one magister for the *Registrum bullarum*, and eight registrars."[40] The multitu-dinous entourage of a single Vatican emissary offered a less imposing sight than the ambulant Grand Court of the Staufer emperor. Administration had become unrepresentable. Files were no longer surrounded by an an-gelic aura; ecclesiological signifiers had lost their power; theological and juridical spheres no longer mutually coded each other. The mystery and the ministries of power had become two separate worlds. As a result, the chancery around 1500 no longer represented itself; it served to represent. Instead of all the maneuvers in the medium of presence, the pompous display of the chancery's activities, the liturgical annunciations, and the administrative monstrosities that Frederick II used to take along on his processions, the chanceries now performed their invisible tasks behind the closed doors of the town halls or in the back rooms of the court. Charged with cultivating the appearance of power, they supplied incom-plete allegories, arbitrary signs that, unlike the fully allegorized order of the Staufer state, were not derived from the Roman canonical, scholastic signifier machines.

Under the rule of Maximilian I, the secular leader of the Christian world, the sphere of representation was differentiated from administrative institutions: highly visible tournaments, theater, and dancing on the one hand, administrative details removed from sight on the other. The latter were now characterized by a new technology: print. Typography demystified files and relegated them to the shadow world of power. Moreover, since it desacralized the work of the chanceries as much as it formalized it, it became part of Maximilian I's government program to resacralize serially produced printed letters. The new nonmanual writing and its profane use in chanceries were outshone by an excessive cult of pictorial letters. However, the strategy employed under Maximilian I to save the old magic of writing availed itself of precisely the technology of reproduction that had brought about this exorcism in the first place. His backward-looking policy of letters presupposed the latest level of print technology. The squiggly letters, which seemed to come from a calligrapher's hand, in fact originated in print shops. They concealed the seriality of typographic writing by shrouding it in secrecy, or rather in secret designs. They contained no arcane knowledge but hid a lost mystery underneath the ornamental surface. It is not known whether the court of Maximilian I used the cryptic signs for any practical purposes, such as to encode diplomatic missives. What is known is that the pseudo-Egyptian *litterae sacrae* were deployed in the sphere of representation. The emperor put to use a "mystery of ancient Egyptian letters handed down from King Osiris"—for example, for a pictorial representation of the dome in the Portal of Honour.[41] Egyptian hieroglyphs—the prized object of humanist research—turn into partial allegories of his power. They represent the mystery of power reduced to letter size. Mysterious letters from ancient times, they contain no overview, rather they condense into an image the ethico-political style of the ruler.

Max Weber has alluded to the irony that "the early stages of the development of modern administration" were subject to Maximilian's "tendency to go over the heads of his officials and to issue orders . . . with every momentary whim."[42] The chancery was forced to adapt to the emperor's movements, ideas, and preferences. His majesty's zeal dictated the work hours: scribes were on standby day and night to take dictation. A government so inimical to delegation, and based on such close fusion of the ruler with a staff that is at his constant beck and call, embodies a type of rule that later will be associated with Josef Stalin. It manifests itself in the "administration that never sleeps,"[43] as emblemized by the solitary illuminated window of the Empire State Building.

There was, however, a conflict between the increase of administrative tasks and Emperor Maximilian's demand to be involved in everything. The sheer size of his sovereign territory made it impossible to satisfy his desire to be informed about everything that was going on within his realm. As a result, things appeared confusing, which, in turn, aggravated Maximilian's distrust. He tried to overcome his well-known "absent-minded restlessness" with a frantic travel schedule. His itinerary is a testament to his struggle to maintain the upper hand. "In a period of less than ten years, we see the emperor roaming about the country like a wandering scholar. The places in which he stayed for less than a day number in the hundreds. Frequently they are small villages, lost hamlets, castles that have long since vanished."[44] His distrust left no room for exceptions; even the most remote backwater aroused his suspicion. The gaze of a ruler intent on inspecting everything himself is as paranoid as it is despotic. Nonetheless, precisely this distrustful style of government was acclaimed as a virtue in a fictional talk between royal father and son in Maximilian's *Weisskunig* (The White King). It starts with the paternal question, "Son, do you understand the *reason why government is based on writing*?" To which the son responds with a gem of governmental wisdom: "Should a king put his trust in a person, and should the king come to believe the beautiful speeches uttered by that person, then that person is the ruler and not the king."[45] A king who aspires to rule had better place no trust in chancellors, for that will merely serve to increase their power. With regard to matters of government, therefore, the basic axiom must be: write yourself, do not believe what chancellors say. The sovereign distrust which demanded that everything be put down in writing shaped the basic policy of literacy that was gradually established at the European courts around 1500. This was also the time in which "municipal administrative operations, which hitherto had been performed without the use of files, are increasingly based on writing." Files increase to the degree that administrations demand written evidence. Subsequently, there were fewer files wherever the demand for accountability was handled in a more relaxed fashion. In the seventeenth century at the latest, Max Weber's principle of *Aktenmäßigkeit*—the principle that "administrative acts, decisions and rules are formulated and recorded in writing, even in cases where oral discussion is the rule or is even mandatory"[46]—becomes an indispensable element of bureaucratic rule. In the dialogue between father and son quoted above, Maximilian I traces the contours of a perfect text-based government: "And when the young White King grew in years and assumed power, he had many secretaries whom he had trained according to his will since his youth and to whom he gave plentiful work. He also never allowed a letter to be sent off, no matter how important or slight its content, without checking it himself, and he signed all the letters with his own hand. . . . Also, he was so unsurpassable when it came to composing and remembering letters that he frequently dictated individual letters to nine, ten, eleven or twelve secretaries. He alone was in command of his entire dominion and all its territory, just as he was of the great wars that he led against other lands and nations."[47] Here, the great wars are joined by small wars and the means to fight them: simultaneous dictation, counterchecking, and signature.

COPIES, CUPBOARDS, AND FILING CABINETS

The gray power of files gradually takes shape in the shadow of dazzling ornamental letters. Around 1500 they were no longer part of a mystery. They were disenchanted—that is to say, they started to resemble today's files. A relatively simply internal administrative change concerning the handling of drafts revolutionized administration. In Maximilian's imperial court chancery, drafts were no longer canceled. For the first time they were preserved *in addition to* being registered. In other words, they were copies instead of cancels. According to Max Weber, this new technique of collecting rather than merely registering issued documents provided the foundation for the modern age. "The modern management of the office," Weber writes in his grand analysis of bureaucracy, "is based upon written documents (the 'files'), which are preserved in their original or draft form."[48] This is how files in today's conventional sense came about. The "unauthenticated, frequently corrected drafts" that are preserved "belong to the files instead of the documents."[49] The sixteenth century, therefore, is "that important epoch in which the modern filing system arises."[50] The latter owes its existence to the differentiated administrative structure that materialized in growing files. "The way in which records were assembled into ongoing files . . . corresponds to the way in which the underlying administrative acts solidified into the continuous function of specific offices."[51] Files are the mirror stage of any administration. Subsequently, they become the object of desire for a positivist historiography that uses files to deduce their administrative as well as their political background. In the words of the file-obsessed historian Ranke: "Those who want to fathom what really happened (chiefly in the late Middle Ages) have to deal with files."[52]

Whatever was preserved in files for subsequent reuse had to remain legible and was therefore to be neither crossed out nor written on erasable slates or scraps of parchment. But once erasure is itself erased, the hierarchy of textual stages, according to which a single original presides over and legitimizes its copies, breaks down. Around 1500, in the realm of typography as well as in file-based administration, all texts were legible and testified to the presence of an origin. All reproduced texts were similarly authentic products without precedent. One text from the *copia*, the wealth of disposable texts, had to be elevated to the status of original and be designated as the official version. Canceling the canceling act entailed a further problem: the preserved drafts could be retroactively altered. Parchment erasures or pencil-written drafts allow for countless undetected corrections that leave scarcely visible marks. Because these techniques of erasure are themselves erased and cannot be proven, they require special supervision. The suspicious administrative style that characterized the chancery of Maximilian I explicitly required that official permission be obtained for any erasure. "Furthermore, regarding letters, in particular public letters and those written on parchment, no names and no numbers indicating day and year or other such sensitive items may be changed or erased. If honest mistakes were made during the writing of the letter, deletion is permitted, but only after consultation with our chancellors or secretaries, and they have to be performed by the same hand that wrote the letter."[53]

Whenever drafts are collected, files come about. The latter in turn change the function of registries. Registry entries are now based on revised drafts. "Item, forthwith the registrar will without demur also enter such copies into his book."[54] An entry containing information on the issued document (date, summary, and addressee) no longer replaces the draft, as was the case with the Sicilian register. It is not a substitute but an index for the copies. In the face of this integrated and independent system of recording, registries can do no more than fulfill a simple referral function. They are pointers, just like computer data that consist solely of an address. With this function in mind, they were called *repertoria, remissoria* or *registra*, or *slossil, slötel, slotel* (all related to the German *Schlüssel* or key) or *claves*. Centuries later, the U.S. military defines *database* in such media-historically precise terms that the definition contains this diachronic development of files from registries. Entries are deduced from files, thus taking on a double function as key and data:

1. A database is a set of files.
2. A file is an ordered collection of entries.
3. An entry consists of a key or keys and data.[55]

A registry is literally and metaphorically the key to a thesaurus, as is evident in a fifteenth-century preamble to land rights. Its praise for the organization of the registry reveals an acute sense of how it is able to order the symbolic. It makes it "easy to open the chest that contains the disorderly treasures of imperial and common law and to take out what you need."[56] The registries were responsible for order. Once the differentiation had occurred that separated files (the "material") and registries (their "indices"), the former were free to lapse into a state of complete disorder. The file registries compiled under Frederick II still contained their own ordering principles—they were, in other words, both signifier and signified—but once the two were severed, problems of order were bound to arise. There no longer was a virtual reference to material texts. Preserving drafts resulted in a corpus of texts that did not correspond to the way it was arranged by the registry. Removed from the symbolic apparatus of the registry, heaps of preserved drafts were kept as files in boxes and chests, even after they were—as pointed out in the preamble quoted above—coupled to the registry. The order imposed by the registry had nothing to do with any orderly appearance. Material files don't care whether they are registered or not. Merely by looking at it, no eye can tell "la différence entre une cassette enregistré et une cassette vierge [the difference between a registered file and an untouched file]."[57]

But registries did not always manage to order the chaos of files. With its system of multiple checks, signing and countersigning, the chancery of Maximilian I separated the writing, issuing, and registering of documents to such a degree that synchronous registering, and with it chronological recording, became impossible. Documents that were begun simultaneously were registered at different times. An alternate approach to documents, registered according to place rather than time of origin, was hampered by continuous interruptions in the shape of random entries. There was "a haphazard rather than an orderly registration according to place."[58] The "temporal discrepancy between production and issuance as well as the abuse of unsystematic registration process" made it difficult for chancery officials, as well as future historians, to locate files using the register. As a key to locating files, the registries of Maximilian I were a failure. "There certainly were attempts to bring order to the chancery's chaos of files, but they do not appear to be very helpful . . . when it comes to looking things up."[59] The main reason was that the information content of registry entries was unformatted. Lacking a place value system, it offered content devoid of all markers. But in many cases the significance of an entry could only be deduced from its position, date, context, or frame, as in Frederick's registers. Without this stereotypical format the information content of an entry fades and eventually vanishes in the course of time. Summarizing his failed efforts to bring order to registers of the Maximilian chancery four hundred later, the historian Gerhard Seeliger concluded: "Understandably, under these conditions it is impossible to disentangle the chronological disorder and to arrange the individual register entries in the order in which they were actually written down."[60]

When files are confined to the real and registers to the symbolic, the need for systematic ordering arises. That is to say, if the production process—as was the case with the chronologically ordered register entries—no longer follows an inherent ordering principle, other principles may be imposed. For the registers compiled around 1500, *time* ceases to be the guiding principle of arrangement. Rather than adhering to a chrono-serial principle, they were arranged according to *subject*. After having been used by the papal chancery for their subsequently compiled general registries, the latter principle slowly gained ground. By the eighteenth century, registries were organized almost exclusively in terms of subject matter.

"The two principal ordering elements, time (date) and reference (subject, place, person), change parts."[61] Continuous chronological self-registration gave way to an order based on criteria of pertinence or subject matter. If technologies of power are no longer oriented toward a temporal continuum, but instead toward semantic categories, however, this indicates a change in the conceptualization of power. A territorial principle imposes itself on a chronological one; geography is more important than temporal duration. Around 1500, registries did not serve to ensure continuity, especially if they were private rather than official. Their reach did not extend beyond their own term. In most cases, once the term ended, files were no longer transmitted. Apart from the chancellor himself and the chancery personnel, continuity between dynasties only came about when old files and registers were found and used. They became the last leverage of deposed rulers, who treated them like hostages. "King Ruprecht of the Palatinate unsuccessfully negotiated with his predecessor Wenzel for the release of the imperial registries."[62]

Registries that only take note of issued documents and preserve mere drafts are a one-sided administrative recording technology; they amount to a monologue of power that installs itself as absolute. A more dialogic form of governance arises only when retention of drafts is complemented by preservation of incoming missives. Only then can we speak of files in the modern sense of the word. Not coincidentally, German adopts the Latin loan word *Acten* to replace older terms like *hendel* or *händel* at the moment when files (*Akten*) start to bundle incoming and outgoing texts in ways that are still in use today. The combined registration of ingress and egress was already part of the early accounting practices of the Italian municipalities. In sixteenth-century German cities, outgoing and incoming writs were collected in such a way as to make up a file. Accordingly, the monological rule changed and became—for all its asymmetry—dialogical. The sovereign turned into an interactive unit that acted and reacted, either in person or by proxy. As the regent, he was in the position of either receiver or emitter. Once incoming writs were registered and preserved, the buildup of documents facilitated control procedures: issued commands and incoming reports could be examined to determine whether the commands had been obeyed. This feedback enabled the government to assume control and guidance functions. The bilateral collection of correspondence in files turned it into a cybernetic structure, a government that intervenes and is able to trace, check, and improve upon the effects of its interventions.

The incoming/outgoing arrangement of files is reminiscent of mercantile accounting practices. It can also be viewed as part of a postal system, like the relay between Innsbruck and the Netherlands established in 1489 by the Habsburg Empire as an extension of the chancery.[63] Postal service and chancery were two sides of one and the same communication network. The *exchange* of letters in files was a sediment of the postal circulation. A letter may not reach its destination, but at least its draft has been filed. They are nothing but inverted letters. The alliance of chancery and postal service that separated the regiment into senders and addressees also structured foreign policy. The organization of embassies and delegations reveals how a military-chivalric dispositive was replaced by an informational-diplomatic one and occasional missions abroad turned into permanent institutions.

Registering outgoing documents, taking notes, and collecting drafts and letters led to an exponential growth of written matter. As files increased in weight and took up more space, they demanded a room of their own. The "rapidly growing files . . . had to be accommodated differently. For the most part they were no longer locked away in chests but kept in bins and drawers and on shelves; sometimes they were hung in sacks on the wall to keep them safe from mice."[64] The closeable, compartmentalized file furniture—"big chests with many boxes . . . a key . . . to lock away the seal and other secret matters . . . and the great chest which houses the many small boxes must have a good lock,"[65] to quote Maximilian's chancery orders—changed its function. Hitherto, the "wardrobes with their shelves, desks with their drawers, and chests with their false bottoms"[66] acted as hiding places or dungeons, a *cachot* (cf. *carcer*), whose purpose was to conceal. But in accordance with the need for feedback mechanisms, cupboards—that is, furniture made up of cupboards—were now supposed to facilitate the retrieval of old files. They were to order as well as store the pages that were lying around like a treasure amid the general disorder. Record shrines, in short, turned into orderly furniture.

"In the wardrobe there exists a center of order that protects . . . against uncurbed disorder,"[67] Gaston Bachelard writes in *The Poetics of Space* about the ordering function of shrines equipped with shelves and boxes.

FIGURE 4.   Bookstore and archival cabinets in the old archive, Lüneburg city hall, built 1521. Louis Leitz Firma, ed., *Schriftgut und seine Aufbewahrung: Aktuell seit 5000 Jahren*, Stuttgart, 1980, 6.

Starting with little boxes, the "oldest unit in the registry,"[68] cupboards developed a layered interior. Increasingly, the order of the registry in the symbolic attached itself to the administrative micro-spaces.

Around 1600, registries that hitherto had acted as specially designated keys to specific little treasure boxes start turning into independent agencies that connect records and their users, the chancery personnel. The registry was an interim zone in which circulating records turned into retired files. In this "registrar zone"[69]—to quote archival scholars—the file

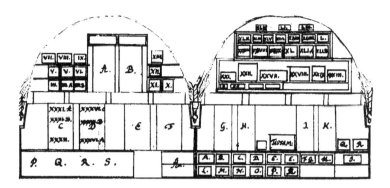

FIGURE 5.   The written material was arranged alphabetically. Louis Leitz Firma, ed., *Schriftgut und seine Aufbewahrung: Aktuell seit 5000 Jahren*, Stuttgart, 1980, 6.

material was ordered in such a way that furniture turned into addresses, that is, into pointers for the retrieval of records that were counted by chests. But only as long as they were in use did files follow the registry's symbolic order. As soon as they fell into disuse, they also fell back into infinite disorder, for unlike documents, they were defined solely by usage. If sources around 1500 mention *Acten*, they refer exclusively to used ones. Once removed from the orderly furniture, they were outside the reuse system of the chancery. "Whatever . . . had been lying around the shelves of the chancery in disorderly fashion, and was subsequently moved to the attic to create space, was no longer accessible and, in most cases, left to decay."[70] Precious texts, on the other hand, were guarded like gemstones. Thus, whether a piece of writing was trashed or treasured depended on whether it was classified as a file or as a document. Only the latter found their way into the *armaria*, the armories or treasure chambers. Their storage removed them from circulation and prepared them for an undetermined eternity. "Documents as embodiments of legal titles turned the archive into an arms chamber (*armarium*) of dynastic and state sovereignty, which is why they were for a long time kept strictly separate from the files."[71] Maximilian I had precious codices and documents brought to the Hofburg, the imperial palace in Vienna. Files, however, were left to fend for themselves. What until the seventeenth century was known as an "archive" was in most cases nothing but a depot with no access facilities. The fortress of Simanca is said to be Europe's first file archive after Emperor Charles V had his cabinet records stored there in 1542. In many cases, however, archives containing files came about due to lack of space and money: the file archive around 1500 is a by-product or waste product of the chancery. With all the partitioned shelves, cases, and boxes, the furniture designed to house files "was so costly and used up so much space that it was not stored with its content; rather, the latter was removed and carried upstairs into the attic with baskets and sacks while the cupboards and shelves remained in use."[72] Reuse of files literally meant the recycling of file boxes, not of their content. Thus, location and type of storage determined the difference between current and stored records. Whatever is dangling from the ceiling beyond the reach of rodents relates to ongoing business that is still *hanging in the air*, while files laid to rest in chests are *closed cases*.

Initially, then, an archive was nothing but a file repository. In Brandenburg-Prussia, the files were "delivered" at the end of each year to a castle cellar known as "the vault."[73] Since they were removed from cupboards and thrown into baskets, they could hardly be reused. As a rule, in the fifteenth and sixteenth centuries there were no procedures in place for reusing retired files; if at all, they seem to have been deposited for possible but as yet undetermined future cases. It took a long time for the practice of referring to old files to assert itself. One indication of its emergence is the establishment of an *archives office*. From the mid-seventeenth century on, Prussian officials were charged with the care of files no longer in circulation, something they had hitherto performed as an aside. They were to register—that is to say, to sort incoming files regardless of their content. Registrars and archivists, however, were not supposed to read what they administered; they were to provide file and shelf marks to prepare their archival reuse. The first Prussian archivist responsible for registering files, Christoph Schönebeck, was also the last secretary of the chancery to peruse records. He stood at the threshold of the decoupling of archiving and administering. For archival purposes, he was the very last to read the files that he registered, so that no one else had to read them after him. "Schönebe[c]k had not simply taken administrative control of a registry, he had truly built an archive."[74] In 1639 he took control of the files, not without the archivist's constitutive complaint about their "exquisite disorder."[75] "The archive was in a state of disorder, almost everything was faulty, indices were all but nonexistent, an official handover was out of the question. . . . Everything was lying around in a mess, many precious items had been nibbled at by mice. There was no sense in enlisting the help of the registrar (Langenheim) who due to his advanced age was blind as well as deaf. . . . Matters were getting worse by the day, not only because new files were coming in from all around the country but also because the acquisition of new provinces added to the rush."[76] Schönebeck was confronted with every archivist's nightmare—that heaps of files grow faster than they can be registered—at precisely the moment when he had decided to rearrange retired files according to subject matter—that is, according to the same criteria that were used in ongoing administrative matters. "The archive contained several hundred small boxes with unordered content. . . . Schönebeck set out to bind together the records pertaining to matters of the Reich. . . . The provincial records, however, which hitherto had only been arranged chronologically, he set out to order according to subject, place family, etc., and to list them accordingly."[77]

The disorder afflicting records is an effect of their belatedness. Their chaotic origins are to be overcome by *orders* that precede material files—orders that are preambles for real, physical files, designed to create order in advance. They are supposed to control the work of the chancery and ensure that files already assume an orderly shape when they are being compiled and not just afterward. The goal is to direct the work in the chancery in such a way that files are compiled and ordered *uno actu*, with no need to tidy them up later. As a result, the focus of the chancery's activities shifted from archival cleanup to planning ahead. The ideal of synchronous collecting and ordering that would come to occupy the fantasies of modern administrative reformers has its origin in an early modern age that viewed administration as a "dirigible apparatus." The state steers or governs by means of regulations or *orders*. Increasingly, "courts, councils, chanceries, chambers, and revenue offices" were subject to orderly procedures that "serve to introduce the uniform and precise handling of files, the documenting and archiving of correspondence, and the issuing of decrees."[78] Files are no longer the end product of administrative acts attached to regulations and technologies determining preservation and reuse. They are the training ground for administrative routine, and thus provide a more stable power base. Administrations that once had created disorder are now to process order. Within the restricted confines of the chancellery, as well as across the entire regimental system, order will assert itself as orderliness, as the inevitable effect of orderly kept files.

§ 4   Governmental Practices

State Practice

Around 1700 the chancery's activities were no less ceremonious than other courtly performances. "When the barriers of the theater and those of the legal courts become indistinguishable,"[1] all that was issued by the chancery turned into a *theatrum juridicum*. Rhetorical devices—that is, language-based ceremonials—took the lead in representing law and power; and once the latter adopted semiotic procedures it was no longer possible to stage parades of material files. Sovereign power was now embodied by rhetoric. Increasingly, "the rulers' bias toward representation turns diplomatic receptions and negotiations, chanceries and cabinets, state assemblies and courtly festivities into opportunities for displaying rhetorical splendor."[2] A rhetoric reduced to questions of representation and style regulated the appropriateness of discourse in terms of occasion and addressee. The many diverse "chancery compositions"—decrees, rescripts, laws, edicts, rules, instructions, patents, promemoriae—represent nothing less than a pragmatic anthropology of the chancery, given that each genre was assigned to a scribe possessing the suitable temperament: sanguine persons were to be responsible for petitions for clemency, melancholics were supposed to handle negative decisions, and cholerics were entrusted with negotiating contracts.[3] This match of style, temperament, and occasion spread into all domains, until in the seventeenth century everyday life had been divided into a patchwork of quasi-institutions: "occasions," which endowed speech with the characteristics of action.[4] Thanks to the "sovereignty of words,"[5] these quasi-institutions could truly represent what they say. The politics of performance, as practiced at European courts around 1700, was based on linguistic pragmatics. There was no divide between words and the actions they referred to: "The . . . ceremonial determines how actions are to be performed," and it also "determines how actions are to be performed in writing."[6] The coding of politeness and diplomacy transferred the domains of the political into written language.

Following the devastations of the Thirty Years War, language had become a sanctuary for political action. Words are more easily ordered than territories, and they are more obedient than mercenaries. "Here, in the tableau of language, words acting as word-warriors could move around in columns, conduct drills, inspect parades, and attack each other's word-bodies. In the empire of the word-people, any disciplinary infraction is punishable by death or torture; syllables are butchered and left to bleed dry. The result of such carnage is simply another word."[7] This substitute world of words was the world of Baroque secretaries. By extolling the word as sovereign, they ennobled themselves as poets and presented their poetic labors as a unification of language and, in consequence, of the disintegrated realm. Organized in language societies, the patriotism of secretaries practiced politics with speech acts. But the *teutschen secretarii*—to use Baroque language—were also fighting for their own existence. After the Thirty Years War, dispersed soldiers were most likely to find employment in chanceries, in which there was an increased demand for scribes. They were "subaltern civil servants of territorial chanceries, charged with handling the correspondence of the privy council. They took notes, recorded decisions and drafted resolutions, which then had to be submitted to the chancellor. Within the administrative structure, they were responsible for functionally differentiated domains, such as the chamber, secret affairs, fiefdom, and the courts."[8] But secretaries were not trained jurists. To be sure, jurists did work in chanceries, sometimes even without payment, in secretarial positions as auditors, registrars, or forwarding clerks, but ultimately they occupied these positions only in order to bridge the obligatory gap before becoming articled clerks.

In the chanceries, there was an ongoing competition between jurists and secretaries. Universally deployable secretary machines considered themselves superior to one-sided jurists. "Poets saw themselves as the moral arbiters of jurists."[9] Kaspar Stieler, known as "The Late One" because he was the latest to join the so-called Fertile Language Society, endowed his fellow members with a new pride of rank: in 1678, he wrote in the *Teutsche Advokat* that while jurists may be able to obtain a doctoral degree, secretaries are good "orators, masters of language, and knowledge-able in the affairs of state."[10] Secretaries convinced themselves that they were the superior jurists. As rhetorically schooled "constitutional lawyers," they strove to render superfluous all unnecessary specialized legal experts. In preparation for the widespread deployment of secretaries in "all chanceries, bureaus, and offices,"[11] they compiled handbooks with form letters for every conceivable occasion. "It was not a matter of providing erudition and insight into the art of government, but of storing forms for copying."[12] From the safe vantage point of ready-made letters, that is, from a collection of samples, it was safe to criticize jurists. For secretaries, deriding intellectuals became a new genre.

The secretaries devoted themselves to matters that from a jurisprudential point of view were not worthy of discussion. They inaugurated the discourse of a practical "legal art" that focused on the less visible work in the chanceries. Administrative tasks that hitherto had received little attention and had been passed on through imitation, were now raised to an art of governmental practice eager to join, if not to replace, jurisprudence. The new discourse of statecraft referred to a ceremonial science that was in turn attached to a courtly ideal, and thus had not yet turned into a university-based academic discourse. Relying on the argument that there was a greater need for practical training for government services, Johann Jacob Moser had justified his goal to establish an academy for future state and chancery officials. The project was guided by the vision of a state that "year after year would employ in its cabinets and chanceries so many men that they could make up several regiments; and yet nobody has thus far been able to show how this can be accomplished."[13] The governments of several duchies had to step in and organize the schooling of their employees if their numbers were to equal that of the army. What was expected from an ideal secretary corresponded to the requirements made of civil servants in the seventeenth century: they had to possess the right manners and a general education, as well as experience and knowledge of history and languages. Legal expertise, however, was not that important. Subsequently, the goal of educating government officials entailed a reorganization of higher academic knowledge. The universities, too, made practical knowledge of chanceries, of which "legal theory remains ignorant,"[14] part of its curriculum. It became "a test case for practice orientation" in law faculties.[15] Under the guise of administrative premises, the Baroque *ars dictaminis* returned as a pragmatics of governmental writing and speech acts in the academic world. It made up a new genre called "state practice" (*Staatspraxis*): the "ability in all matters of state to speak, write, and conduct oneself in a skilled manner worthy of one's origin."[16]

The textbook by Johann Stephan Püttner, professor of *Polizeywissenschaften*, the newly created university discipline designed to teach state practice, in Göttingen, already spelled out in its title what "state practice" entailed: "Juridical Instruction as to how in Germany Legal Matters and other Matters of Concern to the Chanceries, the Empire, or the State, be they subject to Legal Procedures or not, are to be Handled Orally or in Writing and Stored in Archives." A comprehensive knowledge of matters of importance to the state, *pragmata*, it comprised questions of rhetoric and style, as well as "mechanical services."[17] With the new science of state pragmatics, the registering and archiving of files became part of university education. In the mid-seventeenth century, Veit Ludwig von Seckendorff, author of the *Fürstenstaat* (The prince's state), had decreed with Protestant meticulousness that chancellors and counselors should "diligently read, ponder and provide comprehensible and faithful summaries of all the incoming news, documents and records that are stored in the . . . archives."[18] In the new treatises inspired by the institutionalization of a *Polizeywissenschaft*, this instruction was divided into individual operations. The use of court files from actual trials served to demonstrate what thus far had not been dealt with on a university level: "how to read files," "how to present them" (Pütter), what paper to use, how to bind, staple, and store them, and so on. The practical instructions were also mindful of the details of the work in the chanceries and provided advice on working as economically as possible. One example of working economically is the "berserk graphomaniac,"[19] Moser's revelation of "why I was able to write so much." He recommends his method of working with "slip boxes" and provides an exact account of their appearance, size, and arrangement: the boxes in which he stores the octavo sheets "have a length and breadth of one shoe, and are four fingers in height"; the sheets contained "in systematic order the names of all the subject matters of German state law, as well as all the other subject matters that I plan to elaborate upon."[20]

Files had been used in universities even before they became objects of presentation and instruction for regulations concerning correct "file maintenance."[21] The distinctly German institution that, depending on the media and means of transmission, is known as "file expedition" (*Aktenversendung*) had already in the preceding century bequeathed large numbers of files to the law faculties. These files contained case records sent by the various courts to law professors for appraisal and decision. The practice of seeking expert advice in legal disputes was already established in the sixteenth century. The more extensive the case recorded, the more the individual missives turned into entire files. As a rule, two or three volumes of records belonged to one case. When the records became so voluminous that—to quote the copious writer Moser—"a horse was hardly able to remove them,"²² law professors dispensed with reading entire files and instead appointed referents to present their content orally. In the eighteenth century, the art of summarizing records became a subject taught at universities to prepare law students for work as appraisers and adjudicators in court proceedings. Like many other experts in *Polizeywissenschaften*, Moser, who had received his doctorate with a dissertation on file expedition, drafted guidelines for summarizing and adjudicating legal records. These techniques have ever since been part of the standard education of assessors.

In addition to subject matter pertaining to state law and administrative procedures, the instruction books for *Polizeywissenschaften* contained treatises on questions of style and rhetoric. Pütter's handbook, for instance, included an "addendum for instruction in juridical practice—especially with regard to orthography and linguistic correctness as well as to the ceremonial chancery style."²³ It didacticized the whole casuistry of courtoisie, that is, what form of writing was to be used on which occasion indicating what distinction of rank. In contrast to the sample letters illustrating the ceremonial style of Baroque secretaries, which in the eyes of state scientists were "ridiculous stuff,"²⁴ the new chancellery style was far more sober. "The writing is short and unaffected and not overly ceremonious." In those cases where chancery writs did not serve to represent sovereign power but were primarily designed to regulate "the communication with civil servants,"²⁵ the exasperating "disputes of rank and ceremony"²⁶ had for the most part been overcome. From this point on, administration would only recognize three distinctions in the traffic among state officials: a superior office avails itself of a *rescript* to address a subordinate, a subordinate office *refers* to a superior level, and two offices of equal rank file *requisitions* to each other. The elaborate ceremonial of the chancery was reduced to a "linear courtesy," a vertical line drawn in the margin of a letter that was designed to replace the verbal display of effusive obeisance. The length of the "devotional line" indicated the difference in rank between sender and addressee—in the most extreme case, it could extend along the entire page.²⁷

Frederick Wilhelm I, king of Brandenburg-Prussia, who was renowned for his lapidary first-person style, was intent on persuading the chanceries to abandon the mannered secretarial style cultivated by the practioners of *Polizeywissenschaften*, in favor of the new ideal of simplicity. Given the standard per-word payment scheme, verbose secretaries had become a financial drain. Hence the order "Chancery employees are to stick to the proper number of words and not ramble on for the sake of making a profit!"[28] To enforce Prussian word economy, Frederick II resorted to paying by style rather than by volume. Not surprisingly, the secretaries remained unimpressed and threatened to sabotage such deceremonialization initiatives, defending themselves by pointing out, among other things, that with loss of the old secretarial arts, official correspondence would lack the standard forms of politeness; besides, nobody would be able to understand the old records anymore. The king responded with an endowed public essay contest: "Why is the old chancery style, execrated by Frederick the First, prohibited by Joseph the First, and baneful to king and people alike, still being practiced in so many places; and how can it be eradicated?" In 1794 the consistorial secretary Carl Christian Link provided the lapidary response: "Chancery employees are incapable of introducing a new chancery style." It was not chancery employees but "the good authors of a nation who shape the language." Faced with the greatest possible differentiation between poets and civil servants, universal Baroque poet-secretaries had become obsolete. In the face of the new, enlightened style of writing they were "suspected of aestheticism."[29]

But despite this—attempted—expulsion of all belles-lettrism from administration, the chancery style retained special characteristics. Though scribes were compelled to employ a less ornate style in external correspondence—"You are to avail yourselves of a clear, straightforward, succinct, and pithy style devoid of long clauses"[30]—certain distinctions between inside and outside were to be maintained. It was the function of the *stilus curiae* to cultivate a distance between civil servants and subjects. The absolutist state always operated with a special language, for "both in speech and in writing, matters of the state and the chancery have their own words, phrases, formulas, abbreviations, signs, and numbers."[31] The insight of Deleuze and Guattari that "grammaticality . . . is a power marker before it is a syntactical marker"[32] literally applies to absolutist speech acts. The exclusivity of the linguistic expression, arising from its distance from everyday language, is a source of authority. Because it is linked to the "interest of the state," there has to be a fundamental distinction between the discourse of the state—which is to be employed almost "contrary to everyday usage"[33]—and everyday language. The secret language of diplomacy could be learned at European courts as a "state grammar" with its own signs and syntax. Those who mastered it not only signaled their linguistic competence but also qualified as civil servants. Because Johann Jacob Moser attached considerable importance to such a state grammar, he was prone to dramatize the dangers of its abuse, drawing up a list of possible linguistic pitfalls: difficult case changes, confusion of feminine and masculine word gender, the correct use of plural and singular, and the fact that the chancery language at times does not allow for comparative adjectives, while in other cases one has to employ "state super-superlatives," which have no equivalent in everyday language. The decision to use either *hic* or *ille* was of pivotal political importance, as was the correct form of address: "thou," "he," "it," or "you." A mix-up of verb tenses could result in "the greatest confusion."[34] In short, there was hardly any grammar rule that Moser's instruction did not identify as a source of danger on the diplomatic terrain. Subsequently, he turned these warnings into a systematized "state grammar" that turned spelling, punctuation, calligraphy, and etymology into disciplines of importance to the state, "because in the language of those versed in matters of the state, all words carry their special weight."[35]

The exclusive and excluding chancery style was part of an arsenal of arcane technologies designed to cordon off the chanceries from their environment. A different kind of barrier function, one not operating on the rhetorical terrain, was performed by the latticed windows that served to exclude—to create an outside world—but at the same time allowed for submission of petitions. To ensure that the traffic between cabinet and chancery remained secret, the wording of all administrative instructions was classified as a "state secret."[36] But secret matters are only really secret as long as they are not understood by officials. Chancery employees were therefore required to be in possession of a "fine hand" but otherwise be of "limited understanding."[37] The ability to reflect, which was to be beyond the mental faculties of subaltern scribes, became the exclusive provenance of secret counselors, or as they are now called, high-portfolio ministers. As already indicated by the similarity of *mysterium* and *ministerium,* ministers are to administer a mystery. The gap between ministers and scribes, angels and working angels, widens under the premise of state secrets. "Civil servants working in an office have to possess a certain expertise; those working in chanceries just have to be reliable calligraphers."[38] As a result, ministers treated "secretaries like privately employed lackeys."[39]

The secretaries were no longer responsible for keeping things locked and secret; they were themselves locked away.

Prussia: Philosophy of the State-Act

PUBLICITY AND SELF-ADMINISTRATION

The enlightened demands of 1789 were aimed at tearing down the barriers that separated people from the mysteries of the state, including those state-imposed barriers that prevented disfranchised subjects from maturing into full-fledged citizens. In 1800, Prussian chancellor Karl August von Hardenberg (1750–1822) recommended that in view of the advances made in other governmental domains, the Prussian administration adopt a "common style."[40] The other ministers were opposed and resorted to the same arguments that in earlier days had been used by secretaries: they feared a loss of courtesy and authority. It is not difficult to discern behind their refusal an obvious desire to remain fully and visibly in power and to speak *nomine regis* (in the name of the king). It was only ten years after Hardenberg had triggered the debate on the deceremonialization of governmental speech and writing that the last resistance to his proposals was overcome. The curial style was abolished per decree. Henceforward the entire country, from schools to bureaus—as the former Baroque chanceries were now called—was characterized by one and the same *gemeine Styl*, or common style. The epoch of a particular state practice based on special discursive rules was over. Special instructions for civil servants in "matters of state" were rendered superfluous. As of 1815, the old disciplines of cameralistics and *Polizeywissenschaften* were no longer required subjects at Prussian universities. What they had taught was either abandoned or reconfigured in other disciplines, such as statistics, demography, economics, public finance, or anthropology. Material files ended their brief career as illustrative material in university courses on state practice. In 1808, Karl Sigmund von Altenstein, later Prussian secretary of culture, recommended in a letter to Hardenberg that file-keeping techniques be removed from the curriculum: "The so-called practical lectures at universities are for the most part nothing but practical instruction. As such, they have a certain importance, but they are of no value to the sciences. They deal primarily with formal matters."[41] Universities no longer taught their students how to compile and archive; such skills were presupposed. Likewise, ever since grammar, orthography, rhetoric, and poetics, formerly the domain of secretaries, had become part of the school curricula, the ability to write and speak was already being taught to children.

By demanding that everybody should be able to read and write, the Prussian school reform of 1812 finalized the shift from the poet-secretary to the common individual. A *particular* state practice became part of the education state. The old corporatist access restrictions to public discourse were abolished, ensuring that all were equally integrated into the body of the state. According to Friedrich Kittler, this incorporation resulted from the way state exams linked up the education system and the civil ser-vice.[42] Karl Marx defined the state exam as the "choice of the determinate individual for civil servant appointment,"[43] paraphrasing a passage from Hegel's philosophy of right, according to which all state exams and high school graduations are a "sovereign act" providing "the individual [with] an official vocation."[44] The integration of all members of the state—all male members, that is—finally achieved the goal of turning all subjects into citizens. The new guiding concept was self-administration, which Baron Karl vom und zum Stein (1757–1831) in his Nassau Memor memoir directed against "formulaic junk and mechanical service."[45] The principle of self-administration, championed by reformers such as Stein and Hard-enberg for the creation of an effectively functioning civil service, resulted in self-control and self-optimization based on "feedback."[46] Civil servants that administer themselves begin to function smoothly within govern-mental administration.

The state, then, is no longer recognizable by a particular state practice. It acts through its civil servants and thus ideally through every citizen. As if it were a supersubject composed of subjects, the state is credited with all its administrative operations and utterances. Once civil servants embody the state, there is no administrative act, no matter how trivial, that does not carry the sovereignty of the entire state with it. Whatever civil servants do and whatever instruction they pass on to citizens, every-thing amounts to a sovereign act. The latter are administrative acts *avant la lettre.* "In all governmental orders that are passed on to citizens there resides, as it were, the 'concept' of the administrative act, which, brought to light, claims legal force."[47] Derived from the French *acte administratif,* the term *administrative act* moves governmental activities into the sphere of validity. In German, the formation of the state as a sovereign indi-vidual can be glimpsed in the switch from the feminine plural *die Akten* (the files) to the masculine singular *der Akt* (the act). For the illustrious singular of the sovereign state act to come about, files (*Akten*) had to lead their unglamorous life in murky Prussian offices. On their own, they are not worth talking about. The daily commerce with the many files that are still produced by subaltern officials on a daily basis is of no interest to the philosophical and theoretical discourse on the transcendental signified of the state.

And indeed, more files than ever accumulated. The main reason for this proliferation around 1800 was the principle of self-administration. Feedback technologies resulted in heaps of files. By institutionalizing the principle of self-administration, Prussia succumbed to the entropic principle. "Because . . . a lot had to be written, even more had to be written"[48]—that is the iron logic of the self-recursive file apparatus. Excessive writing paralyzed the administration. Because letters could kill the living spirit, officials were not supposed to hold on to them. "It is our will that the actions of our high-ranking officials should be based on their own opinions and on local investigations rather than on dry reports . . . to ensure that the life and spirit of our administration is not lost under all the writing."[49] As Frederick William III had already intended, mindless scribes were to make way for independent-minded civil servants. The Stein-Hardenberg reforms, too, aimed at creating civil servant subjects who administered themselves. In the eyes of vom Stein, increasing numbers of files were a sign of lack of independence; to him, "working with files and pretending to work" were synonymous.[50] The officials he encountered appeared to resemble "unthinking chancery employees" from former days. As was the case with Bartleby, the entire existence of these meticulous recording entities was consumed by mechanical writing—a betrayal of the ideal of self-administration that incurred the ridicule of Hardenberg's campaign "against bureauism."[51] Since he expected nothing from a "constitution, albeit so necessary and beneficial for the Prussian state," he pinned his hopes on the powers of administration, especially on civil servants who acted in autonomous fashion. The latter, however, would remain scarce as long as

we are ruled by *salaried, bookish, disinterested, and unpropertied bureauists.* This may go on forever. These four words sum up the spirit of our governing machinery and others like ours: *salaried,* that is, striving to maintain and increase the numbers of those receiving a salary; *bookish,* that is, living in a world of letters rather than in reality; *disinterested,* that is, devoid of any connection with any of the classes that make up the citizenry of the state and instead forming their own cast, the caste of scribes; *unpropertied,* that is, oblivious to the fate of property, rain or shine. . . . [A]ll that is of no concern to them, they draw their state salary and write, write, write in silence in their offices behind closed doors, unknown, unnoticed, unpraised, and raise their children to be equally useful writing machines. I saw the military machinery fall on October 14, 1806; maybe the writing machinery will have its October 14.[52]

Vom Stein is referring to the decisive defeat of Prussia at the hands of Napoleon at the twin battles of Jena and Auerstedt on October 14, 1806. Nothing can express the hope of the reformers for author-subjects more emphatically than his depressing image of its exact opposite: the writing machines (*Schreibmaschinen*) or typewriters that made their German debut in this 1821 letter.[53]

KEEPING RECORDS AND BECOMING A SUBJECT

Subjects produce themselves by administering themselves, by establishing a feedback with their own actions. The imperative of the Enlightenment to reflect one's own actions comes from the very end, from the notion of a Last Judgment at which "like at a trial the records of our life are read out."[54] Our conscience is a court that has been moved into a *forum internum*; it demands accountability. Once the demand for accountability applies not only to merchants and their shenanigans but to the most banal chores and most secret ideas of an individual, the bookkeeping practices common to business offices are transformed into diaries, autobiographies, and other such accounts. The permanent imaginary tribunal forces us to frame our goals and intentions as a statement of accounts. The Swiss writer Johann Kaspar Lavater demanded from himself in his *Secret Journal of a Self-Observer* to keep a meticulously honest and complete diary "as carefully as if I were to read my journal to God: so carefully, that on my deathbed I shall be enabled, by these records, to give to myself an account of my life, like that which will be laid before me, when my spirit shall have taken its flight to better regions."[55] The self-observations are phrased as a plea in response to the general indictments of the Last Judgment. Autobiographical writings, then, are a way of accounting for one's own life in order to have enough material to match the evidence accumulated in heaven. They provide a view of one's whole life—a perspective that centers on life as limited time. Time is a precious commodity; it is imperative to provide a clear account of how it is used.

In record-keeping nations like Prussia, where every citizen was his own civil servant, public and private records became indistinguishable. They both amounted to files compiled by the "administration of the interior"

(Ranke) or, literally, the ministry of the interior. The *mysterium internum* is what is revealed in writing: the secret of the soul. It became accessible to the public when selected files were published, for instance in Karl Philipp Moritz's 1782 *Archiv für Erfahrungsseelenkunde* (Archive for empirical psychology). But when Prussian ministers of state—the state's most exclusive civil servants-subjects—set pen to paper, the state-run ministry of the interior was directly involved in producing subjects by way of record-keeping. It had the right of first access to ministerial records. Immediately following "the death of a minister, several high-ranking officials appeared and sealed his office, in order to be undisturbed while sorting his files and confiscating everything of an official nature."[56] Whether or not ministers were posthumously transformed into "great men of administration"[57] was up to the ministry of the interior. Upon his death in 1822, State Chancellor Hardenberg left behind widely scattered documents, bills, invoices, receipts, cabinet files, letters, and memoranda that he had composed as a Prussian representative, accounts, notes from other ministries, fragments of memoirs, diaries, and a kind of "expanded itinerary," all of which were seized. "This paper estate, located in Genoa and Verona, in Hardenberg's official residence in Berlin, and in Glienicke near Potsdam, was sealed, inspected, and put into safekeeping by Karl Georg von Raumer, the director of the state archives."[58] "Hardenberg" became classified information. According to an untraceable but nonetheless obeyed ruling, his files were to be kept safe from public inspection for fifty years from the time of his death. A temporal barrier was set up between secret and public—the retention period.

Only what is no longer volatile can become history. An edict of 1776 clearly spelled out that only such matters may be made public whose release from the archive "has no adverse effect on state and government."[59] In time the potential for jeopardizing the state decreased, with the result that restricted files could be made public without any risk. When an editorial series was established in 1877 to turn the founding of the empire into a discursive event, the retention period imposed on Hardenberg's records had just elapsed; his records had aged sufficiently to become harmless, state-supporting history. Hence it was possible to launch the new series with the "Commentaries of State Chancellor Prince of Hardenberg."[60] The sealed files were opened by none other than the minister at the time, Otto von Bismarck. The task of editing them was entrusted to the historian Leopold von Ranke. Given his ambition to "base historiography exclusively on documentary records and reports," Ranke was uniquely qualified for the job; indeed he hoped that Hardenberg's commentaries would allow him to apply the file-based principles of historiography "in even greater measure than before."[61] These introductory aspirations were followed by five volumes of published records of the former chancellor. In combination with the corresponding files from the other ministries, they amount to history.

Following a rigorous policy of self-administration that renders Ranke superfluous, Johann Wolfgang von Goethe bequeathed his literary inheritance to posterity already in the shape of a thoroughly ordered archive. The shift from the alleged paper chaos of the author of *Faust* to the ordered archive of the poet occurred in the year of Hardenberg's death.[62] The first complete edition of Goethe's works had appeared, marking a caesura that demanded introspection. Goethe noted on the occasion of the publication: "For his remaining years, the author directs his attention to editing, tidying up, and securing the amassed papers."[63] Such time management requires ordering and archiving old files rather than writing and planning new books. For a man of seventy-three, it is high time to take stock of his life. After all, even "a man of forty, if he believes that he has achieved something noteworthy and has led an important life, should start writing an account of his life."[64] At this stage, life is still a detailed registry and hence "still close enough to our mistakes and faults." Goethe's survey, too, proceeds in this synoptic fashion; the unedited notes are used "to draw up a balance sheet and see what was successful and what wasn't." This inner court, however, has less moral bias than Lavater's. The "world-child" Goethe is more prone to accuse his life's work of being "scattered and dismembered." His ultimate goal is a literary estate that will arrange the patchwork of life in such orderly and coherent fashion that it can assume its rightful place in the Elysium of world literature. This concern about his literary afterlife focuses on ordering his amassed papers, in an attempt to "prepare as well as possible the work of friends who will dedicate themselves to my estate."[65] At this point in time, the latter would not be able to cope "with the masses of paper that surround me, and which, though arranged in orderly fashion, can only be used by myself." To create an immediately obvious order, Goethe penned a "suggestion for a complete edition of Goethe's literary estate, conceived by himself."[66] To preclude any abuse of the poet's files at the hands of helpful friends, it reveals and communicates the tacit knowledge of his private record-keeping. A transparent file order will defend the dead poet from posthumous distortions. It programs future readers, ensuring that the literary achievement will be acknowledged on its own grounds.

It is Goethe's explicit goal that "after completing the archival ordering, he may survey his own life,"[67] as early modern rulers clearly surveyed their domain. In 1822, however, his gaze still encounters a disorderly mess. "Whenever I looked upon the large mass spread out in front of me and perceived the printed matter partly ordered, partly scattered about, partly sealed, partly in need of completion . . . I was afflicted by wistful confusion . . . from which I tried to escape as resolutely as possible." Order is the sole means of escape from this melancholia. "Of pivotal importance was the separation of the shelves, which I had kept fairly tidy . . . and a thorough, orderly compilation of all papers . . . in which nothing was to be neglected or dismissed as unworthy." Since even the smallest scrap may contribute to the understanding of a life, Goethe took measures to ensure "that not only printed and unprinted, collected and disseminated writings should be arranged in perfect order, but that diaries and letters sent and received should find their way into an archive that, in addition, has been ordered and registered according to all manner of rubrics, letters, and numbers."[68] Ordering and archiving are tantamount to combining the unbridled instincts into "active life."[69] The active life is that which operates by written feedback. One's own archive contains the *vita activa* in the aggregate state of orderly files.

Ordering papers is usually the task of clerks and secretaries. Theodor Kräuter, "a young, sprightly man well-versed in library matters,"[70] is hired by Goethe to record his testimonies. In stark contrast to the detailed accounts he provides of his own activities, Goethe rarely talks about the work of his secretaries. By adopting a secretarial demeanor, Goethe subdued real-life secretaries: "In much the same way as he mimicked secretaries, he was not afraid to play dispatcher, building inspector or any other such part. . . . He was flattered when this subaltern versatility did not go unnoticed."[71] This mimetic strategy, which turns a writer into a secretary, calls for yet another amanuensis to provide a fitting account of these subaltern activities. A work published in 1834 in Jena, entitled *Goethe's Official Activities: Based on his files and on the correspondence between him and Grand Duke Carl August, Privy Councilor Voigt and others, presented by his last assistant, Dr. C. Vogel,* subjected Goethe's administrative habits to professional scrutiny: "I have as much as possible endeavored to depict Goethe's peculiarity by means of his files. . . . True human greatness is not diminished by revealing its shortcomings, it is rendered more credible. It is for this reason that I have not concealed Goethe's mistakes."[72] The ingrained duty of the copyist to provide exact replicas results in a verdict on the imperfections of the poet: "And thus he who was so inclined to record

FIGURE 6.   Sealed files of Goethe's political activity. Stiftung Weimarer Klassik, Weimar 1998.

everything, even matters pertaining to his private life, was anything but that which we call a man of files. Despite Goethe's indeed singular love for order, his files, which he kept in utmost tidiness, were in fact never in a state that allowed for practical use."[73]

Such bureaucratic criteria are sidelined once literary scholars rather than clerks start to write about "Goethe as Administrator." The essay by this name, written by Ernst Robert Curtius five years before his death, adopts the point of view of a fellow author. It follows the birth of the poet from his files, highlights the chancery discourse employed by Goethe to give accounts of his active life, and quotes diary entries: "Looking through the capsules. Older and more recent manuscripts"[74] (March 5, 1818). "Prepared rubrics for varia and outlined schemata" (August 15, 1821). "A number of drafts of letters, fair copies, and the like. Filed and arranged them differently. Drew up a schema for the agenda" (June 5, 1828). "Fascicles newly laid out for incoming and outgoing letters"[75] (December 30, 1816). And so on. These quotes prove the poet to be a civil servant-subject; they refer his accomplishments as a poet to dealings with files that Goethe had learned and cultivated as a member of the Weimar Privy Council.

Goethe adopted the administrative techniques of a chancery clerk to provide a foundation for the author function. The act of canceling, which he refers to as "disposal" (*Beseitigung*), relocates his writings into the legal domain of authorship. Pondering the ambivalence of the frequently used verb *to dispose*, Curtius remarked that it is a "sovereign act" oscillating between "destroying" and "getting things done," for example in these entries: "Preparations for spending the day in the lower garden. Disposed of several things" (May 5, 1830). "Selected some poetic material for Wendt. . . . Disposed of other things" (May 6, 1830).[76] Whatever is disposed of lands in paper bags—but it is not garbage, it is the biographic base of the literary inheritance. As Curtius points out, Goethe performs self-administration in an increasingly literal sense of the word: "Goethe has long since ceased to merely administer affairs of state. He administers his own existence. And when he lacks the energy to do more, he finds contentment in the well-regulated course of self-administration."[77] In the idle motion of files, life creates itself as a regulated administrative procedure: "Rose early. Soon lay down again. Awaited the arrival of Privy Councilor Vogel. Once more futile attempt to get up. Meanwhile I continued to work. Wrote, dictated, had fair copies made, so that by evening I had everything satisfactorily accomplished" (June 22, 1839).[78]

Secret State Archive

Just as the techniques of file-based self-administration around 1800 constitute the subject as an individual and citizen, the *archive* becomes the constituent element of the nation. The archive—more precisely, the type of archive that coincided with the formation of the nation-state— was initiated by the French Revolution, which for a brief moment in history struggled with the alternative: *respect aux fonds*, or clearing of all memory. From an archival perspective, the revolution presented itself as the liberation of huge piles of paper from regional file depots that the revolutionaries, in order to effectively or at least symbolically destroy the ancien régime, wanted to burn, thereby continuing the "tradition" of storming or incinerating archives that reaches back to antiquity. The struggle against the old powers was effective insofar as "a lot of archival matter was destroyed in July and August 1789."[79] But before serious gaps could emerge, the file-destroying fury gave way to new archival projects. The tendency toward preservation became noticeable just two weeks after the storming of the Bastille, though at first it focused on the revolutionary activities themselves. The fact that they were still involved in daily scuffles did not keep the revolutionaries from taking a historical view of their own notes and minutes and considering them worthy of being included in an archive. Later this option of *respect aux fonds* also prevailed when it came to the documents of the vanquished regime. In a meeting of the National Assembly on 7 Messidor in Year 2 (June 25, 1794), the deputy Dubois defended the records of the old absolutist regime from impending destruction. His argument reached far back into history and invoked the alleged refusal of the Romans "[de] livrer tous les titres aux flammes et de faire disparaître jusqu'aux moindres vestiges des monuments d'un regime abhorré [to give up all the books to the flames and make disappear all vestiges of the monuments of a detested regime]."[80] The French, too, ought to preserve some of the documents of the hated regime, to convey to posterity the nature of the reign of terror they had overcome. Subsequently, rather than destroying the records of the ancien régime, the National Assembly declared them to be public property, *propriété publique* (*et particulière*).[81] The archive was handed over to the public and became just as accessible as, for instance, the Dôme des Invalides.

Mikhail Bakunin later delivered a harsh critique of the revolution's conserving, and conservative, treatment of files. In his "Programme and Purpose of the Revolutionary Organization of International Brothers," he attributed the failure of the French Revolution to the fact that it put more trust in the guillotine than in incinerating files. The anarchistic program, on the other hand, intends to complete the stalled revolution by taking aim at the very heart of the state: its administrative infrastructure, which resides less in its operatives than in its paperwork:

> Power stems far less from men than from the positions made available to privileged men by the organization of things, in other words the institution of the state. . . . In order to launch a radical revolution, it is therefore necessary to attack positions and things and to destroy property and the State, but there will be no need to destroy men. . . . As we see it, the revolution must set out from the first radically and totally to destroy the State and all State institutions. The natural and necessary consequences of this destruction will be: . . . the abolition and incineration of all title-deeds, wills, bills of sale and gift, legal papers—in other words all legal and civil red tape.[82]

Those versed in the workings of bureaucracy, however, are little inclined to support anarchistic dreams of destroying files while sparing people. Max Weber, for one, rejected Bakunin's ideas: "The naive idea of Bakuninism of destroying the basis of 'acquired rights' together with the 'domination' by destroying the public documents overlooks that the settled orientation of *man* for observing the accustomed rules and regulations will survive independently of the documents."[83] Weber's critique of the anarchistic faith in files raises the crucial question of whether power is tied to persons or to administrative structures. Human inertia, the sociologist Weber diagnoses, resists innovations in the administrative realm. A kind of Clausewitz of bureaucracy, he emphasizes that this inertia can be used strategically as a continuation of administration under a changed command to secure continuity during regime shifts (which, of course, does little to answer Bakunin's question of how such continuity might be interrupted—at least it does not lead necessarily to the conclusion that the only way a successful regime change can be brought about is by exchanging the administrative personnel). "A rationally ordered officialdom continues to function smoothly after the enemy has occupied the territory; he merely needs to change the top officials."[84] This insight barely refutes Bakunin's "naive" ideas, for the notion that the bureaucratic machine will "survive independently of documents" solely because of the "settled orientation of man" is itself an effect of files. In the words of the anarchist, a filed-based administrative structure will function only and as long as "the organization of things" remains intact, that is, as long as official procedures and the circulation of files continue to be in operation. Thus the "settled orientation" (Weber) of the administrative personnel follows from the "organization" of administrative things (Bakunin). In other words, the inertia of the personnel is itself an effect of files.

If we were to combine the theses of Bakunin and Weber by arguing that it is the union of files and officials that provides the basis for continuity of power, Prussian history could serve as a proof. Following the French occupation, Prussian administrative activities momentarily ceased. The continuity of the state was interrupted. In October 1806, the production of files dropped to a low, which in a state that takes note of all its movements *in actis* points to an event *in mundo*—namely, the fall of the military machine that vom Stein would like to have seen followed by the fall of the writing machinery. The defeat at Jena and Auerstedt was not put on record. In the administrative domain, it found its meager expression in the no more than twenty-one files that were compiled between October 14, 1806, and a few weeks before the Peace of Tilsit in June 1807. Nonetheless, the Prussian writing machinery was only temporarily out of joint. As the last official act of the general directory, the files were handed over to "Secret Counselor Sack," yet after the peace treaty Prussian bureaucrats resumed their "activities under the supervision of officials from the occupying power,"[85] File output soon returned to former levels. Making use of all the old paperwork Bakunin had set his sights on, the administration continued to operate smoothly, even under an occupying power.

Prussia becomes the subject of the state by administering itself. By anticipating how it will be viewed by future history, the state becomes a subject of history. Archiving its files amounts to the administration of an estate on a state level. When, following a suggestion by vom Stein, the administrative apparatus was restructured around ministries rather than provinces, territorial distinctions gave way to the idea of the state: the reorganization turned the multitude of Prussian states into the Prussian State. From then on, the state acts as its own originator. It makes history and is thus able to write itself into history. Whatever happens is worthy of being archived; records of ongoing procedures already turn into history. Droysen's description of his own, historically conscious present expresses what was already practiced at the beginning of the nineteenth century: "No business of public life is conducted without an awareness of its historical context. . . . At every moment business is immediately transformed into history and history, in turn, is applied to business."[86] Administrative acts reveal themselves to be historical anticipations.

Prussia bequeathed an ordered archive to posterity. No longer was it a depot created with the vague purpose of being "of use for future times";[87] unlike the leftovers from bygone times that, according to Droysen, first had to be duly processed by historians, Prussian records "are, and want to be, sources."[88] The Prussian state archive was a premeditated agglomeration of the forces of history. Its basic capital was the pre-1770 records that had been bought up or captured from "ceded provinces for the good of impoverished officials."[89] These were supplemented by the records from Prussia's ongoing administrative proceedings. Thus the repositories of the archive were made up of files from the old regime and new ones supplied by the central administration. At the end of the ancien régime stands the beginning of a rule based on, and imbued with, history. The *state* archive becomes the power dispositive of the Prussian state. The "historical bureau" administers history just as the statistical bureau administers the population. The former was no archive with dead files; rather, it mediated between the present and the future, thus keeping the past from being over. Hence an *archivarius* is no longer a man who must "take pleasure in files";[90] he is a historian working in the interest of the state. In highly self-referential manner, the "secret archival assistant" Carl Wilhlem Cosmar penned not the history of this or that dynasty but the history of the Royal Prussian Secret State and Cabinet Archive itself. Its end coincides with that of the old kingdom in 1806. "Based on archived records," he narrated the history of files that they themselves do not contain: the origin of their order, of the chancery and registry practices, of the changing archivists, of the subsequent rearrangements, and so on. The new state archive acted as a guide to such reports from the world of the archival preconscious, when archives were mere depots rather than the memory of the state.

The reformed Prussian Reform State no longer simply found and arranged empirical data into tableaus; it created itself by way of writing and recording. It generated itself in files that did not merely accumulate but grew *organically*. Prussian files are, have, and institute the life of the state. To write the history of Prussia, then, requires only retrieving the administrative procedures that have been laid *ad acta* and reviving the history deposited in the lower strata of the archive. That is how the Protestant historian Ranke proceeded. He penetrated the cordon of official writing to find traces of life and political entanglements, to track down biographical details, moods, errors, and intrigues. Unlike his colleagues, he was no longer satisfied with simply retelling the documented history of great events; he was focused on their origin, on things as they were evolving. It was not possible, Ranke wrote, "for the rich active life, of which these texts capture mere moments, to already regard itself as an object of historical reflection. Who has not felt, or heard expressed, the desire to obtain more detailed and comprehensive information about Prussian history and Frederick II in particular than he himself volunteered? It is a commonly held conviction that matters can be observed more closely, that new perspectives and more profound historical insights may be gained, if one has the opportunity to research the archives harboring the documents and letters which contain the most immediate knowledge of events. . . . In accordance with my objectives I had to fully immerse myself in the extensive records."[91] As in the case of Goethe, the "rich active life" creates and validates itself in the act of writing things down. Even in the ideal notion of "administration as an actively engaged constitution,"[92] propagated in the mid-nineteenth century by Lorenz von Stein, written feedback becomes the very signature of activity—*administratorii vel activi*, as it was said of the angels in Sicilian chanceries. And this active life, turned into writing, is now conserved in archives, awaiting its revival at the hands of historians.

Ranke's quest for active life is the historiographical pendant to the archival politics of State Chancellor Hardenberg, who, following the centralization of all state archives in the Prussian chancellery in 1810, became, as it were, the minister of history.

The *state* archive was tied to the central organization of administration; its arrangement "mirrors the historical evolution of the central authorities."[93] The archived records did not merely store specific contents. Every single detail concerning the official channels was wholly inscribed by the reorganization of Prussian bureaucracy. "The 'rationalization' granted to bureaucracy since Hegel and Weber," Bruno Latour writes, "has been attributed by mistake to the 'mind' of [Prussian] bureaucrats. It is all in the files themselves."[94] Latour's insight merely recapitulates what Prussia had imposed upon itself: a way of handling files contains its own bureaucracy. It was not the mind of Prussian officialdom that gave rise to the rationality of bureaucracy, but rather phantom bureaucrats, the invisible hands of file notes and control characters. But because historians search for the essence of the state behind profane administrative techniques, they do not dwell for very long on the files themselves. Rather, they deduce the spirit of Prussian bureaucracy from the imprint it left on its administrative structure.

Prussia itself is responsible for this faulty conclusion. By locating "the soul of all public state business"[95] in the archive—by having files imbue the state with a soul in much the same way as private records bring about an active subject—the micrologistics of record-keeping presents itself as a narratable story. The result is not an overview of the development of controlling administrative algorithms, but a story of the spirit of officialdom materialized in files. The archive, however, contains both possibilities: it enables us to analyze the birth of the state either from the sprit or from the control signs of Prussian bureaucracy.

§ 5   From the Bureau to Data Protection

The *chancery* is replaced by the *office*. With the switch from the nineteenth to the twentieth century, the organization dispositive shifts from administrative techniques to office technologies. The new reign of the office manifested itself in Bismarck's Reich Chancellery, which was a chancellery in name only. In the 1886 official handbook of the German government, it was already defined as the "Central bureau of the Reich chancellor," charged "with conducting all official exchanges with individual department heads."[1] Just like the Roman *ab epistulis* office, it was responsible for official communications throughout the Reich; hence it was also in charge of the postal and telegraph system. But like all channels and relays, the office remained indifferent to the messages transmitted, with the result that the historically decisive advent of the Weimar Republic hardly affected the internal organization of the chancellery. From its inside perspective, the end of the monarchy in 1919 amounted to no more than a simple distribution problem: According to the memoirs of Arnold Brecht, a former secretary of the Reich Chancellery, it merely became a bit more difficult to distribute incoming letters, because in many cases the secretaries were no longer personally acquainted with the senders.[2]

Max Weber used the principle of bureaucratic rationality to capture the remarkably smooth way the administration continued to function after 1918. The rationality of the bureaucracy is the *ratio* of the office, which, following the recommendations of 1910, increasingly came to depend on modern means of communication, such as telephones and typewriters. Since the turn of the century, reformers had been trying to introduce these technologies, which were already in use in the private sector, to public offices. The suggested reforms of 1910 and 1919, however, were only gradually implemented; in part they were included in the Common Rules of Procedure for the Administration (1926) and the Common Rule of Procedure for Higher Reich Offices (1928). The war-induced break in the transmission of tacit administrative knowledge made it necessary to explicitly formulate rules of procedure to replace Bismarck's legendary file marks, which until then seem to have been a sufficient basis for the Reich administration after 1870. In 1912 they were compiled and published for official use (quoted in what follows as *Compilation*). Though it continued to apply these administrative means, the National Socialist regime put an abrupt stop to the suggested reforms before they could be fully realized. There was no sympathy anymore for the principle of municipal self-administration that reformers had inherited from the Stein-Hardenberg reform. Its implementation was forestalled by the centralist and authoritarian elements of the administrative structure, as is evident from Arnold Brecht's description of administrative procedures after 1933: "Ultimately, the reason for the demise of the office reform was the amalgamation of the Reich ministries and the Prussian ministries under Hitler. Given the large preponderance of files in the Prussian ministries, the reform was stopped in its tracks; nobody had the energy to introduce the proposed changes to the Prussian sector of the new combined ministry."[3] While this may have spelled the end of the reforms (with the result that all historical accounts dealing with them end in 1933), it did not mark the end of bureaucratic innovation. On the contrary, when it came to the census and subsequent selection of the population, the Nazis made full use of office technologies, such as index cards and the tabbing system (i.e., tabs affixed to identity cards for purposes of classification).[4]

There are very few accounts that reflect this continuity and focus on the administrative aspects of the Nazi policies of colonization, deportation, and extermination. In 1959, Hans Günther Adler, a German writer and expert on National Socialism living in exile in London, analyzed, at the behest of the Munich *Institut für Zeitgeschichte*, the deportation files of the Würzburg Gestapo. The results were published in 1974 as *Der verwaltete Mensch* [Administered man]. The study offers a perspective on the National Socialist regime beyond all ideological analyses. It inquires into administrative efficiency and the practical implementation of legal power. What is lacking, though, is a comprehensive history of administrative techniques that reaches from the modernized administration of the

Weimar Republic and the Nazi administration to the Federal Republic of Germany, highlighting in particular the manufacturers of office technologies as well as the careers of administration experts who were influential in all three time periods. Only Götz Aly and Karl Heinz Roth, in their study *The Nazi Census*, researched precisely these aspects of Nazi selection and extermination politics by dwelling on modern office technologies from the 1920s to the 1980s. The main focus of their work was on population statistics. Their analysis, which in turn was indebted to Raul Hilberg's comprehensive study *The Destruction of the European Jews*, is the point of departure for the following remarks on the normality of the bureaucratic machine.

Reflecting on the sources he used for fifty years, Hilberg himself has drawn attention to the continuity of Nazi bureaucracy: "The whole of the voluminous internal correspondence produced by the bureaucracy . . . conformed to established patterns. It was fashioned in time-honored ways and transmitted through channels hollowed out by generations of functionaries. Formats were adopted. . . . In the creation and distribution of documents, form follows form, and routine perpetuates routine."[5] To conduct its policies, then, the National Socialist regime relied on the established bureaucratic forms and procedures that it inherited from the administrative reforms of the 1920s, without, however, sharing any of its reformist ideals.

Office Reform around 1920

TELEPHONE, TYPEWRITER, CARBON COPIES

But before these reforms took hold, the Second Reich had to deal with the unstoppable proliferation of files. Bismarck was forced to decree that "henceforth no file may weigh more than two kilos."[6] Such weight restrictions—which resulted in lighter, though not necessarily fewer, files—were accompanied by selection procedures that had been in effect since the 1830s and were designed to counteract the rapidly growing number of public files. "The registry periodically rids itself of its old files by selling them as scrap paper."[7] When it comes to processing files, then, chancellery and archive were joined by a third entity: waste paper traders.[8] These three agencies corresponded to the official designations of the aggregate state of files: "indispensable for ongoing business," "currently not in use

but qualified for further storage," "to be destroyed without further notice." The classification of the files according to these categories was undertaken by the office responsible. To counteract the temptation to consider all clerical work worthy of archival storage, incentives were offered
for the destruction of files. If low-ranking officials responsible for sorting
out the files and selling them as scrap made a profit, they were entitled
to 25 percent of the proceeds. Once files had been cleared for pulping, an
official certificate attesting to their complete annihilation precluded any
abuse of the documents. The fact that discarded files gave birth to new
files dealing with the discarded ones is part of the paradox of a "government in writing." Even the "transmutation of records into wastepaper"
has to be recorded.[9] It appears that nothing on file can ever really disappear. It leaves a trace, be it only in the shape of a registered gap. In the
1920s files were so closely linked to their physical destruction that the entry on files in the handbook of the Prussian administration concentrates
almost exclusively on this aspect. Strategies for mastering the incessant
growth of files ranged from rules determining their selection to instructions geared toward preempting records. The first legally binding contributions were the 1910 Outlines for Simplified Governmental Procedures,
which had been worked out by a commission appointed a year earlier.
The civil servants' verdict on this reform was short and devastating: the
files concerning the 'reduction of paperwork' had reached an alarming
size. The only successful part of the reform was the adoption of a neolo-
gism: *Weglegesache* (discardable matter). But since a mere term could not
make files disappear in the real, the recommendations issued in 1917–19
once again focused on how official paperwork could be minimized. They
not only adopted simplification and rationalization techniques that had
been imposed by the austere wartime economy, but an efficiency expert
imported more effective administrative and organizational means and
procedures from the front.

After 1933, the Nazi government made use of the rhetoric of simplification, but it was directed at legally guaranteed procedural matters rather
than bureau-technical details. In fact the reform-oriented selection of files
for physical destruction was explicitly revoked, since the new emphasis
on research into ethnic and racial ancestry had increased the importance
of retired records. Records were to be stored and reused rather than destroyed. This tendency to rule with the help of old files—more precisely,
with the aid of the population data contained therein—became evident

soon after the Nazis came to power. The first step was to integrate church registries, which contained data on members of the community reaching back several generations, into the ongoing administrative process. These were analyzed by Protestant theology students in order to issue a certificate of racial descent, which since 1935 was a condition for employment in several party and administrative offices.[10]

The bureaucratic innovations of the 1920s, which were indebted to no small degree to the technology transfer of the First World War, had already been anticipated by General Field Marshal Alfred von Schlieffen's vision of a fully bureaucratized military. In his essay "War Today," he depicted a future commander-in-chief "in a house with a spacious office, where telegraphs, telephones, and signal apparatus are to hand."[11] In *Economy and Society*, Max Weber confirmed Schlieffen's scenario: The "modern higher-ranking officer fights battles from the 'office.'"[12] Postwar offices took over the telephone from the battlefield offices of the First World War. The reformers' hope of curbing governmental file production now focused on this oral medium. Phone calls, however, are prone to further paper trails, not only because announcing the call has to be done in writing, but also because the conversation itself has to be recorded and put on file to verify that it really took place *in mundo*. Weber defined the paradox of orality in writing as the basic rule of bureaucracy: "Administrative acts, decisions, and rules are formulated and recorded in writing, even in cases where oral discussion is the rule or is even mandatory."[13] In a frequently quoted passage, Weber elaborated this rule of procedure: "The combination of written documents and a continuous operation by officials constitutes the 'office' (Bureau) which is the central focus of all types of modern organized action."[14] In defiance of a "naïve Bakuninism," then, the link between files and officials secures continuity. In the domain of instrumental reason, files become the means for the modern, rationalized exercise of legal power. Governmental acts *must be*—not just *can be*—documented in writing: "To each official action there corresponds the act of putting it on record."[15] Under these circumstances, the proliferation of files was all but inevitable. Constant reminders to curb stylistic exuberance were insufficient. There was a need for a new Stein or Hardenberg, who would resume and update the reforms shelved after 1848. According to a cabinet resolution of January 19, 1917, Bill Drews, one of the last ministers of state appointed during the Second Reich, and president of the Higher Administrative Court and Prussian state official until 1937, was charged with preparing an administrative reform. Drews, who wrote a short biography of Stein in 1930, introduced his reforms with a promise that echoed pledges made by Stein, namely to "turn dead pieces of machinery into independently thinking individuals working in an official capacity."[16] His measures for discourse reduction, however, were aimed less at the abolition of soulless writing machines than at the ubiquitous deployment of their mechanized descendants. *Typewriters*, not civil servant-subjects, were to be the bearers of postwar reforms.

By the end of the 1920s, typewriters had become standard equipment for governmental agencies. And with them women, who were more likely than men to be trained in stenography, entered the domain of public administration. The civil service had been open to women since 1897, though only to unmarried ones. Women thus had the choice of either becoming or marrying a civil servant. According to a recommendation by Heinrich von Stephan, the postmaster general, the latter was the preferable alternative, given the low wages for single employees. The celibacy clause rested on the assumption that one cannot be married to the state and a state official at the same time—a logic that remained unchanged even when women and typewriters merged into an effective working unit. Typewriters, after all, cannot enter into a nuptial relationship with the state. Secretaries were and still are not eligible for civil servant status; they are restricted to a terminable employment relationship.

The link between typewriter and stenographer brought about the switch from chancery to office, rendering all basic chancery activities obsolete. The act of preparing a draft was replaced by a combination of dictation and shorthand. Likewise, preparing press copies became unnecessary after typewriters were equipped with carbon paper. The latter in fact predated the typewriter, but it was only due to the link with the typewriter that it became a staple of public administration around 1910. Inserted into the machine, it simultaneously created one or more copies of the clean copy. In short, "shorthand notes and typewritten carbon copies supplant the draft"[17] as well as the press copy. Furthermore, the use of forms rendered copies unnecessary. Transcribing and comparing, those "very dull, wearisome and lethargic" tasks (to quote Bartleby's employer) became a thing of the past. To introduce machines is to exclude scriveners like Bartleby. The chancery had already lost some of its material and media-technological power base around 1500, when the act of canceling was supplanted by storing drafts, but with the loss of its principal activities, drafting and copying, the very institution disappears. Without a draft, there is no cascade of controls, no revision, and no cancellation.

What is filed is no longer a draft but a carbon copy—that is, an identical copy—of the posted document. But once draft and final version no longer differ from each other, once there is nothing in the files that does not also find its way into the world, all hermeneutic enterprises that frolicked in the interpretive space between the various textual stages and delighted in the marginal notes on records are rendered just as obsolete as a historiography that drew its material from these differences. Historians and archivists deplore what administrative reformers acclaim: "The multiplication of texts that already gained momentum in the nineteenth century, and subsequently of course the employment of typewriters as well as the increased use of forms and print of all kind, divests the content of a file of all uniqueness."[18] The increasing formalization of administration, which since the days of the printing press resulted in the loss of all reference to an original, breaches the last bastion of secrecy, the mystery of files. They forfeit their privileged position in the universe of writing and thus lose their archival and historiographical significance. Archivists do not know where to store the "uniform mass of single-case files," and above all they do not know why they are storing them for future generations at all.[19]

VERTICAL FILES AND PLANS FOR RECORD-KEEPING

Though not directly involved in the reform debate, Max Weber offered some theoretical observations by reflecting on the degree to which bureaucratization was linked to the emergence of the modern office: "The decisive reason for the advance of bureaucratic organization has always been its purely technical superiority over any other form of organization. . . . All advances of the Prussian administrative organization, for example, have been and will in the future be advances of the bureaucratic . . . principle."[20] The bureaucratic principle is, upon close inspection, a bureau-technological one. It was the technological superiority of files and their ordering systems that inaugurated and secured the reign of the office; no wonder, then, that "of all the parts of a German ministry, the section that was subject to the most particular attention on the part of the reformers was the record and the filing system."[21] A new type of ring binder, as consequential to modern bureaucracy as was the plow and stirrup to the

Die Entwicklung des Briefordners

Biblorhapte

Die Briefe werden auf 5 Nadeln aufge-
spießt. Wenn der Apparat voll ist, wird
die Einlage mit den Briefen herausge-
nommen und eine neue eingesetzt.

Biblorhapte-Registrator

Die Nadeln sind durch 2 Röhrchen mit
aushebbarem Stecker ersetzt, dadurch
können an jeder beliebigen Stelle Briefe
eingefügt und entnommen werden.

Steckordner

Der Einband hat im Gegensatz zu Bild 2
einen steifen Rücken. Voraussetzung hie-
zu ist die von Louis Leitz erfundene Be-
weglichkeit des abgesetzten Unterdeckels.

Shannon-Registrator

Erster Ordner mit Umlegebügeln; sie
öffnen sich durch die Drehung nach aus-
wärts. Den Shannon-Registrator gab es
nur auf zweifarbigen Holzbrettchen.

Leitz-Ordner Vorläufer

Nach langwierigen Versuchen entstand
dieses Übergangs-Modell, das erste mit
nach links zurückklappbaren Bügeln. Der
Hebel befindet sich zwischen den Bügeln.

Leitz-Ordner mit Hebel

Der letzte entscheidende Schritt ist ge-
tan, der Hebel nach außen verlegt. Zur
Erzielung eines leichten Ganges ist die
kleine Rolle eingefügt.

FIGURE 7. The evolution of the file binder. Reprinted with the permission of
Jörg Schmalfuß (Department Head, Historisches Archiv, Deutsches Technikmuseum Berlin).

Middle Ages, turned out to be the center of the reform: the vertical file. Its invention coincided with the founding of the Second Reich.

In 1871, Louis Leitz, scion of an old Suebian family of craftsmen, opened a manufacture for the production of loose-leaf binders called *biblorhaptes*. In designing his new office gadget, he made use of an expired Parisian patent as well as of the Shannon Arch File. The latter was a contraption consisting of "a finely polished, well-glued wooden tablet, to which the bronzed metal part, including the small nickel tube and the arch, have been attached *sideways*. Inside the tube is a movable, separable and almost indestructible registry or alphabet insert that is imprinted on both sides. The parchment compressor cover has a nickel metal coating that comes equipped with a bolt. . . . Opening and readjusting arch and bolt secures whatever is inserted."[22] True to the combinatorial law of all innovations, the encounter of *biblorhapt* and Shannon File in the small workshop in the vicinity of Stuttgart resulted in something new, "the now ubiquitous, well-proven lever mechanism that closes and fixes the clamp."[23] The so-called Registrator-Sammelmappe A was not only the synergic product of the determined, goal-oriented Suebian inventor, it was also the well-contrived result of a legal circumvention in the face of the eagerness of the German owners of the Shannon patent to go to court. Starting in 1885, Leitz acquired a couple of patents related to what was later to become the Leitz binder, but the binder itself—a combination of rods, clamp, pins, rivets, lever mechanism, pull-out hole, nickel fitting, and stiff cover—is not patented.

First, however, the core—a complex "tin case," to quote the patent of 1885—was put under legal protection. By 1893, it had been refined to such an extent that it gave rise to the arch lever. In 1896, the lever, which hitherto had been placed between the arches, was moved to the outside, and with that improvement the perfect design still in use today had been found. But the success story of the Leitz Binder was not over yet. It reached its peak in a third fundamental innovation of office technology: the vertical file. Thanks to wooden, and later cardboard, covers, papers that traditionally would have been laid flat could now be placed upright, thus presenting the appearance that is today automatically associated with the word *file*. As is usually the case with epochal media innovations, there followed a series of changes designed to make the technology more user-friendly, such as improving the compressor bar or adding slits to the cover to prevent undue pressure on the clamps. In 1911, a finger pull hole was

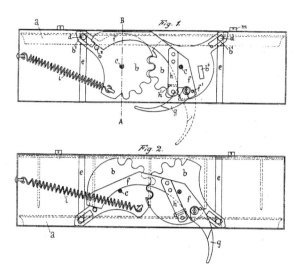

FIGURE 8.   From patent 36552/class 11 (18 July, 1885; figures 1 and 2).

added to make it easier to remove a file. A further, subsequently patented improvement ensured that the clamp lever mechanism—which, to protect the paper, could not be oiled—always worked without friction.

Two worlds coincide in the binder: the mechanized world of the ordering apparatus and the alphabetical world of letters. To quote a prospectus that offers a virtual tour of the Leitz firm, "Metal on the one hand, cardboard and paper on the other . . . unite and give rise to a technological organism, the binder."[24] It clearly states that with the metal container inside the binder, the alphabet-based medium file has turned into a technological-industrial product. Leitz, "mechanic *and* manufacturer producer of factura books,"[25] combined precision mechanics and account ledgers into a third object, the letter binder. Its outside appearance is derived from books—in particular, the vertical arrangement showcasing the inscribed back cover. But unlike books, the inside contains, in addition to mere letters and numbers, a gripping mechanism attached to the cover that spears, staples, and if required, releases papers, "making it possible to alphabetically order the individual pages at any other given place."[26] The contraption inside the binder, which started out as a tin case before it was turned into a refined holding device, mechanizes the paper world of the order of letters. According to the production logic of the Stuttgart Workshop for the Manufacture of Metal Parts for Ordering Devices, not only are mechanical and alphabetical worlds effectively united, but the alphabet itself has been mechanized. The order created by the binders is already present in their production. A "machine automatically takes one leaf from every pile of paper and combines it in alphabetical order with the other lettered pages, so that in the end the whole registry has been artfully combined."[27] Once the alphabetized inlays are supplied beforehand, it becomes unnecessary to retroactively arrange the papers in alphabetical order. The entire order of the bureau can now rely on prefabricated ordering automatisms.

The file mechanism, the miraculous order-creating contraption on the inside, prompted Leitz's philosophers to emit utterances that bring to mind the words of Prussian state archivists around 1800. Whereas the latter praised the archive as the soul of the Prussian state, a Leitz leaflet from around 1900 claims: "The mechanism is the soul of the binder."[28] Here, the gaze has become microscopic. It is no longer directed at the state, but rather at its smallest unit, the metal clamps of file and letter binders. Out of this module, the whole of the state emerges, as if to confirm Goody's trinitarian formula of bureaucracy: "The state, the bureau, and the file." In the course of governmental reforms around 1929, the triad was arranged in such a way that the entire order could be derived from the smallest element, that is, the state from a single file.[29] The bureau mediated between the two. According to reformers, administrative restructuring had to begin with the microcosm of the state: the desk of the civil servant. But the reformers' campaign to put vertical filing systems to use ran into stiff resistance from traditional work habits. Leitz's Registrator-Sammelmappe A, which had made a triumphant entry into the offices of private enterprise, was rejected time and again by the public administration of the German League. What merchants immediately grasped—namely, the rationalization benefits that could be derived from variable forms of bundling papers—was lost on state bureaucrats.

Not coincidentally, the adoption of the new file binders took about as long to spread as the ubiquitous typewriter. Both innovations required new containers. The first prerequisite was that official books and ledgers be composed of unbound individual pages, for only the latter can be inserted into typewriters. To bundle them, the slip box, which had been in use since the days of the *scrinia* to store loose papers, was reactivated. The

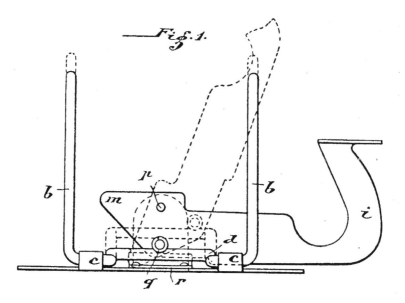

FIGURE 9 (a).   Fig. 1 from patent 153 568 Class 11e (27 July, 1902).

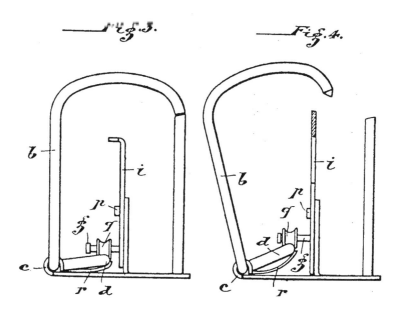

FIGURE 9 (b).   Figs. 3 and 4 from patent 153 568 Class 11e (27 July, 1902).

Genuine Shannon Sectional Cabinets

THE Shannon Arch method has been for twenty years, and is today, the safest way to file letter or cap size papers.

Prices quoted include stock index (please specify in your order the *style* of indexes desired).

Price *"with lock"* means the *"I and A"* combination locking device described on page 6.

Compressor on cover keeps papers compactly together; printed form shows record of transfers for locating back correspondence.

No. 1020. 3-Dr. Letter-size Shannon Half Section with Document or Utility Vertical File. $10.40. No. 1018. Cap-size, $10.65.

No. 19. 3-Dr. Letter-size Section, $6.50.
No. 22 3-Dr. Cap-size Section, $6.75.

No. 20. 9-Dr. Letter-size Section, $16.25
No. 18. 9-Dr. Cap-size Section, $16.75.

FIGURE 10. Genuine Shannon Sectional Cabinets. JoAnne Yates, *Control through Communication: The Rise of System in American Management* (Baltimore, London: 1989), 36.

boxes evolved into binders, which, like slip boxes, first were made of wood before being replaced by cardboard. As a container, therefore, the new binders were simply deconstructed file furniture, single parts of wooden cabinets made up of drawers and boxes, the likes of which had been used around 1500 to bring order to the archive. In short, we are dealing with modules made up of slip boxes, which combine to form file cabinets.

JoAnne Yates's *Control through Communication* offers a genealogy of the vertical filing system, from the letter boxes of the Amberg File and Index Company and the wooden file sections with drawers to the cabinets of the Shannon Arch method. Yates pinpoints the debut of the vertical system in the very same year when Leitz first marketed his lever mechanism-equipped legendary Leitz Binder "A": 1893, when the World Fair for the first time presented vertical card files for librarians.[30] Just like in Germany, vertical filing systems got off to a rough start in the United States. Here too, the bureau-technological combination of vertical files, typewriter, and carbon paper, first deployed in private enterprise, was only gradually adopted by the state bureaucracy. Yates points out that railroad companies were the driving force behind the adoption of the new communications technologies. The United States, too, charged a commission with overseeing the administrative reforms that had begun around the turn of the last century. First convened in 1910 and named after President Taft, the commission did not pursue its goal with the zeal of the Prussian reformers. Rather, it began its work by distributing questionnaires designed to find out how government officials handled and filed their correspondence in order to make recommendations based on the findings. Unexpectedly, the very act of filling in the questionnaire already had a certain reforming effect: "The self-examination that the questionnaires forced upon them caused some offices to undertake immediate correction of their faulty practices." Though there was no German counterpart to this case of administrative self-improvement, the skepticism engendered by the new filing systems and their ordering methods was similar. In the United States, too, offices clung to the old-fashioned habit of folding papers and storing them in document containers; hence the commission's first recommendation was "that all correspondence should be filed in flat vertical files."[31] It was the first recommendation because it entailed all subsequent innovations. As in the case of the German reform of the 1920s, reorganizing the entire administrative apparatus hinged on the smallest module, the mechanized vertical file. Names like Wilson and Jones are the American equivalent of Leitz. What eventually emerged around the turn of the last century as the ring binder was composed of various patents.[32] Notwithstanding all the similarities between the pioneering inventiveness in Stuttgart and Chicago, however, the differing mechanical details of the clasp entail an ongoing clash of cultures: "Europeans cannot understand, why the unnatural two-hand-pushing-on-the tongues movement would be preferred to the simple natural pulling motion needed to open two rings. Americans insist on the tongue and three rings."[33]

The promoters of the vertical filing system mobilized all possible arguments to stress the technological superiority of the new file type. Their campaign is reminiscent of attempts by historians to explain why the codex won out over scrolls. In much the same way, the superiority of codices was linked to the fact that they allowed users to quickly look up and retrieve specific passages, German administrative reformers listed the advantages of vertical files for daily usage: "(1) Each file remains at its place in a defined order; (2) it can instantly be recognized and removed, without (3) disturbing the other files; and (4) there are no pasteboard markers or other visual indicators anymore, which used to facilitate the finding when records piled up."[34] Hoping to alleviate the fears of his colleagues, one proponent of the new filing system offered a description of the new system that is almost touching in its accuracy: "Binders now replace our loose files. . . . They are extremely easy to handle. The binder contains clamps designed to hold the papers in place. Simply pressing down on a so-called hole puncher is enough to make holes in a piece of paper that can then be inserted before closing the binder again."[35] If this official handling of texts, involving typically female work with "needle and thread,"[36] turns into a thoroughly male activity, it binds officials all the more strongly to their working appliances—that is, to *files*, a word derived from *filum* (Latin for thread) that entered the English language via French *filer*, "to string documents on a wire for preservation or reference." "Once the administrative employee is made responsible for his own records, he will immediately realize that his small world of files, too, can only be governed by order."[37] As intended by the official reform proposals, the intimate intercourse with files will necessarily create order. Hence tidiness is no longer a job requirement for civil servants: They become orderly when they are given their own files. The concept of creating a close link between officials and records in their "small world of files" reveals the Protestant mentality at work on the level of new office technology. The old goal of avoiding the conflict that arises from scraps of paper lying around everywhere is replaced by an instrument, the self-binder. It puts an end to the reign of loose slips. It is no longer necessary to issue step-by-step instructions on how to handle records. The file itself prescribes the necessary activities. Starting with the punch, its individual physical parts predetermine a clear order: *punch, open, fix, insert, close.*

Once the automatism of working appliances guarantees order, those who work with files can easily be granted autonomy in their small world of files. In a letter circulated by the Ministry of the Interior, administrative reformers decreed that offices were to be in charge of handling their own affairs, with the result that the "expediter stores and administers the files in his own office."[38] Sovereignty made its entrance into bureaus and offices. "All the files pertaining to a specific sector of administration are to be stored in the office of the administrator responsible for that sector."

As envisaged by the reform proposals of 1919, the topological classification according to *areas* of operation amounts to self-administration in the form of "working officials" who are to be "their own file administrators."[39] The vertical filing system shapes "intelligent and understanding self-administrators . . . in the spirit of Stein."[40] Or, expressed without the reformers' enthusiasm: a processor, a file—and Prussia has attained its normal level of despotism, "for every civil servant left to his own devices is a potential despot."[41] With the bureau reform of the Weimar Republic, however, civil servant despotism attained its true object: files that contain punched, readily available texts. When civil servants rule their own small world, the tension between responsibility and arbitrariness is solved by granting the greatest possible autonomy to individual clerks. Their alleged autonomy, however, is merely the flip side of their subordination to a filing system that automatically generates order. The danger of bureaucratic despotism is thus contained by an automatic ordering system.

The automation of order brought about by the self-processing of files promotes the records rather than their human processors to agents of bureaucracy. Folders instructing users where they should be brought next literally get files on their way. They move themselves from department to department. The addresses on the cover replace commands, obedience, and control by officials. To quote the pertinent 1932 guidelines: "The regular circulation of a written document within the administration is not supervised; there is no need for any switchboard; each office immediately passes on the document to the next." And should this transmission by an invisible hand be sidetracked because a document "has to be submitted to an official . . . in a department that is not part of the regular chain of transmission, this can be noted by the office responsible." Address, location, and hold-file notes belong to the arsenal of operators that process the automobility of files. The nonmathematical algorithmic guiding regulations, without which no file could circulate, are noted on index cards that know and control, remember and steer what happens inside the administrative apparatus. These modern *laterculi* reveal and disclose files by channeling and recording their movements.

The reformers never doubted that such an organized system would speed up the circulation of files far more effectively than imperial decrees ordering things to be handled *cito, cito*, or *citissime*. Faced with the possibilities of acceleration provided by the means of modern bureaucracy, reformers advocated—to use Paul Virilio's term—a veritable dromology of files: Arnold Brecht, the former secretary in the Reich Chancellery and until 1932 department head in the Prussian State Ministry, estimated that if the reform proposals were to be accepted, the time it would take for documents to be filed would be reduced by five to seven days.[42] In 1927, Brecht, chief protagonist of the office of administrative reform, wrote a textbook on this very topic addressed to the German administration. In 1940, having emigrated to the United States and joined the New School of Social Research in New York, he published an abbreviated English edition in collaboration with one of his students, the administrative expert Comstock Glaser. What was intended to be an incentive "for reorganizing governmental agencies"[43] in the United States became the basis for the denazification trials in Germany after the war. According to Brecht, the Allied authorities derived their understanding of the German administrative apparatus from his book. Underneath its triple goal (administrative and bureau reform in the Weimar Republic, restructuring of government agencies in the United States, and denazification), Brecht outlines a dromology of files as a result of time-saving measures:

> The number of moves necessary for answering a letter was reduced from fourteen to eight or six, that is by 43 or 57 percent. The time saved thereby included not only the actual time of performance of clerical steps, but also backlog (waiting time) and transportation. In an average German Division, which may be supposed to receive 25,000 communications a year, the saving due to elimination of steps amounts to an aggregate of 250,000 communication-hours and 4,000 job-hours.[44]

Once files act like people by staying overnight and spending extended time in corridors, that is, once files take on the habits of their users, a new time has begun—the time of files. The circulation of files dictates both work time and work routine. It is in the face of such imposed behavior that Niklas Luhmann, the theorist of administration, later emphasized the autonomy of the worker, which manifests itself in the fact that anybody "can pick up a difficult file and look up a co-worker or their superior to talk things over."[45] But from an organizational point of view, such individual deviation from the files' regular pattern of circulation is irrelevant. Codes of procedure and official instructions issued during the time of office reform treated and designated officials as *Aktenstelle*[46]—literally, "file place"—that may be subject to "removal."[47] Their subordination under files "in the service of record keeping"[48] implements the progress of files as

a "self-command" to "rationalize itself," as indicated by the title of a frequently reissued manual by Gustav Grossmann that was first published in
1929.[49] A rationally organized circulation of files operates independently
of individual processing times. To avoid unnecessary delay, reformers such
as Herman Haussmann, the founding director of the College of Administrative Science in Speyer, Germany, made use of Taylorist principles
worked out in the context of industrial production, and applied them to
record keeping. As in the cases of Taylor and Gilbreth, the analysis was
based on close examination of the work sequence. In this Taylorized file-
based administration, the "determination of the psychological and mental
restraints"[50] that had been applied to secretaries and clerics yielded to the
goal of "removing restraints from business procedures."[51] Psycho-tech-
nological issues turn into organizational problems. Following reformist
ideals, smooth processing of files eliminates clerks as a source of irrita-
tion. Administration experts like Morstein-Marx transferred this indus-
trialization of file processing to administrative dimensions that equaled
that of a small town. Eventually, a cybernetics of files was to conjure up
nothing less than an automatized administration that can do without any
employees.

From the point of view of the officials, however, the automation of
work routines has no impact on their increasingly close relationship with
their work means. On the contrary, with the envisioned abolition of the
central registry, this relationship becomes all the more intimate. In the
words of the reformers, doing away with the registry, thus creating an immediate relationship between files and officials, amounts to reestablishing
an administrative "state of nature."[52] It spells a return to the initial state
of records, the self-indexing registry files of around 1200. Indeed, for the
U.S. reform commission, "self-indexing" is the magic formula which will
ensure "that with the installation of modern filing systems in Government
offices the necessity for book or card registers would disappear."[53] Aiming for the same goal, German reformers suggested that the processing
of records should be entrusted to a single person and literally be transferred into the file itself. Registrars would be rendered superfluous, to be
replaced by a simple cover page that summarizes the content of the files.
This incorporated register is to replace the multiphase registration system
composed of daily ledgers, central register, and file release date record.

But the abolition of registries envisaged by the reformers means the
abolition of all central control. That is the price—the very high price—

Der gesuchte Brief

springt Ihnen förmlich entgegen,

wenn Sie Leitz=Registerserien in Ihren Leitz=Ordnern verwenden.

Alle Buchstaben des Alphabetes sind nach den Regeln der Häufigkeit zergliedert. Die Abbildung zeigt den 9. Ordner der 12 teiligen Serie mit den Buchstaben R - S.

Vorteile: Schnelles Ablegen — Sofortiges Finden
            gefüllte Ordner

Bedarf: Sie brauchen in einem Jahr so viele Leitz-Ordner, wie Sie im Durchschnitt täglich Briefe abzulegen haben.

Auswahl: Es gibt Leitz-Registerserien für jedes Bedürfnis. Die kleinste Serie besteht aus 2 Ordnern (A-L, M-Z). Die größte Serie umfaßt 600 Ordner.

Ihr Schreibwarenlieferant wird Sie gerne beraten!

FIGURE 11. "The letter you are looking for jumps out at you." Reprinted with the permission of Jörg Schmalfuß (Department Head, Historisches Archiv, Deutsches Technikmuseum Berlin).

that has to be paid for the sovereign rule of each official in his file world. Observers concluded that while clerks may "find their way in their own particular domain, the overall confusion has increased."[54] Subsequently, the reform proposal of 1919 was itself revised: decentralization—that is, individualization and intimization of file processing—was countered by the introduction of uniform guidelines to ensure that all individually processed files were dealt with according to the same principles. The basic prerequisite was the *file plan*. "All simplifications regarding the administration of written matter depend in one way or other on the file plan."[55] Functionally speaking, a file plan is a registry in reverse. It imposes order upfront, while a register does so afterward. To use one of the reformers' favorite expressions, file plans are "thought out in advance."[56] Once such a plan is in existence, records are assigned a specific place even before they enter the system. Much like laws, file plans require an abstract form capable of anticipating as yet unknown specific cases. Administering files, then, is raised to the status of a quasi-juridical endeavor, reputedly "an intellectual penetration of file matter, an ongoing conceptual separating and summarizing, abstracting and subsuming."[57] File plans give birth to a transcendental order of files prior to all content.

The new vertical files implement this order in the physical domain. What distinguishes them from older systems is that their installation precedes the compiling of records. Their standardized breadth limits in advance the amount of incoming material, whereas traditionally a file, the size of which had depended simply on whether or not it could be handled, came about solely by amassing individual sheets. Empty vertical filing systems are hollow bodies, containers; as such, they are the media-technological realization of the twentieth century's bureaucratic dispositive of order, the plan. The distinction between a retroactively imposed order and one that is planned ahead cannot but have an impact on ordering activities: instead of tidying up and registering, we have advance planning and systematizing.

But reformers like the American librarian Melvil Dewey were not satisfied with a plan restricted to one administrative division only. They demanded a unifying plan that applies, if not to the entire administration of the German Reich, then at least to one ministry. There was hardly any author of a book or treatise on the organization of bureaus who did not pose as an administrative legislator offering new general record-keeping principles for the Reich administration. At the beginning of the twentieth

	250 teilig (für 250 Ordner)						
1	Aa-Ad	66	Hamm-Haq	131	Mes-Met	196	Scham-Schaz
2	Ae-Alk	67	Har-Hat	132	Meu-Mez	197	Schea-Schek
3	All-Aq	68	Hau-Haz	133	Mia-Mim	198	Schel-Schez
4	Ar	69	Hea-Hed	134	Min-Miz	199	Schia-Schim
5	As-Az	70	Hee-Heh	135	Moa-Mok	200	Schin-Schk
6	Baa-Bah	71	Heia-Heil	136	Mol-Mor	201	Schla-Schle
7	Bai-Baq	72	Heim-Hek	137	Mos-Mud	202	Schli-Schly
8	Bar-Baz	73	Hel	138	Mue-Muf	203	Schma-Schmi
9	Bea-Beq	74	Hem-Hen	139	Mug-Muq	204	Schmo-Schmy
10	Ber-Bez	75	Hep-Her	140	Mur-My	205	Schna-Schne
11	Bia-Biq	76	Hes-Hez	141	Naa-Nar	206	Schni-Schny
12	Bir-Bl	77	Hia-Hir	142	Nas-Naz	207	Schoa-Schok
13	Boa-Bok	78	His-Hof	143	Nea-Nek	208	Schol-Schoz
14	Bol-Boz	79	Hog-Hom	144	Nel-Net	209	Schra-Schri
15	Bra	80	Hon-Hr	145	Neua-Neul	210	Schro-Schry
16	Brea-Bret	81	Hua-Huk	146	Neum-Nez	211	Schua-Schul
17	Breu-Bri	82	Hul-Hy	147	Nia-Nil	212	Schum-Schuz
18	Bro	83	Ib-Il	148	Nim-Niz	213	Schwa-Schwep
19	Bru-Brz	84	Im-Iz	149	Noa-Not	214	Schwer-Schy
20	Bua-Buk	85	Ja	150	Nou-Ny	215	Staa-Star
21	Bul-By	86	Je-Ju	151	Oa-Oe	216	Stas-Steh
22	Ca-Ci	87	Kaa-Kah	152	Of-Oo	217	Stei-Steo
23	Cl-Cz	88	Kai-Kam	153	Op-Oss	218	Step-Stez
24	Da	89	Kan-Kas	154	Ost-Oz	219	Sti
25	Dea-Des	90	Kat-Kaz	155	Paa-Pam	220	Sto
26	Det-Di	91	Kea-Kel	156	Pan-Paz	221	Stra-Stri
27	Do	92	Kem-Kez	157	Pea-Pes	222	Stro-Sty
28	Dr	93	Kia-Kiq	158	Pet-Pfi	223	Ta-Ter
29	Du-Dz	94	Kir-Kiz	159	Pfl-Ph	224	Tes-Th
30	Ea-Eh	95	Kla-Klim	160	Pi	225	Ti-Tra
31	Ei-Ek	96	Klin-Km	161	Pla-Pog	226	Tre-Tz
32	El-Em	97	Kna-Kno	162	Poh-Poz	227	Ua-Ull
33	En-Eq	98	Knu-Kod	163	Pr-Pt	228	Ulm-Uz
34	Er-Es	99	Köa-Kön	164	Pu-Qu	229	Vaa-Vl
35	Et-Ez	100	Köp-Kof	165	Raa-Rae	230	Vo-Vy
36	Fa	101	Kog-Koo	166	Raf-Ral	231	Waa-Walk
37	Fea-Fel	102	Köp-Koz	167	Ram-Ras	232	Wall-Waz
38	Fem-Fez	103	Kra-Kres	168	Rat-Raz	233	Wea-Weik
39	Fi	104	Kret-Kro	169	Rea-Reh	234	Weil-Weq
40	Fla-Fli	105	Kru-Kug	170	Rei	235	Wer-Wess
41	Flo-Fo	106	Kuh-Ky	171	Rek-Rer	236	West-Wh
42	Fra	107	Laa-Lag	172	Res-Rh	237	Wia-Wier
43	Fre	108	Lah-Lan	173	Ria-Rier	238	Wies-Wil
44	Fri	109	Lap-Laus	174	Ries-Rim	239	Wim-Wis
45	Fro-Fry	110	Laut-Laz	175	Rin-Roc	240	Wit-Wl
46	Fu-Fy	111	Lea-Lef	176	Rod-Rok	241	Woa-Wolf
47	Ga	112	Leg-Lel	177	Roi-Rosem	242	Wolg-Woz
48	Gea-Geq	113	Lem-Leq	178	Rosen	243	Wr-Wuq
49	Ger-Gi	114	Ler-Lez	179	Roser-Rud	244	Wur-Wy
50	Gl-Gn	115	Lia-Lim	180	Rue-Rz	245	Y-Zam
51	Goa-Gok	116	Lin-Ll	181	Saa-Sah	246	Zan-Ze
52	Gol-Goz	117	Loa-Log	182	Sai-Sar	247	Zia-Zil
53	Graa-Gral	118	Loh-Loz	183	Sas-See	248	Zim-Zl
54	Gram-Graz	119	Lua-Lug	184	Sef-Sem	249	Zo-Zu
55	Grea-Gres	120	Luh-Ly	185	Sen-Set	250	Zw-Zz
56	Gret-Griz	121	Maa-Mae	186	Seu-Sh		
57	Groa-Gron	122	Maf-Mak	187	Sia-Sil		
58	Groo-Groz	123	Mal-Man	188	Sim-Sn		
59	Grua-Grun	124	Manr-Marz	189	Soa-Som		
60	Grup-Gs	125	Mas-Mauk	190	Son-Soz		
61	Gua-Guo	126	Maul-Maz	191	Spa-Spi		
62	Gup-Gy	127	Mea-Meh	192	Spl-Ss		
63	Haa-Had	128	Mei	193	Sua-Sus		

FIGURE 12. Probable frequency of letters arranged in alphabetical order. Reprinted with the permission of Jörg Schmalfuß (Department Head, Historisches Archiv, Deutsches Technikmuseum Berlin).

century, the Dewey decimal system was introduced in the United States to replace the over 250 different filing systems in existence with one uniform ordering system.

But file plans not only create order, they also give rise to new ordering problems. First, whatever is thought out in advance has to anticipate unexpected events. To accommodate them, filing plans must contain a catchall subdivision, such as Dewey's "000 General." Second, the filing system has to be able to accommodate unplanned and as yet unforeseeable developments. Since it is difficult to decide beforehand whether or not an incident should be officially recorded, or whether an exchange of letters is significant enough to be put on file, there is a need for an interim category. Otto Frank, author of several studies on classification and ordering, and charged with implementing the Dewey decimal system in Germany, labeled this phase as "pending classification."[58]

This intermediary category is informed by an ordering system based on probabilities. It is designed to ward off the danger that periodically threatens every file user: the need to reclassify and reorder files after sections that were "thought out in advance" turn out to be useless or the classification grid proves to be too coarse. Leitz, who was as interested in binder mechanics as he was in their content, had anticipated the problem. He had already conceived of the alphabetic arrangement of loose papers, which the Shannon File, too, had partly realized: "The entire system is so well thought out that the distribution of the alphabet is fully sufficient, because the letter-based subdivisions are worked out in accordance with the statistical distribution of German names, ensuring that the individual sections fill up at similar rates."[59] To assess the probable frequency of letters of the alphabet, office reformers have to do what has been the task of decoders since the beginning of the sixteenth century: they have to count letters.

The expected frequency of individual letters determines the subdivision into alphabetical sections. The greater the number of folders, the more detailed the subdivisions. In the 1920s Leitz offered letter series made up of 2, 14, 36, 50, 75, 100, 150, and even 250 folders. Increasing the number of folders resulted in lengthening the letter combinations, which on occasion could turn into whole syllables. A set of 250 folders offered combinations like *Rosen, Roser-Rud; Schall, Scham-Schaz; Wies-Wil, Wim*, which are reminiscent of declensions and, contrary to their function, create a new order of meaningful signifiers resulting in words and names.

These Markoff chains read like the bureaucratic subtext of early Dadaist "ur"-sonatas that, according to their composer, Kurt Schwitters, were indeed indebted to such "abbreviated labels."[60]

Sign systems that operate on the basis of statistically determined letter frequencies, however, are of little use to administrations that classify their records according to events and occurrences rather than personal names. Their classification system replaces Dadaist syllable chains with *reference numbers* made up of a sequence of numbers or letters containing information about the file's content, location, and year of origin, as well as the office responsible. In addition, the reference number is to mirror the entire taxonomy of administration, from the individual dossier to the encompassing architecture; the overall order is to be apparent on every level. A sign code becomes the systematized address of a file, thus rendering the register superfluous.

Based on the reformist ideals of self-indexing, self-evaluating, and self-interpreting, the micro-order consisting of the systematized signifiers of business and reference numbers is to reproduce the administrative macro-order—the topography of shelves as well as the spatial arrangement of offices—until the entire administration is nothing but one big filing plan. Micro- and macro-order are interlocked in such a way that the individual file represents the entire universe of an office, while a twentieth-century office building, in turn, turns into one "enormous file."[61]

Such visualization fantasies have their basis in the files themselves. Vertical folders with inscribable backs indicate a higher order in far more persuasive fashion than makeshift ordering devices like pasteboard markers. And it is precisely the visibility of vertical files that excited the fantasy of planners intending to create an administrative panopticon. Above all, the arrangement had to be "transparent."[62] The entire system of order had to be visible at one glance. The technologies that created administrative transparency and control were first used in the economic sphere, where "charts and Planboards for Visual Control systems that indicate facts and forecasts, loadings and progress, costs, stock and production relationships can be seen, understood and acted upon."[63] Visibility and accessibility of records are the result of the same optical organization, up to and including the attached signs that control the resubmission of files.

The reformers' emphasis on visibility and clarity put an end to the technologies of secrecy. In the eyes of the reformers, the office was a chancery without barriers. It was accessible; when, for instance in Berlin, "all offices in the buildings on Wilhelmstrasse 74 and Luisenstrasse 33/34 are to be equipped with notices indicating which pieces of equipment are located in the rooms by referring to their inventory number,"[64] the public was able to immediately grasp what was going on inside the administration of the Reich capitol. The interior of the office is the inventory turned inside out. Modern technologies of visualization ensure that administrative procedures are subject to a logic of representation: A tidy desk stands for an orderly administration. Within an administrative context, Niklas Luhmann argues, the "ceremonial of accompanying symbols, seals and letterheads, and especially the usage of . . . written bureaucratese" possesses "a symbolic value for the ideal presentation of administrative work results."[65] This dogma of transparency, however, also entailed new means of concealment. Special devices are created for truly secret records.

In the epoch of the office—and this distinguishes it from the time of the chancery—censorship occurs *before* things are put on record. Most files no longer contain any secrets, or at least none of "our errors and mistakes," which Goethe had entrusted to them. "If possible, no mistake or misconception, and none of the efforts to correct them, is to be put on file."[66] This is how the sociologist of organization, Luhmann, describes the materialization of files under the gaze of the other, that is, under the gaze of a public that is thought to be reading along. As a result, "anybody who has something to say that he wants to put on record will consider what he has to say and how he will express it."[67] From now on, offices are characterized by a certain reticence that has nothing to do with the technologies of secrecy practiced in chanceries. What is secret is neither that which is screened off by barriers nor that which has been put on file, but that which is off the record. This restructuring of secrecy from a defined and recorded arcanum to an off-record concealment[68] stems from the fact that everything that is put on file threatens to turn against those who keep the records. In case of doubt, the file testifies against the clerk. The more transparent and accessible the records, the more reticent the officials. Weber may have had in mind this tendency to hide and conceal when he claimed that "bureaucratic administration always tends to exclude the public, to hide its knowledge and action from criticism as well as it can."[69] It is in this discursive domain that, following the Second World War, the struggle for making records public will be carried out.

Surveillance and Information Society:
Access to Files (Inspection of Records)

Ever since the publication of records could create a *public*, that is, ever since the historian August Ludwig von Schlözer (1735–1809) called for an end to state secrecy (and followed up on his demands by founding a journal dedicated exclusively to publishing records), files have been the medium instrumentally involved in the differentiation processes that pit state against society and administration against citizenry. The state compiles records, society demands their disclosure. Alongside these struggles over access to files, society arises as a discursive unit, a political force antagonistic to the state. Whereas nineteenth-century debates had centered on free access to archived records, the twentieth century expanded the demands to include the right to inspect current and active files. But a society that wishes to be informed about matters of government is poised to trespass on one of the last arcane domains of the state: the state secret. No longer protected by physical barriers, chests, and keys, it has become virtual and exists solely on the basis of a declarative act that something is "secret" or "top secret." This classification, however, remains hidden from the public. Secret services by definition work with secret records, hence constitutional oversight is only possible in part. The state secret, therefore, belongs to the state "taboo-protected phantoms"[70]; uncontrolled, it flits about and arouses suspicion. As a result, elaborating a legal framework that guarantees the right to inspect one's files becomes a touchstone for a functioning democratic rule of law.

In Germany, the debate over where to draw the line between "official secret" and "public records" erupted in the 1970s in the wake of the U.S. Freedom of Information Act of 1967, which was itself the juridical result of a social struggle over the public access to government records. Once the latter were perceived to be means of "social control, identity-giving and memory-tracing," they moved into the public eye and become an object of widespread public concern. "Because records . . . affect both the course of an individual's life and the course of society, they present a problem of social significance."[71] The public debate over the decisive power of records found immediate confirmation in the official information politics of the Vietnam War. In the wake of the almost total blackout imposed on U.S. military activities, the public was compensated with a guaranteed right to obtain information after the fact on all governmental activities. In justifying the Freedom of Information Act, then Secretary of Justice Ramsey Clark emphasized that the realization of the ideal of democratic self-determination presupposes an "informed public." By linking self-government (to quote the First Amendment to the U.S. Constitution) to the idea of an "informed public," the secretary of justice officially recognized the public as a body with the right to control government activities.

Despite efforts to amend the situation, the people's right to know, as guaranteed in the United States by the Freedom of Information Act, was for a long time not implemented in Germany, where the notion that access to government records is part of a general right of the public to obtain government information lacked a basic prerequisite. In the wake of the Second World War, administrative proceedings became public property in the United States, but not in Germany. On the contrary, the Federal Constitutional Court left no doubt that "in principle private individuals cannot ask the public administration for access to their files or to provide copies."[72]

Up until the passing of the Federal German Freedom of Information Act (on January 1, 2006), it was only in the individual domain that subjects were granted the right to access their records. This was not, however, so much the legal implementation of the ideal that all should participate in the business of government as a statement of the right of the individual to defend herself against the state. Thus article 29 of the German Administrative Procedures Act grants only the party concerned the right to access pertinent records. Other parties, whose basic rights may or may not be infringed upon by the administrative circulation of government files, do not enjoy that right. Framed as a subjective right to inspect one's own records, the social demand for public transparence is transformed into an individual's claim to valuable assets. From then on, two interests confront each other: the government's interest in keeping things secret and the individual desire to be informed. Given this particular arrangement, the interests of both sides appear to be equal, making it possible to weigh the pros and cons. Section 2 of the article 29 anticipates this balancing act by listing the grounds on which government may deny the individual's right of access.

Files and Filing Systems

In the individual context, the demand for greater access to records manifests itself as concern over the protection of one's own data. In the United States, as in Germany, the increased efficiency brought about by electronic data processing has placed special emphasis on this personal dimension and fanned the fear of increased state surveillance. "The single most important factor leading to the emergence of concern for record-keeping systems is the computer and the possibilities it presents not only for the extremely rapid and efficient processing of huge amounts of information on people, but for the sharing of information from a variety of sources."[73] The fear that computer technology will increase files' usefulness as state surveillance technologies translates into a critique of computerized files, which are perceived as instruments of state incursion into the private sphere. Prior to their automation, the power of conventional files was expressed metaphorically. The shock of finding one's life on record, of being thrown into a labyrinthine administrative system, was highlighted by an antibureaucratic rhetoric in which mountains of files became a popular metaphor for *too much* bureaucracy and, more generally, an inhumane bureaucracy.

The complicity of technologies of government record-keeping and the examination of the population only became a topic of public discussion when administrations switched to electronic data processing. Although the micro-census that was carried out in Germany in the late 1960s could well have triggered a public confrontation with the power of records, the awareness that such a census may easily infringe on individual rights did not arise until files were transformed into data. The debate emerged in the face of the electronically optimized statistical surveys, rather than after the end of the Second World War, when the potential for destruction that resides in government record-keeping had become all too evident. The highly effective census apparatus implemented by the Nazi regime gained the attention of historians in the wake of the boycott of the 1983 German census.

Jurists transformed the concern over one's own data into a right. From the basic right to free development of one's personality, they derived a right for the protection of "personal data" that is in some respects reminiscent of a claim of ownership. When in late 1972 the German Department of the Interior, reacting to the concern over personal data, presented the first draft of a Federal Data Protection Act (which came into force six years later), several such laws were already in effect on the state level. A leading expert on data privacy described the aim of the law: "With the data protection act the legislature clearly rejects any tendency to perceive and treat the individual as a mere object of information."[74] This goal indicates a closure. The genealogy of the subject from records returns to its point of origin: after census technologies have for centuries provided information that turned humans into an object of knowledge, this very same knowledge is returned to them as their personal data, of which they may dispose as they wish. In the eyes of the law, the census object becomes the sovereign of its data.

Humans, then, are researched and raised to a status where they enjoy the *right to informational self-government*. When the German Federal Constitutional Court centered its 1983 boycott verdict on this particular right, it followed the lead of existing data protection acts suggesting that the individual should not be a "mere object of information." The court, however, did not concur when it came to establishing the range of data protection. Data protection, it argued, begins not with processing but with the collection of data. Both federal and state data protection laws followed the lead of the constitutional court by placing the collection of data on the same level as other steps, thus ensuring that it too comes within the purview of applicable laws. The court located its decision in a time of change. A relatively harmless time of files, it argued, was giving way to an epoch of electronic data processing that threatened self-determination. No longer are data manually collected on index cards and in files; they have become "infinitely storable and, regardless of the distances involved, instantly retrievable."[75] By taking on the issue of the unlimited data processing capabilities at the end of the age of files, the court reiterated the discursive conditions that had lead to the debate over data protection in the first place.

The rupture between manual and electronic data processing on which the Federal Constitutional Court had based its census boycott decision is already apparent in the Federal Data Protection Act of 1978, which starts with a basic distinction between paper files (*Akten*) and electronic filing systems (*Dateien*). It only protects data that can be processed electronically. The nonprotection of data in old-fashioned *files* is a result of the emergence of data protection from the increased capabilities of electronic data processing. But since files can also be automated, they too fall under the protection of the law, as is evident from later versions of the law, which under certain circumstances puts files and databases on an equal footing: "A filing system is a set of personal data that can be evaluated according to specific characteristics by means of automatic procedures. . . . This shall not include files and sets of files unless they can be rearranged and evaluated by means of automated procedures."[76]

Stasi Records

One year after the amendment to the Federal Data Protection Act, another law was passed. It too deals with files and filing systems, but in this case the difference between the two was of less importance. The Stasi Files Act (*Stasi-Unterlagen-Gesetz*) is not concerned with the technological standards of data processing because it does not focus on protecting personal data. It regulates access to one's "own dossier" but refers back to the terms used in the Data Protection Act to define its object of regulation. Article 46 (2) of the Data Projection Act specifies that a file is "any document serving official purposes. . . . [T]his shall include image and sound recording media. It shall not include drafts and notes that are not intended to form part of a record." The Stasi Files Act alters the Data Protection Act by turning the word *document* (*Unterlagen*) into a heading that now subsumes both files and filing systems. As specified in the first sentence, subsentence a, of Section 6 (1), the term "Records [*Unterlagen*] of the State Security Service" includes "in particular files, data files, documents." This commonality established between files and data files is only suspended in the context of special technical procedures, such as erasing data.

The Stasi Files Act regulates a specific right to access records. It refers exclusively to the files of the Ministry for State Security of the former German Democratic Republic (Ministerium für Staatssicherheit, or MfS). Since no secret service would ever willingly grant access to its own records, we are obviously dealing with an office that has gone out of business. The events that led up to this legal regulation were extraparliamentary in nature; it is a story of street-level brawls and scuffles. Of the many versions of the events that took place outside the Ministry for State Security on January 15, 1990, only that related in the first activity report of the Federal Commissioner for the Records of the State Security Service of the former German Democratic Republic has gained official status. It begins with a preambular narrative of the "civic protest and revolutionary change of Winter 1989/90": "When in late November and early December of 1989 black clouds of smoke rose from the State Security district offices in Erfurt, Dresden, and other cities, signaling that fulltime employees had begun to 'deal with the past' in their own way, enraged citizens started to blockade and occupy the buildings. They attempted to put a stop to the activities of the largely defunct but still unruly State Security and to secure its holdings. This development culminated in the storming of the headquarters in Berlin in mid-January 1990."[77] The security of the state was no longer an issue; the rush was aimed at securing State Security's records.

Banners and slogans indicated the goals of the protest actions: "Security for our records," "I want my record," and "Freedom for my file." Given the long history of occupying government buildings, pillaging archives, and trashing files, this collective concern over records, especially over one's own, may present something completely new. The actions were geared to accessing records rather than destroying them, even though there were reports of a more or less symbolic destruction of the insignia of the hated state apparatus: "Office furniture was vandalized, files were shredded." Such vandalism notwithstanding, what was spared was precisely that which was to turn into the founding myth of a new government agency: *Truly important* records were left unharmed, that is, they were transferred to secret locations."[78] They were not only to be out of the reach of East German civil rights activists and U.S. spies, but the principal aim was to withhold them from posterity. For days and nights, members of the State Security Service fed files to their shredders until the latter had glutted themselves to the point where they had to be replaced with superior Western models; these too were unable to cope with the loads of papers. Yet it wasn't possible to destroy the files in other ways; the smoke from burning paper, for instance, would quickly have alerted outside observers.

Only a small portion of the removed and shredded files was later found. These cancels, as it were, were to be rendered legible again by a Project Group for the Reconstruction of Destroyed Documents. Their task was to view and paste together "17,200 sacks or 25 kilometers"[79] of shredded files. A lengthy procedure, no doubt, for while computers may assist in the reassembly of Babylonian potsherds (see chapter 6), the reconstruction of Stasi files still proceeds manually. The Stasi Files Office assumes that the former State Security Service was following a "paperwork destruction tactic,"[80] in which the shredded files ranked highest. In short, the destroyed files were the "truly important" ones. A list of the files that were erased or rendered illegible uses a V for *Vernichtung* (destruction) to indicate their value. Thus the negative registration of the V-files takes on the function of a *signifiant barré*. The significance of the legible text derives from that which has been canceled. In some cases, the contents of the files were also recorded on decodable magnetic tapes that escaped destruction.

With the dissolution of the Ministry for State Security and the East German Bureau for National Security, the now homeless records are caught in that strange limbo between administration and archive where archivists also locate the registry. Bereft of an agency, they are no longer administrative records. At the same time, however, they are not archived records since they are not subject to any archival retention period and are constantly being reused. They are discarded records that can be reactualized at any given moment—archival quasi-objects of a quasi-office. After all, the Office of the Federal Commissioner for the Records of the State Security Service, itself the product of a historical rupture, is organized like a government agency, yet it does not have its own area of responsibility. Legally, it is part of the Ministry for the Interior. It is a concentrate of the dissolved East German ministries, with one purpose only: to administer files *as files*. In this respect, it once again resembles an archive, whose main task is to guard the files that originated in spatially and functionally disparate agencies. To quote a commentary on the Stasi Files Act, "The Commissioner is an independent archival office." Section 37 (1) obliges the commissioner to take custody of, evaluate, and administer the records "according to accepted principles for maintaining archives." Which means, above anything else: not according to political principles. Like an archive, the Office of the Federal Commissioner is charged with collecting records, locating "rogue files," and disclosing the located and reacquired files upon request. The office, then, is a relay for the collection, distribution, and filtering of records, with the single task of storing and registering files and making them accessible to those who wish to inspect them.

The many goals to which these records hovering between archive and procedure are put to use—scholarly, administrative, legal, biographical— are very different from those once pursued by the former Ministry for State Security. The records attain archival status when used for scholarly research; they turn into forensic documents when used in a civil or criminal procedure; and they assume the status of public administrative records when transferred to another office that extracts information for an ongoing administrative procedure. Finally, the files in limbo turn into their own record the moment they are submitted to a private person. They contain a knowledge that, if reactivated in a different context, exhibits uncontrollable and unanticipated results.

This *personal inspection of records* forms the core of the Stasi Files Act. In the discussions surrounding the introduction of the bill, it was stated that the primary goal was to allow people "insight into the documents that concern them so that they may catch up with their life's story."[81] Translated into legalese, Section 1 (1) of the Stasi Files Act states that its purpose is "to facilitate individual access to personal data that the State Security Service has stored regarding him, so that he can clarify what influence the state security service has had on his personal fate." If understanding one's fate is legally facilitated by the right of access to one's records, then the nineteenth-century autobiographical principle of record-keeping has undergone a remarkable change: the law envisages that the Stasi files (which were kept to enlighten about the individuals observed) can be used for the purpose of self-enlightenment in much the same way as keeping and reading a diary. The legally granted access to records merges these texts (comprising anonymous informer reports, file notes, and Stasi instructions) with the life of the file subject. The result intended by the law is to clarify one's "fate." This remarkably nonjuridical goal—expressed with the equally nonjuridical term *fate*—is based on the assumption that the Stasi files are capable of storing individual life stories. The same applies to the protesters outside the Ministry for State Security: they too unquestioningly assumed that "my records" and "our files" exist, and with their banners and slogans they prepared the ground on which the Stasi files could become their own.

According to the Stasi Files Act, the right to inspect records is accorded to anybody who, in the language of the law, was a "data subject." This classification is in turn based on the file the concerned party is applying to inspect, as are other classifications that may impact the right to inspect the records: "The classification of citizens as victims, informal collaborators, or full-time employees of the Stasi is not based on any hearing but solely on the information derived from the written documents of the Ministry of State Security."[82] In other words, to regulate access to the records, the commissioner's office is forced to adopt the perspective of the ministry that compiled the records in the first place. "It is of no relevance which classification is, from today's point of view, the correct one."[83] This circular reasoning effectively seals itself from all extra-administrative criteria that may be involved in classifying those who demand access. With this legally effectuated elimination of the outside world, problems arise, if at all, only in connection with internal contradictions. In a hearing prior to the introduction of the Stasi Files Act, former attorney general Alexander von Stahl pointed out that he was familiar with files in which "an individual first appeared as a victim, then as a beneficiary, and then again as a victim."[84] This, however, obliterates the classic archival rule of "one subject—one file."[85] Given that one and the same person can have different functions in different contexts, Article 6 (8) of the Stasi Files Act states that it is not the file in its entirety but the individual item of information that determines the status of the party demanding access: "It shall be ascertained for each piece of information if the person involved was an employee of the State Security Service, a beneficiary, a data subject, or a third party. The determining factor for ascertaining the above shall be the purpose for which the information was documented in the records."

If the goal of clarifying what influence the State Security Service has had on her personal destiny is to be achieved, and if the "data subject" is to establish a relationship to "her" file, there has to be a third party that brings the two together. "*Pour être deux, il faut être trois* [To be two, it is necessary to be three],"[86] as the legal historian Pierre Legendre introduces the logic of the Parasite into the administrative realm. This intermediary position is taken by the Commissioner's Office. It negotiates between file object and file subject. That is to say, the personal inspection of one's file is only possible after it has been read by a third party. "The clerks of the Commissioner's Office acquire a complete and in part intimate knowledge of the data subjects."[87] This first, official reading is not just, in the commissioner's words, an initial "getting to know"; it is also the first intervention in the file. The "prerogative to preprocess the file"[88] precedes the right to inspect it. It grants the government that inherited the Stasi files the privilege of preparing the records for private viewing. In the interest of protecting the privacy of others, certain information will be deleted, names rendered illegible, duplicates made. The context of the record is erased; hence the file that is handed over for private viewing is invariably depersonalized, devoid of any reference to other files or individuals. It is a text that is tailored exclusively to the individual making the request. The context that in the opinion of archival experts is the indispensable precondition for the making of the true file is missing. The preread file that is deemed safe for inspection is, ultimately, a canceled file.

These cancellations trigger a desire for one's own real file. The latter is not just an idée fixe; the very fact that the records have been officially precensored leads to the inevitable conclusion that there must be a real file. Apart from the visible deletions, the indisputable proof that the released file has been tampered with and is therefore incomplete is the *envelope* that accompanies it. It contains the pages that for legal reasons are not to be read by anybody else after having been read by officials. The envelope is fastened with a paper clip; it may not be removed from the premises, and the data subject may only open it in the presence of a supervising official. However, the very act of physically handling this envelope, of turning it on its head, results in an identification with the released file. Focusing on what has been withheld from them, indignant readers exclaim: "But that's my file!"[89] As part of the Ministry for the Interior, the Office of the Commissioner for the Records of the State Security Service knows how to administer secrets of the soul. It has entrusted the envelope with the secret that attracts all kinds of phantasms. The envelope is an "envelope idéale, qui les [les textes] contient tous [ideal envelope, which contains all (the texts)]."[90] It fuels the suspicion that the legible file is nothing but an inferior, secondary text lacking the truly important pages. It does not hold the *whole life*. Rather, it is the forbidden envelope that contains everything. Subsequently, one's own life story turns out to be illegible, something that can only be found in the *complete* file. Like the heavenly book, it alone contains all the pages of life.

No wonder, then, that the inspection of records generated a new literary genre: the file-based autobiography, designed to add what is missing from the canceled Stasi records. The historian Timothy Garton Ash, himself accustomed to working with files, demonstrated how studying files leads to literature—more precisely, how inspecting files promotes the literary genre of the file-based autobiography. Following a first perusal, he accepts his Stasi file as "a gift to memory"[91] and thus pursues the very activity spelled out in Article 1 (1) of the Stasi Files Act. Aligning his life story to the contents to the file, he sheds light on his fate and produces, as announced by the subtitle of his book, a *Personal History*. Ash's *The File* is a book based on a file, his "own" file. It is the result of the effort to reconcile file and memory. The writing of the biography is prompted by a counterstatement: the authorial file, that is, the autobiographical book, is a denial of the inspected file. Written into the gaps and omissions of the inspected records, *The File* is not the one that was handed over but the revised one that was confronted and made to coincide with the subject's life story.

The autobiographically validated record reenacts the Goethean principle of keeping records to become a subject. "The Stasi is my Eckermann"[92] is a line from a Wolf Biermann song frequently quoted in connection with the Stasi Ministry, though the ministry resembled a party general secretary more than it did Goethe's private assistant. The comprehensive recording of all works, deeds, and intentions was undertaken for pastoral reasons, to guard the population and keep the flock united. The Protestant clergyman Joachim Gauck, the first commissioner of the Stasi Files Office, did not completely condemn that ministry's attempt to meticulously record life. Resorting to Biermann's line, he confessed that "even the most perfidious account contains something of the profound will of large parts of the population."[93] Why shouldn't the principle of heavenly accounting also work in secular hands? Even "infernal files," Gauck continues, are capable of "providing evidence."[94] They give evidence of a subject, and the more recalcitrant the latter, they more they provide. "We do not arrive . . . as white, blank pages," the commissioners warned the old Federal Republic. His office has indeed contributed countless written pages to the process of unification, initiating a wave of file-based subject constitutions—a seemingly anachronistic mixture of divine bookkeeping, Protestant governmentality, and Eckermannization that has permeated the republic since its official reunification. A defunct state that left behind huge numbers of personal dossiers, an opposition fixated on records, and a government agency that was created by a Files Act and is responsible for nothing but files—all came together to enable this historically extraordinary case of allowing masses of individuals to inspect their files.

Regardless of whether the Stasi files were released in response to a request by a data subject, for administrative or legal procedures, for purposes of documentation, or to provide historiographical material, in each case it has to be assumed that they are capable of transmitting the truth. But with the dissolution of the Ministry for State Security, they lost the institution that guaranteed their veracity. The Commissioner for the Stasi Files cannot occupy this position, since he does not have the power to make legally binding decisions on the files' truth content. Instead, he is left to publicly reflect on their truth content by borrowing the voice of those who inspected their files: "The citizens who inspected their records frequently confirmed that the Ministry for State Security correctly . . . recorded facts," and that their files "accurately mirrored their lives." Based on these subjective impressions, the commissioner concludes in his activity reports that the files are "credible"—a quality that is usually ascribed to witnesses.[95] In the legal domain, however, those who inspect their own files have no say in determining their truth content; the courts alone are qualified to reach a decision that can turn files into facts on file. At most, Article 14 (1) of the Stasi Files Act endows data subjects with the right to request that "their personal data and the evaluation aids used to find records shall be erased and depersonalized" and thus removed from this world. The right to request such erasure, however, does not extend to beneficiaries and Stasi employees: they will continue to be judged by the truth preserved in their files.

This nonerasable file—reminiscent of the repertoire of punitive measures in Kafka's *Trial*—remains the final threat for the functionaries of the Stasi apparatus. Their last and only hope is that their files may be canceled on Judgment Day, when our sins are erased (*exaleíphein*) from the divine record that registers all our deeds. A similar hope, though one unrelated to any specific crimes, was expressed in a note left by the philosopher Hans Blumenberg: "Bluntly put, it could be that it is only the file of the condemned that contains his identity, while the 'Book of Life' that is opened on Judgment Day is marked by an abundance of deletions made by overly zealous angels,"[96] those heavenly chancery employees.

In the face of earthly accounting procedures, however, such hopes for merciful cancellations are most likely in vain. The question arises of what would come about if everything were indeed registered, once and for all? A perfect order? Striving for the latter has given birth to the well-known organization and control technologies that turn meticulously arranged files into the measure of all order. They ensnare clerks and officials, until those officials start to administer themselves, asking for deliverance from the circulation of official papers with the magic formula *tbf* (to be filed), and transmute into a part of the stratified order, just like other office furniture. Ten years prior to its dissolution, Heiner Müller used the Ministry for State Security to trace this progressive mimesis of files in "Volokolamsk Highway," which takes the governmental ideal of the unification of clerk and file at its word, leading to a literal fusion between the two.

Müller's teratology of the socialist obsession with records begins with a myth. Its point of departure is the old administrative dream of perfect order. Here it finally has been realized. As a result, all matters of administration have come to a stop, and the end of civil servants is at hand. Only a consciously committed *breach* of the rules is able to defer the collapse into total order and thus grant the civil servant-comrades a last lease on life. In the name of order, they act against it. Covered by an official command, the inferior comrade is to drive through a red light. The maneuver proves fatal. Shortly afterward, the victim returns as an angel-like revenant to where he came from: the desk of the official who gave him the order to breach the order.

> I had a dream last night. It was a nightmare
> Then I woke up and all things were in order.
> Comrade Super everything's in order
> No incident no disorderly conduct
> And not a single crime . . .
> We have done it after all Comrade Super
> Ten years of day and night shifts not for nothing
> Security and order that was it
> What we were taught and that was our goal . . .
>
> For in-house-use I'll tell you We produce
> Security and order
>   And awareness,
> Yes and awareness Right And the mother
> Of order is disorderly conduct
> The father of State Security is
> None other than the same State's Enemy . . .
>
> Who would need us if all things were in order
> I'd go and hack my desk to firewood
> And use the staff files here to kindle it . . .
>
> First you will make amends for your mistake
> You did retreat when you were facing facts
> And soon lost sight of our sacred truth
> By your blind faith in what your eyes were seeing
> A fact is not a fact if we won't say so . . .
>
> And when you have corrected your mistake
> You needn't hang yourself when you're off duty
> A medal's what you get And a bonus
> Now go and drive across the intersection
> When all the lights are red.
>   At red across
> The Intersection I.
>   And you'll be
> In uniform. And that is an order. . . .
>
> He drove at red across the intersection

In uniform On duty In rush hour . . .

We'll have to hush up and dress up his death
A statue for the Unknown Keeper of
The Law . . .

   And suddenly there stood
Right on my desk top our honored corpse
Brand new the uniforms the epaulets
Already sprouted into angels' wings
Comrade Super everything's in order
The dialectics have been reestablished
And all systems are now back to normal.
He stooped down and sang into my ear . . .

Got up and turned on toes a pirouette
Flew out the window flapping twice his wings
And when I tried to get up tried to see
How he took to flight something like lightning struck
Me down with pain like from a welding torch
I and my desk had grown to form one body
Into one body grew my desk and I . . .

Was this my desk or was this I myself
Who told you so Old Prussian my friend . . .

I am my desk Who is Who's Property
The desk is people's property And what
Am I Below a desk above a human
No human but a humachine
A furnitureman or a manfurniture
The staff files are my abdominal organs
I'm an occurrence. To be put on file. [97]

§ 6   Files into Icons

In the 1970s an antique archive was discovered on the Athenian agora that to all appearances had remained undisturbed for millennia:

The archive consists of lead tablets rolled up with a single name on the outside. Inside each tablet we usually find the same man's name with a description of his horse and its price. There is no date. Some tablets are from the fourth century, some from the third. Thus apparently every cavalryman had his own lead roll with a brief description of his horse and its value. What is most peculiar about these tablets is that all have been tightly rolled up and were found in their original state (as one can tell because they are made of lead). It is thus very doubtful if any had ever been consulted. . . . Perhaps they only recorded what everyone knew already. Or the records were in fact too crude (and they are very crude indeed) to be of much use as records without other information that could be supplied orally. Or it was simply felt inappropriate to have a record of each horse (which included its value) and of its owner, even if the record was not going to be consulted much. . . . They seem never to have been opened.[1]

In the 1980s the German artist Anselm Kiefer completed *The High Priestess*, the largest work in his series of lead books.[2] *The High Priestess* is composed of 126 giant folios arranged on vast steel bookcases. Here, lead does not appear, as Gutenberg would have it, as print technology's *res metallica*, in the shape of letters on almost weightless paper; rather, the very books themselves are made of lead. As a result, their weight renders them unusable. The immobile tomes are their own tombs. Their content can only be accessed if it is transferred into books that are easy to handle and read—for instance, photographic reproductions contained in an illustrated book on *The High Priestess*. From the point of view of the technology of production, the folios are not books; instead, they resemble files: "The first of these books consisted of sheets of paper with images stuck to them, stapled together; gradually more and more materials were incorporated, and the books became thicker and heavier." Like files, they may incorporate anything that can be impressed on lead, arranged in layers, and finally bound together by wire. The incorporated objects and materials go beyond the usual scope of any book designed for reading purposes. "Since the advent of printing we have come to see a book as something meant for ease of use, designed to impart its information content quickly; in Kiefer's hands it has progressively transformed itself into a weighty tome"[3]—a tome so heavy that it takes several men to lift a single book. Unlike files—and this is what ultimately distinguishes files from Kiefer's work of art—the near-unmovable books do not circulate through buildings and corridors, and nobody accesses their information or refers to individual pages. The immobilization amounts to a musealization, creating a work of art out of files.

As a unique museum artifact, Kiefer's lead books are as unused and unusable as the lead tablets of the Greek cavalry archive. The latter, too, are files at a standstill, an archaeological monument as much as Kiefer's books. Equally devoid of signs of reuse, they are an aesthetic monument. They represent nothing less than the alphabetic media. For what is one to do with these unreadable tomes other than venerate them as icons of writing and literacy? They preclude all use and reuse, and it is precisely this dysfunctionality that highlights their literal function. Whatever is not in use, or is altogether unusable, turns into a memory sign (a monument). The external appearance of the tomes recalls the origin of the book from file-*codices* and refers to Greek lead records.[4] The metal they are made from alludes to the printing press, and the peas they contain may be an allusion to the fact that reading, as already evident in the etymology of *lex*, is rooted in sorting and counting. Last but not least, *Zweistromland*, the German title of Kiefer's lead files, has a memory function. Though ancient Mesopotamia used clay tablets rather than lead books, both media serve the same purpose: they organize transmission processes. According to Max Weber, "the rivers or canals of Mesopotamia" play a role similar to that of "the contemporary means of communication";[5] they transport goods as well as data. By naming his composition *Zweistromland*, Kiefer is translating the communication flows of the Babylonian empire into a territorial order. The rivers flow into a topographic arrangement of tomes in steel shelves. The left shelf is called "Euphrates," the right "Tigris."

The opposite of this artful arrangement is the strenuous task of deciphering. To learn to read Babylonian clay tablets, the Free University of Berlin started a decades-long project of compiling catalogs that list the frequency of signs and recurring sign combinations. The decoded text and the process of decoding are compatible in that they both operate in a nonsyntactic language. "The basic data structures this 'language' refers to are 'lists' of 'words,'"[6] and the catalogs for deciphering this language are themselves composed of lists. Using INTERLISP, a dialect of LISP (list processing), the clay tablets are transferred onto electronic media, thus fusing the oldest and youngest "revolution in data processing."[7] This historical splicing together of clay tablets and silicon chips brackets the ends of a genealogy of files. Between Mesopotamia and LISP, between millennia-old lists and their computer-based deciphering, are the epochs of nonmathematical, merely quasi-algorithmic techniques for controlling transmissions and the life of files.

But what could be a clearer indication of the closure of the epoch of files and their dispositive than the reappearance of files as stylized icons on computer screens, designed to visualize the computer's operating instructions? At the interface of computer and user, material files turn into icons, which a mouse, replacing the hand, "opens" and "closes" with a click. The very terminology of computer surfaces is designed to remind users seated before screens of the familiar world of files. The menu tab offering options like "list," "format," "thesaurus," "table" and the instructions *copy, delete, save* turn users into virtual chanceries or chancellors. By condensing an entire administrative office, the computer implements the basic law of bureaucracy according to which administrative techniques are transferred from the state to the individual: from the specialized governmental practices of early modern chanceries to the "common style," from absolutist administrative centers to individual work desks, from the first mainframe computers in defense ministries to the desktop at home.

The current copresence of digital and paper files results in an intermedial competition that has prompted archivists and administrative experts to reflect on the near-extinct medium of files. Old, hitherto overlooked filing techniques are now subject to analytical evaluation. Rather than appearing as mere pictographs on user interfaces, filing techniques are to be turned into discursively analyzed *principles* that can be applied to computerized data processing. For a simple "1:1 on-screen depiction of shelves, binders and folders does not capture the previous functions. It erodes old forms by giving rise to vibrant e-mail communication that leaves no trace, neither in the files nor elsewhere."[8] Faced with electronic facilities of communication, the bureaucratic principle of filing things—which was first explicitly spelled out during the emergence of another fleeting communications technology, the telephone—is once again emphasized. Auto-protocol features save data from complete decontextualization and immaterialization, thus retaining the filing principle, even in the digital domain.

But the history of files is not only apparent when it comes to data processing or the one-to-one graphic rendition of the old world of files and paper. In highly unmetaphorical fashion, files and their techniques organize the very architecture of digital machines. As processors, they have become part of the hardware of the transmission, computing, and storage machine called a computer; they ensure access to all internal operations by controlling both instructions and data, as well as their addresses. A central processing unit, whose register controls all that goes on within a computer, retrieves the old universal function fulfilled by files in the days of the Staufer emperor Frederick II. The history of files therefore also contains a prehistory of the computer. Not because old filing principles are consciously transferred to the new medium but because administrative techniques of bygone centuries are inscribed as *stacks, files, compiler,* or *registers* in a digital hardware that remains unaware of its historical dimension. And with this media-archaeological reference to files, it finally becomes possible to determine where their power resides today.

Notes

Preface

1. Heinrich von Kleist, "The Broken Pitcher," in *Five Plays*, trans. Martin Greenberg (New Haven, CT: Yale University Press, 1988), 94.
2. Cf. the official U.S. definition of files as recording devices for "preservation or appropriate for preservation" [U.S. C 366 (1964)], quoted in Rehbinder, *Die Informationspflicht der Behörden im Recht der Vereinigten Staaten* (Berlin: Duncker & Humblot, 1970), 61.
3. Classen, "Zur Einführung," in *Recht und Schrift im Mittelalter* (Sigmaringen: Thorbecke, 1977), 8.
4. Bernhard Siegert, *Relays: Literature as an Epoch of the Postal System*, trans. Kevin Repp (Stanford, CA: Stanford University Press, 1999); and Wolfgang Ernst, *Im Namen von Geschichte: Sammeln - Speichern - (Er)Zählen: Infrastrukturelle Konfigurationen des deutschen Gedächtnisses (1806 bis an die Grenzen zur mechanischen Datenverarbeitung)* (Munich: Fink, 2003).

Chapter 1

1. Jacques Derrida, *Of Grammatology*, trans. Gayatri Spivak (Baltimore, MD: Johns Hopkins University Press, 1997), 126.
2. Claude Lévi-Strauss, *Tristes Tropiques*, trans. John and Doreen Weightman (Harmondsworth: Penguin, 1992), 296.
3. Jacques Lacan, "Fonction et champ de la parole et du langage en psychanalyse," in *Écrits* (Paris: Éditions du Seuil, 1966), 272.
4. Wolfgang Sellert, "Aufzeichnung des Rechts und Gesetz," in *Das Gesetz in der Spätantike und frühem Mittelalter* (Göttingen: PUBL, 1992), 80 and 83.

5. Hanna Vollrath, "Gesetzgebung und Schriftlichkeit," *Historisches Jahrbuch* 99 (1979): 42.

6. Niklas Luhmann, *Law as a Social System*, trans Klaus A. Ziegert (Oxford: Oxford University Press, 2004), 237.

7. Lévi-Strauss, *Tristes Tropiques*, 296–97.

8. Oswald Spengler, "Zur Weltgeschichte des zweiten vorchristlichen Jahrtausends," in *Reden und Aufsätze* (Munich: Beck, 1937), 250.

9. Jack Goody, *The Logic of Writing and the Organization of Society* (Cambridge: Cambridge University Press, 1986), 104.

10. Ibid., 105

11. Angelika Menne-Haritz, "Elektronische Schriftlichkeit und Geschäftsordnungen," in *Neubau der Verwaltung: Informationstheoretische Realitäten und Visionen*, ed. Heinrich Reinermann (Heidelberg: Decker, 1995), 131.

12. Cf. Derrida, *Of Grammatology*, 141ff.

13. Ahasver von Brandt, *Werkzeug des Historikers* (Stuttgart: Kohlhammer, 1992), 106.

14. Kurt Dülfer, "Urkunden, Akten und Schreiben in Mittelalter und Neuzeit," *Archivalische Zeitschrift* 53 (1957): 53.

15. Angelika Menne-Haritz, *Akten: Vorgänge und elektronische Bürosysteme mit Handreichungen für die Beratung von Behörden* (Marburg: Archivschule, 1996), 31.

16. Erhard Blankenburg, "Die Aktenanalyse," in *Empirische Rechtssoziologie* (Munich: Piper, 1975), 198.

17. Thomas-Michael Seibert, *Aktenanalysen: Zur Schriftform juristischer Deutungen* (Tübingen: Narr, 1981), 5.

18. Ibid., 12.

19. Bruno Latour, "Visualization and Cognition: Thinking with Hands and Eyes," *Knowledge and Society* 6 (1986): 28.

20. Seibert, *Aktenanalysen*, 32.

21. Ibid., 39.

22. Blankenburg, "Die Aktenanalyse," 195.

23. Hans Günther Adler, *Der verwaltete Mensch: Studien zur Deportation der Juden aus Deutschland* (Tübingen: Mohr, 1974), 967.

24. Karl Kroeschell, *Deutsche Rechtsgeschichte* (Opladen: Westdeutscher Verlag, 1980), 2: 173. I am indebted to Michael Stolleis for this reference.

25. Heinrich Otto Meisner, *Archivalienkunde vom 16. Jahrhundert bis 1918* (Göttingen: Vandenhoek and Ruprecht, 1969), 127.

26. *Translator's note*: The original heading of this section was "Kafkas Kanzleien." In German, *Kanzlei* refers to a (modern) law office as well as to a medieval chancery; though Kafka himself did not work in a chancery, the bulk of this section is dedicated to the old *Kanzleien* that preceded modern bureaus.

27. Franz Kafka, *The Trial*, trans. Willa and Edwin Muir (New York: Modern Library, 1956), 267–69.

28. Jacques Derrida, "Before the Law," in *Acts of Literature*, ed. Derek Attridge (New York: Routledge, 1992), 195.

29. Jacques Lacan, *The Seminar of Jacques Lacan: Book II, The Ego in Freud's Theory and in the Technique of Psychoanalysis*, ed. Jacques-Alan Miller, trans. Sylvana Tomaselli (New York: Norton, 1991), 301.

30. Ibid., 302.

31. Derrida, "Before the Law," 203.

32. Kafka, "The Problem of Our Laws," in *The Complete Stories*, ed. Nahum H. Glatzer (Schocken: New York, 1971), 437–38.

33. Ibid.

34. Gilles Deleuze and Félix Guattari, *Kafka: Toward a Minor Literature*, trans. Dana Polan (Minneapolis: University of Minnesota Press, 1986), 49 (emphasis in the text).

35. Derrida, "Before the Law," 213.

36. Pierre Legendre, *Le Désir politique de dieu: Étude sur les montanes de l'état et du droit* (Paris: Fayard, 1988), 323.

37. Legendre, *L'Empire de la vérité: Introduction aux espaces dogmatiques industriels* (Paris: Fayard, 1983), 107.

38. Kafka, *Trial*, 74.

39. Hans-Walter Klewitz, "Cancellaria: Ein Beitrag zur Geschichte des geistlichen Hofdienstes," *Deutsches Archiv für Geschichte des Mittelalters* 1 (1937): 78.

40. "Cancelli," in A. Walde and J. B. Hoffmann, *Lateinisch-etymologisches Wörterbuch I* (Heidelberg: Winter, 1938).

41. "Cancelli," *Pauly's Realencyclopädie der classischen Altertumswissenschaft* (Stuttgart, 1894). The English definition for *cancelli* refers to the "screen dividing the body of a church from the part occupied by the minister. . . . Under the Romans *cancelli* were similarly employed to divide off portions of the court of law." "Cancel," *Encyclopaedia Britannica* (1910), 174–75.

42. "Cancellarius," *Pauly's Realencyclopädie*. See also "chancellor," *Encyclopaedia Britannica* (1910), 50–51: "The original chancellors were the cancellari of Roman courts of justice, ushers who sat at the cancelli or lattice work screens of a 'basilica' or law court, which separated the judge and counsel from the audience."

43. Kafka, *Trial*, 149.

44. Ibid., 57.

45. Ibid., 149.

46. Ibid., 159 (translation modified).

47. "Cancellarius," *Pauly's Realencyclopädie*.

48. Derrida, "Before the Law," 204.

49. Kafka, *Trial*, 152.

50. Jacques Derrida, *Archive Fever: A Freudian Impression*, trans. Eric Prenowitz (Chicago: University of Chicago Press, 1996), 4.

51. "Cancel," *Encyclopaedia Britannica* (1910).

52. Anton Linsenmayer, *Geschichte der Predigt in Deutschland von Karl dem Großen bis zum Ausgange des vierzehnten Jahrhunderts* (Munich: Stahl, 1886), 23.

53. Kafka, *Trial*, 259.

54. Ibid., 262.

55. Ibid., 266.

56. Ibid., 264.

57. "Kanzlei," in Grimm, *Deutsches Wörterbuch*, cols. 178–79.

58. Wolf Kittler, "In tiefer Nacht: Franz Kafkas 'Türhüterlegende,'" in *Neue Literaturtheorien in der Praxis*, ed. Klaus Michael Bogdal (Opladen: Westdeutscher Verlag, 1993), 174.

59. See Walter Benjamin, "Critique of Violence," *Selected Writings: Volume 1, 1913–1926*, ed. Marcus Bullock and Michael W. Jennings (Cambridge, MA: Harvard University Press, 1996), 236–52.

60. Walter Benjamin, "Franz Kafka: On the Tenth Anniversary of His Death," in *Illuminations*, ed. Hannah Arendt (New York: Schocken, 1968), 115.

61. Kafka, *Trial*, 267.

62. Marie Theres Fögen, "The Legislator's Monologue," *Chicago Kent Law Review* 70 (1995): 1595.

63. Derrida, "Before the Law," 191.

64. Ibid., 190.

65. Ibid., 199.

66. Jean-François Lyotard, *Lectures d'enfance* (Paris: Galilée, 1991), 35.

67. Joseph Vogl, *Ort der Gewalt: Kafkas literarische Ethik* (Munich: Fink, 1990), 158.

68. Kafka, *Trial*, 267.

69. Vogl, *Ort der Gewalt*, 161.

70. Kafka, *Trial*, 272.

71. Ibid., 270.

72. Ibid., 277.

73. Ibid., 277.

74. Ivo Pfaff, *Tabellio und Tabellarius: Ein Beitrag zur Lehre von den römischen Urkundspersonen* (Vienna: Manz, 1905), 14, 30, 40, 45.

75. Ibid., 3–5, 23.

76. "Cancel," *Encyclopaedia Britannica* (1910), 174–75. See an earlier version of the following passages by the author in "Cancels: On the Making of Law in Chanceries," *Law and Critique* 7 (1996): 131–51.

77. Ernst H. Kantorowicz, "Mysteries of the State: An Absolutist Concept and Its Later Mediaeval Origins," *Harvard Theological Review* 48 (1955): 69.

78. Béatrice Fraenkel, *La Signature: Genèse d'un signe* (Paris: Gallimard, 1992), 52.

79. Derrida, *Of Grammatology*, 109.

80. R. W. Chapman, *Cancels* (London: Constable, 1930), 14n.

81. Ibid., 6, 15.

82. Ibid., 10, 21n.

83. Ibid., 3.

84. Kafka, *Trial*, 104.

85. Ibid.

86. Paul Johann Anselm Feuerbach, *Betrachtungen über die Öffentlichkeit und Mündlichkeit der Gerechtigkeitspflege* (Giessen: Heyer, 1921), 330.

87. Kafka, *Trial*, 111 (translation amended).

88. Ibid.

89. Leo Koep, *Das himmlische Buch in Antike und Christentum: Eine religionsgeschichtliche Untersuchung zur altchristlichen Bildersprache* (Bonn: Hanstein Verlag, 1952), 47.

90. Herman Melville, "Bartleby, the Scrivener," in *Melville's Short Novels*, ed. Dan McCall (New York: Norton, 2002), 3.

91. See Johannes Dietrich Bergmann, "'Bartleby' and 'The Lawyer's Story,'" in ibid., 173–76.

92. Melville, "Bartleby," 30.

93. Hans Magnus Enzensberger, *Kiosk*, trans. Michael Hamburger (Newcastle: Bloodaxe, 1997), 33.

94. Melville, "Bartleby," 3.

95. Max Weber, *Economy and Society: An Outline of Interpretive Sociology* (Berkeley: University of California Press, 1978), 956.

96. Melville, "Bartleby," 10.

97. Klaus Theweleit, *Recording Angels' Mystery: Buch der Könige 2* (Frankfurt: Stroemfeld, 1994), 704.

98. Alan Delgado, *The Enormous File: A Social History of the Office* (London: John Murray, 1979), 72, 44; Friedrich Kittler, *Gramophone, Film, Typewriter*, trans. and intr. Geoffrey Winthrop-Young and Michael Wutz (Stanford, CA: Stanford University Press, 1999), 183–87 and 193–94.

99. Cf. Melville, "Bartleby," 21; and Kittler, *Gramophone, Film, Typewriter*, 189.

100. Melville, "Bartleby," 10.

101. C. Wright Mills, "White Collar: The American Middle Classes," quoted in Delgado, *The Enormous File*, 5.

102. Melville, "Bartleby," 10.

103. "Chancellor," in *Encyclopaedia Britannica* (1910), 853. See also note 51.

104. Melville, "Bartleby," 10.

105. Ibid., 15.

106. Ibid., 10.

107. William Lombard, *Archeion or Discourse upon the High Court of Justice in England* (London: E. Purslowe, 1591), 45–46. I am grateful to Peter Goodrich for the reference.

108. S. F. C. Milsom, *Historical Foundations of the Common Law* (Toronto: Butterworths, 1981), 90.

109. "Chancery," in *Encyclopaedia Britannica* (1910), 836.

110. Melville, "Bartleby," 5.

111. Milsom, *Historical Foundations*, 90.

112. Melville, "Bartleby," 33.

113. Costas Douzinas and Ronnie Warrington, "The Trials of Law and Literature," *Law and Critique* 6 (1995): 152.

114. Gerhard Ebeling, "Geist und Buchstabe," in *Die Religion in Geschichte und Gegenwart* (1958), col. 1291.

115. Melville, "Bartleby," 34.

116. Ibid., 10.

117. Ibid.

118. Gilles Deleuze, "Bartleby; or, The Formula," in *Essays Critical and Clinical*, trans. Daniel W. Smith and Michael A. Greco (Minneapolis: University of Minnesota Press, 1997), 70.

119. Ibid., 68.

120. Sabine Mainberger, *Schriftskepsis: Von Philosophen, Mönchen, Buchhaltern, Kalligraphen* (Munich: Fink, 1995), 189.

121. Melville, "Bartleby," 10.

122. Ibid., 14.

123. Ibid., 23.

124. Ibid., 24.

125. J. H. Baker, *An Introduction to English Legal History* (London: Butterworths, 1990), 379–90.

126. Ibid., 385.

127. Melville, "Bartleby," 23.

128. Herbert F. Smith, "Melville's Master in Chancery and His Recalcitrant Clerk," *American Quarterly* 17 (1965): 739.

129. Deleuze, "Bartleby," 68.

130. Melville, "Bartleby," 23.

131. Ibid., 16.

132. Ibid., 33.

133. Melville, "Bartleby."

134. See W. Kittler, "In tiefer Nacht," 174.
135. Richard Buckminster Fuller, *Ideas and Integrities: A Spontaneous Autobiographical Disclosure*, ed. Robert W. Marks (Toronto: Collier-Macmillan, 1969), 148.
136. Melville, "Bartleby," 33.
137. Ibid., 26.
138. Theweleit, *Recording Angels' Mysteries*, 705.

Chapter 2

1. François Hotman, *Antitribonian ou Discours d'un grand et renommé Iurisconsulte de nostre temps: Sur l'estude des Loix, Fait par l'aduis de feu Monsieur de l'Hospital Chancelier de France en l'an 1567* (Paris: Perier, 1603, rpt. Saint-Etienne University, 1980), 120–21.
2. Elizabeth Eisenstein, *The Printing Press as an Agent of Change: Communications and Cultural Transformations in Early Modern Europe* (Cambridge: Cambridge University Press, 1979), 1: 103.
3. Leopold Wenger, *Die Quellen des römischen Rechts* (Wien: Holzhausen, 1953), 592.
4. Donald R. Kelley, *Foundations of Modern Historical Scholarship: Language, Law and History in the French Renaissance* (New York: Columbia University Press, 1970), 69.
5. Quoted in Karl Eduard Zachariä von Lingenthal, "Digesta Justiniani Augusti recognovit," *Zeitschrift für Rechtsgeschichte* 10 (1872): 166–67.
6. Franz Wieacker, *Römische Rechtsgeschichte*, vol. 1 (Munich: Beck, 1988), 154.
7. Ulrich Wilcken, "Hypomnématismoi," *Philologus* 53 (1894): 101.
8. C. H. Roberts, "The Codex," *Proceedings of the British Academy* 40 (1954): 196.
9. Ernst Posner, *Archives in the Ancient World* (Cambridge, MA: Harvard University Press, 1972), 162.
10. Bruno Hirschfeld, "Die Gesta municipalia in römischer und frühgermanischer Zeit," PhD diss., Marburg University, 1904, 16.
11. Franz Wieacker, *Textstufen klassischer Juristen* (Göttingen: Vandenhoeck & Ruprecht, 1960), 94.
12. Harold A. Innis, *Empire and Communications* (Toronto: University of Toronto Press, 1986), 112.
13. Wieacker, *Textstufen*, 111.
14. Ibid., 114, 117.
15. Wieacker, *Römische Rechtsgeschichte*, 118.
16. Hotman, *Antitribonian*, 124; Kelley, *Foundations*, 69.

17. Wieacker, *Römische Rechtsgeschichte*, 117, 118n28, 120.

18. Heinrich Otto Meisner, *Urkunden- und Aktenlehre der Neuzeit* (Leipzig: Koehler and Amelang, 1950), 36.

19. Legendre, *L'Empire de la vérité*, 140.

20. Zachariä von Lingenthal, "Digesta Justiniani," 172–73.

21. "Commentarii," *Pauly's Realencyclopädie*, cols. 748–50.

22. Wolfgang Kunkel and Roland Wittmann, *Staatsordnung und Staatspraxis der römischen Republik (Die Magistratur)* (Munich: Beck, 1995), 106.

23. Hans-Georg Gadamer, "Unterwegs zur Schrift," in *Schrift und Gedächtnis*, ed. Aleida Assmann and Jan Assmann (Munich: Fink, 1993), 15.

24. Eduard Böcking, *Über die Notitia Dignitatum Utriusque Imperii: Eine Abhandlung zur Literaturgeschichte und Kritik* (Bonn: Marcus, 1834), 84.

25. Posner, *Archives*, 196.

26. Thedor Mommsen, *Römisches Staatsrecht* (Tübingen: Wissenschaftliche Buchgesellschaft, 1952), 3: 1035.

27. Kurt Dülfer, "Urkunden, Akten und Schreiben in Mittelalter und Neuzeit: Studien zum Formproblem," *Archivalische Zeitschrift* 53 (1957): 19.

28. Adler, *Der verwaltete Mensch*, 964.

29. Otto Roller, *Das Formular der paulinischen Briefe: Ein Beitrag zur Lehre vom antiken Briefe* (Stuttgart: Kohlhammer, 1933), 86.

30. Ibid., 220.

31. "Acta," *Pauly's Realencyclopädie,* col. 285.

32. Weber, *Economy and Society*, 969–70.

33. Martin Schanz and Carl Hosius, *Geschichte der römischen Literatur bis zum Gesetzgebungswerk des Kaisers Justinian* (Munich: Beck, 1966), 170.

34. Detlef Liebs, *Römisches Recht: Ein Studienbuch* (Göttingen: UTB, 1994), 42. See also Mommsen, *Staatsrecht*, 1019.

35. On this distinction, see further Niklas Luhmann, "The Form of Writing," *Stanford Literature Review* 9, no. 1 (1992): 25–42.

36. Livy, *The Rise of Rome, Books 1–5*, trans. T. J. Luce (Oxford: Oxford University Press), 197.

37. Jean-François Lyotard, *The Differend: Phrases in Dispute*, trans. Georges Van Den Abbeele (Minneapolis: University of Minnesota Press, 1988), 126.

38. Roller, *Das Formular*, 54.

39. Viktor Gardthausen, "Protokoll. Text und Schrift," *Zeitschrift des deutschen Vereins für Buchwesen und Schrifttum* 2 (1919): 102.

40. Ulrich Wilcken, "Hypomnématismoi," *Philologus* 53 (1894): 103.

41. Arthur Mentz, *Geschichte der Stenographie* (Berlin, 1920), 21.

42. Quintilian, *Institutiones*, I, 1, 28. Quintilian, *The Orator's Education*, books 1–2, ed. and trans. Donald A. Russell (Cambridge, MA: Harvard University Press, 2001), 79.

43. Sigmund Freud, "A Note upon the "Mystic Writing-Pad,'" *The Standard Edition of the Complete Psychological Works of Sigmund Freud*, trans. and ed. James Strachey (London: Hogarth, 1961), 9: 229.

44. Quintilian, *Institutiones*, X, 4, 1.

45. See further Nicole Loraux, *The Divided City: On Memory and Forgetting in Ancient Athens*, trans. Corinne Pache and Jeff Fort (New York: Zone Books, 2002).

46. Rosalind Thomas, *Oral Tradition and Written Record in Classical Athens* (Cambridge: Cambridge University Press, 1989), 52–54.

47. Freud, "Mystical Writing Pad," 230.

48. Cf. Quintilian, *Institutiones*, X, 3, 31.

49. Paul de Man, *Allegories of Reading: Figural Language in Rousseau, Nietzsche, Rilke, and Proust* (New Haven, CT: Yale University Press, 1979), 277 (emphasis in the original).

50. Jacques Derrida, "Acts," in *Memoires for Paul de Man*, trans. Cecile Lindsay et al. (New York: Columbia University Press, 1989), 96.

51. Wolfgang Ernst, "Kantorowicz: New Historicism avant la lettre?" in *Geschichtskörper: Zur Aktualität von Ernst H. Kantorowicz*, ed. Wolfgang Ernst and Cornelia Vismann (Munich: Fink, 1998), 192.

52. Kunkel and Wittmann, *Die Magistratur*, 106.

53. Wolfgang Kunkel, *Römische Rechtsgeschichte: Eine Einführung* (Cologne: Boehlau, 1993), 80.

54. Böcking, *Notitia Dignitatum*, 81–82.

55. Herbert Lorenz, "Untersuchung zum Prätorium: Katalog der Prätorien und Entwicklungsgeschichte ihrer Typen," PhD diss., University of Halle, 1936, 88.

56. Böcking, *Notitia Dignitatum*, 81.

57. Weber, *Economy and Society*, 980.

58. See Friedrich Preisigke, *Die Inschrift von Skaptoparene in ihrer Beziehung zur kaiserlichen Kanzlei in Rom* (Strasburg: Trübner, 1917), 45.

59. Henrik Zilliacus, *Zu der spätgriechischen Gebrauchssprache* (Helsingfors, 1967), 18.

60. Goody, *The Logic of Writing*, 97.

61. Preisigke, *Die Inschrift*, 17, 63.

62. Peter Classen, "Kaiserreskript und Königsurkunde: Diplomatische Studien zum römisch-germanischen Kontinuitätsproblem," *Archiv für Diplomatik* 1 (1955): 34.

63. Böcking, *Notitia Dignitatum*, 82.

64. Michael Stolleis, "Condere legis et intrepretari: Gesetzgebungsmacht und Staatsbildung in der frühen Neuzeit," *Staat und Staatsräson in der frühen Neuzeit:*

Studien zur Geschichte des öffentlichen Rechts (Frankfurt am Main: Suhrkamp, 1990), 189.

65. See Sten Gagnér, *Studien zur Ideengeschichte der Gesetzgebung* (Stockholm: Almqvist & Wiksell, 1960), 109.

66. *The Civil Law: Including, The Twelve Tables, the Institutes of Gaius, the Rules of Ulpian, the Opinions of Paulus, the Enactments of Justinian, and the Constitutions of Leo*, trans. and ed. S. P. Scott (Cincinnati: Central Trust Company, 1932), 2: 3 [Section (2) of the Preamble to Justinian's *Institutes*].

67. *The Civil Law*, 2: 180 [Section (5) of the First Preface to Justinian's Digest].

68. Ibid., 3–4 [Sections (3) and (5) of the Preamble to Justinian's *Institutes*].

69. Gerhard Dulckeit and Fritz Schwarz, *Römische Rechtsgeschichte: Ein Studienbuch*, ed. Wolfgang Waldstein (Munich: Beck, 1989), 304.

70. Cf. *The Civil Law*, 181 [Section (7) of the Preamble to Justinian's Digest]: "You must also observe the following, namely: if you find anything which the ancients have inserted in their old laws or constitutions that is incorrectly worded, you must correct this, and place it in its proper order, so that it may appear to be true, expressed in the best language, and written in this way in the first place."

71. Dieter Simon, "Aus dem Kodexunterricht des Thalelaios," *Zeitschrift der Savigny-Stiftung für Rechtsgeschichte* 86 (1969): 378.

72. Liebs, *Römisches Recht*, 99.

73. *The Civil Law*, 2: 206 [Section (21) of the Third Preface to Justinian's Digest; translation amended.]

74. Benjamin, "The Task of the Translator," in *Illuminations*, 79.

75. Wieacker, *Textstufen*, 110–11.

76. *The Civil Law*, 2: 197 [Section (22) of the Second Preface to Justinian's Digest].

77. See Pierre Legendre, "Les juifs se livrent à des interprétations insensées: Expertise d'un texte," in ed. Pierre Rassial, *La psychanalyse—Est-elle une histoire juive?* (Paris: Seuil, 1981), 93–114.

78. *The Civil Law*, 2: 195 [Section (18) of the Second Preface to Justinian's Digest].

79. Pierre Noailles, *Les collections des Novelles de l'Empereur Justinien: Origine et formation sous Justinien* (Paris: Larose & Tenin, 1912), 36.

80. Marie Theres Fögen, "Gesetz und Gesetzgebung in Byzanz: Versuch einer Funktionsanalyse," *Jus Commune* 14 (1987): 142.

81. Peter Kussmaul, *Pragmaticum und lex: Formen spätrömischer Gesetzgebung 408–457* (Göttingen: Vandenhoeck & Ruprecht, 1981), 48.

82. Fögen, "Gesetz und Gesetzgebung," 140.

83. Novella 7.1.

84. Otto Hirschfeld, *Die kaiserlichen Verwaltungsbeamten bis auf Diokletian* (Zürich: Weidmann, 1975), 339.

85. Wulf Eckart Voss, *Recht und Rhetorik in den Kaisergesetzen der Spätantike: Eine Untersuchung zum nachklassischen Kauf- und Übereignungsrecht* (Frankfurt am Main: Löwenklau, 1982), 23.

Chapter 3

1. Classen, "Kaiserreskript," 65.
2. *Translator's note*: Through most of this chapter, the German *Urkunde* will be translated as "document." *Urkunde* is somewhat more specific than "document"; it is at times closer to "charter," "deed," or "certificate." In many instances, however, these terms are too specific to be used here.
3. Classen, "Kaiserreskript," 91.
4. Hubert Mordeck, "Karolingische Kapitularien," in *Überlieferung und Geltung normativer Texte des frühen und hohen Mittelalters* (Sigmaringen: Thorbecke, 1986), 47.
5. Peter Rück, "Die Urkunde als Kunstwerk," in *Kaiserin Theophanu*, ed. Anton von Euw et al. (Köln: Schütgen Museum, 1991), 2: 330, 313.
6. Ibid., 316, 318.
7. Classen, "Spätrömische Grundlagen," 84.
8. Fritz Kern, "Recht und Verfassung im Mittelalter," *Historische Zeitschrift* 120 (1909): 34–37.
9. Kantorowicz, "Zu den Rechtsgrundlagen der Kaisersage," *Selected Studies* (New York: J. J. Augustin, 1965), 307.
10. Papritz, "Grundfragen der Archivwissenschaft," *Archivalische Zeitschrift* 52 (1956): 140; on Papritz, see further Götz Aly and Karl Heinz Roth, *The Nazi Census; Identification and Control in the Third Reich*, trans. Edwin Black (Philadelphia: Temple University Press, 2004), 83n.
11. Harry Breslau, Michael Tangl, and Karl Brandi, "Einführung," *Archiv für Urkundenforschung* 1 (1908): 2.
12. Meisner, *Urkunden- und Aktenlehre*, 18–19.
13. Ernst Pitz, *Schrift- und Aktenwesen der städtischen Verwaltung im Spätmittelalter Köln-Nürnberg-Lübeck* (Köln: Neubner, 1959), 25.
14. Kroeschell, *Deutsche Rechtsgeschichte*, 2: S.173.
15. Peter Moraw, *Von offener Verfassung zu gestalteter Verdichtung: Das Reich im späten Mittelalter 1250 bis 1490* (Frankfurt am Main: Ullstein, 1985), 189.
16. Roger of Hoveden, quoted in Klewitz, "Cancellaria," 75.
17. Rudolf von Heckel, "Das päpstliche und sicilische Registerwesen in vergleichender Darstellung mit besonderer Berücksichtigung der Ursprünge," *Archiv für Urkundenforschung* 1 (1908): 454.

18. Weingarten, "Datenbanken," *Schrift und Schriftlichkeit/Writing and Its Use: Ein interdisziplinäres Handbuch*, ed. Hartmut Günther and Otto Ludwig (Berlin, 1994), 164.

19. Adler, *Der verwaltete Mensch*, 968.

20. Fritz Kern, "Recht und Verfassung im Mittelalter," *Historische Zeitschrift* 120 (1919): 22, 34–35.

21. Eduard Winkelmann, ed., *Acta Imperii Inedita Seculi XIII: Urkunden und Briefe zur Geschichte des Kaiserreiches und des Königsreiches Sizilien in den Jahren 1198–1273*, vol. 1 (rpt. Aalen: Scientia, 1964), 736.

22. Friedrich Philippi, *Zur Geschichte der Reichskanzlei unter den letzten Staufern Friedrich II., Heinrich (VII.), Konrad IV.* (Münster: Coppenrath, 1885), 30.

23. Wilhelm E. Heupel, "Schriftuntersuchungen zur Registerführung in der Kanzlei Kaiser Friedrichs II," *Quellen und Forschungen aus italienischen Archiven und Bibliotheken* 46 (1966): 1.

24. Martin Grabmann, *Die scholastische Methode im 12. und beginnenden 13. Jahrhundert* (rpt. Freiburg: Herder, 1957), 85, 87.

25. Mary J. Carruthers, *The Book of Memory: A Study of Memory in Medieval Culture* (Cambridge: Cambridge University Press, 1990), 99–100.

26. See Ernst H. Kantorowicz, *The King's Two Bodies: A Study in Mediaeval Political Theology* (Princeton, NJ: Princeton University Press, 1957), 275–84.

27. Thomas Aquinas, *Summa Theologica* (London: Burns, Oates and Washburn, 1920), Part I (Q. 10, Art. 5), 107 (translation amended).

28. Von Heckel, "Registerwesen," 452.

29. Latour, "Visualization," 28.

30. Report based on an eyewitness account quoted in Paul Scheffer-Boichorst, *Zur Geschichte des 12. und 13. Jahrhunderts* (Berlin: E. Ebering, 1897), 282.

31. See Winkelmann, *Acta Imperii*, 736.

32. Ibid.

33. Hans Martin Schaller, "Die Kanzlei Kaiser Friedrichs II: Ihr Personal und ihr Sprachstil," *Archiv für Diplomatik* 3 (1958): 317–18.

34. Letter reprinted in ibid., 285–86.

35. Walter Seitter, *Menschenfassungen: Studien zur Erkenntnispolitikwissenschaft* (Munich: Boer, 1985), 58.

36. Thomas Aquinas, *Summa Theologica*, Q. 10, Art. 5, 107.

37. A. Michel, "Eternité," *Dictionnaire de Théologie catholique contenant l'Exposé des Doctrines de la Théologie catholique, leurs preuves et leur Histoire* (Paris, 1913), 914.

38. Bernhard Siegert, "Vögel, Engel und Gesandte: Alteuropas Übertragungsmedien," in *Gespräche-Boten-Briefe. Körpergedächtnis und Schriftgedächtnis im Mittelalter*, ed. Horst Wenzel (Berlin: Erich Schmidt, 1997), 55.

39. Kantorowicz, *The King's Two Bodies*, 282.

40. Emil Göller, "Aus der Kanzlei der Päpste und ihrer Legaten," *Quellen und Forschungen aus italienischen Archiven und Bibliotheken* 10 (1907): 321.

41. Quoted in Karl Giehlow, "Dürers Stich 'Melencolia I' und der maximilianische Humanistenkreis," *Mitteilungen der Gesellschaft für vervielfältigende Kunst: Beilage der Graphischen Künste* (1904): 61.

42. Weber, *Economy and Society*, 281.

43. Erich Kaufmann, quoted in Günter Dürig, "Zeit und Rechtsgleichheit," *Gesammelte Schriften: 1952–1983*, ed. Walter Schmitt Glaeser and Peter Häberle (Berlin: Duncker & Humblot, 1984), 309.

44. Viktor von Kraus, "Itinerarium Maximiliani I. 1508–1518: Mit einleitenden Bemerkungen über das Kanzleiwesen Maximilians I.," *Archiv für österreichische Geschichte* 87 (1899): 272.

45. Maximilian I, *Kaiser Maximilians I: Weisskunig* (Stuttgart: Kohlhammer, 1956), 1: 227 (emphasis added).

46. Weber, *Economy and Society*, 219.

47. Maximilian I, *Weisskunig*, 1: 227.

48. Weber, *Economy and Society*, 957.

49. Ahasver von Brandt, *Werkzeug des Historikers* (Stuttgart: Kohlhammer, 1992), 97.

50. Hans Spangenberg, "Die Kanzleivermerke als Quelle verwaltungsgeschichtlicher Forschung," *Archiv für Urkundenforschung* 10 (1926): 525.

51. Pitz, *Schrift- und Aktenwesen*, 463.

52. Quoted in Heinz Quirin, *Einführung in das Studium der mittelalterlichen Geschichte* (Braunschweig: Westermann, 1964), 103.

53. Quoted in Gerhard Seeliger, "Die älteste Ordnung der deutschen Reichskanzlei. 1495. Oktober 3. Mecheln," *Archivalische Zeitschrift* 13 (1888): 4.

54. Quoted in Gerhard Seeliger, *Erzkanzler und Reichskanzleien: Ein Beitrag zur Geschichte des deutschen Reiches* (Innsbruck: Wagner, 1889), 203.

55. J.A. Jones, *Databases in Theory and Practice* (London: Kogan Page, 1986), 33.

56. Quoted in Otto Stobbe, *Geschichte der deutschen Rechtsquellen* (Leipzig: Scientia, 1965), 444.

57. Krzysztof Pomian, "Les Archives: Du Trésor des chartes au Caran," *Les Lieux de mémoire*, ed. Pierre Nora (Paris: Gallimard, 1992), 3: 167.

58. Gerhard Seeliger, "Die Registerführung am deutschen Königshof bis 1493," *Mitteilungen des Instituts für österreichische Geschichtsforschung* (1890), 342.

59. Wilhelm Bauer, "Das Register- und Konzeptwesen in der Reichskanzlei Maximilians I. bis 1502," *Mitteilungen des Instituts für österreichische Geschichte* 26 (1905): 265.

60. Seeliger, "Die Registerführung," 343.

61. Rudolf Schatz, *Behördenschriftgut: Aktenbildung, Aktenverwaltung, Arcivierung* (Boppard am Rhein: 1961), 22.

62. Spangenberg, "Die Kanzleivermerke," 473.

63. See further Fritz Ohmann, *Die Anfänge des Postwesens und die Taxis* (Leipzig: 1909), 109.

64. Hermann Wiesflecker, *Kaiser Maximilian I: Das Reich, Österreich und Europa an der Wende zur Neuzeit.* Vol. 5: *Der Kaiser und seine Umwelt. Hof, Staat, Wirtschaft, Gesellschaft und Kultur* (München: Oldenbourg, 1986), 297.

65. Quoted in Seeliger, *Erzkanzler*, 198.

66. Gaston Bachelard, *The Poetics of Space*, trans. Maria Joals (New York: Orion, 1964), 78.

67. Ibid., 79.

68. Pitz, *Schrift- und Aktenwesen*, 477.

69. Meisner, *Urkunden- und Aktenlehre*, 80.

70. Pitz, *Schrift- und Aktenwesen*, 473.

71. Meisner, *Urkunden- und Aktenlehre*, 87.

72. Pitz, *Schrift- und Aktenwesen*, 475.

73. Carl Wilhelm Cosmar, *Geschichte des Königlich-Preußischen Geheimen Staats- und Kabinettsarchives*, ed. Meta Kohncke (Cologne: Boehlau, 1993), 44.

74. Adolf Brenneke, *Archivkunde: Ein Beitrag zur Theorie und Geschichte des europäischen Archivwesens*, ed. Wolfgang Leesch (Leipzig: Koehler & Amelang, 1953), 402.

75. Georg Wilhelm Raumer, "Geschichte des Geheimen Staats- und Cabinets-Archivs zu Berlin bis zum Jahre 1820," ed. Eckhart Henning, *Archivalische Zeitschrift* 71 (1976): 44.

76. Cosmar, *Geschichte des Staatsarchivs*, 18.

77. Raumer, "Geschichte des Staatsarchivs," 44.

78. Stolleis, *Geschichte des öffentlichen Rechts*, 1: 357.

Chapter 4

1. Ernst, "Kantorowicz," 192.

2. Wilfried Barner, *Barockrhetorik: Untersuchungen zu ihren geschichtlichen Grundlagen* (Tübingen: Niemeyer, 1970), 170.

3. Cf. Friedrich Carl Moser, *Der Herr und der Diener* (Frankfurt, 1759), 100ff.

4. Rüdiger Campe, "Im Reden Handeln. Persuasion und Figurenbilden," in *Literaturwissenschaft – Einführung in ein Sprachspiel*, ed. Heinrich Bosse and Ursula Renner (Freiburg: Rombach, 1999), 9.

5. Michel Foucault, *The Order of Things* (New York: Vintage, 1994), 311.

6. Johann Stephan von Pütter, *Anleitung zur Juristischen Praxi—wie in Teutschland sowohl gerichtliche als aussergerichtliche Rechtshändel oder andere Canzley- Reichs und Staats-Sachen schriftlich oder mündlich beygelegt werden* (Göttingen, 1789), 51.

7. Stefan Rieger, *Speichern/Merken: Die künstlichen Intelligenzen des Barock* (Munich: Fink, 1997), 51.

8. Edith Grether, *Die Poesie der Throne: Die Juristen in der fruchtbringenden Gesellschaft* (Frankfurt am Main: Lang, 1995), 137.

9. Ibid., 119.

10. Quoted in Martin Johannes Heller, *Reform der deutschen Rechtssprache im 18. Jahrhundert* (Frankfurt am Main: Lang, 1992), 52.

11. Cf. Georg Philipp Harsdörfer, *Der teutsche Secretarius; das ist Allen Cantzleyen, Studir- und Schreibstuben nutzliches, fast notwendiges und zum dritten mal vermehrtes Titular- und Formularbuch* (rpt. Hildesheim: Olms, 1971).

12. Hans Hattenhauer, *Zur Geschichte der deutschen Rechts- und Gesetzessprache* (Hamburg: Vandenhoeck & Ruprecht, 1987), 21.

13. Johann Jacob Moser, Preface to *Entwurf zu einer Staats- und Canzley Academie* (Hanau, 1749), n.p.

14. Pütter, *Anleitung*, 6.

15. Miloš Vec, *Zeremonialwissenschaft im Fürstenstaat. Studien zur juristischen und politischen Theorie absolutistischer Herrschaftsrepräsentation* (Frankfurt am Main: Klostermann, 1998), 224.

16. Christian August Beck, *Versuch einer Staatspraxis, oder Canzleyübung aus der Politik, dem Staats- und Völkerrechte* (Wien, 1754), 1.

17. Julius Wilhelm von Massow, *Anleitung zum praktischen Dienst der königlich-preußischen Justizbedienten für Referendarien* (Berlin, 1816), 45ff.

18. Veit Ludwig von Seckendorff, *Teutscher Fürsten-Staat* (Jena, 1720), 94.

19. Michael Stolleis, "Jus publicum und Aufklärung," in *Universitäten und Aufklärung*, ed. Notker Hammerstein (Göttingen: Wallstein, 1995), 182.

20. Johann Jakob Moser, "Ein selbstgezeichnetes Charakterbild," in *Das Leben Johann Jakob Moser's: Aus seiner Selbstbiographie, den Archiven und Familienpapieren*, ed. August Schmid (Stuttgart: Liesching, 1868), 501–2. See further Markus Krajewski, *Zettel Wirtschaft: Die Geburt der Kartei aus dem Geiste der Bibliothek* (Berlin: Kadmos, 2002).

21. Johann Georg Estor, *Anweisung für beambten und adlichen gerichts-verwalter und aussergerichtlichen rechtshändeln auch zu summarischen prozessen* (Marburg, 1762), 50.

22. Quoted in Bernhard Diestelkamp, "Das Reichskammergericht im Rechtsleben des 16. Jahrhunderts," in *Rechtsgeschichte als Kulturgeschichte: Festschrift für Adalbert Erler*, ed. Hans-Jürgen Becker et al. (Aalen: Scientia, 1976), 460.

23. Pütter, *Anleitung*, first edition of 1759.

24. Moser, "Preface," 9.

25. Max Lehmann, "Der Ursprung des preußischen Kabinetts," *Historische Zeitschrift* 63 (1889): 271.

26. Beck, *Versuch einer Staatspraxis*, 95, 97.

27. Meisner, "Aktenkunde," 102–3.

28. Von Massow, *Anleitung*, 74.

29. Martin Johannes Heller, *Reform der deutschen Rechtssprache im 18 Jahrhundert* (Frankfurt am Main: Lang, 1992), 222.

30. Von Massow, *Anleitung*, 71.

31. Beck, *Versuch einer Staatspraxis*, 11.

32. Gilles Deleuze and Félix Guattari, *A Thousand Plateaus: Capitalism and Schizophrenia,* trans. Brian Massumi (Minneapolis: University of Minnesota Press, 1987), 101.

33. Moser, "Preface," 7.

34. Ibid., 13–15.

35. Friedrich Karl (Carl) von Moser, *Versuch einer Staatsgrammatik* (Frankfurt am Main, 1749), 125.

36. Cabinet decree of September 15, 1746, quoted in Hans Haussherr, *Verwaltungseinheit und Ressortrennung: Vom Ende des 17. Jahrhunderts bis zum Beginn des 19. Jahrhunderts* (Berlin: Akademie-Verlag, 1953), 26.

37. Moser, "Preface," 117.

38. Preisigke, *Die Inschrift*, 30f.

39. Bernd Wunder, *Geschichte der Bürokratie in Deutschland* (Frankfurt am Main: Suhrkamp, 1986), 45.

40. Quoted in Herman Granier, "Ein Reformversuch des preußischen Kanzleistils im Jahre 1800," *Forschungen aus der brandenburgischen und preußischen Geschichte* 15 (1902): 171.

41. Quoted in Gottfried Baumgärtel, *Die Gutachter- und Urteiltätigkeit der Erlanger Juristenfakultät in dem ersten Jahrhundert ihres Bestehens: Zugleich ein Beitrag zur Geschichte der Rechtspflege* (Erlangen: Döres, 1962), 65.

42. Friedrich Kittler, *Discourse Networks,* trans. Michael Metteer and Chris Cullens (Stanford, CA: Stanford University Press, 1990), 61.

43. Karl Marx, *Critique of Hegel's "Philosophy of Right,"* ed. Joseph O'Malley (Cambridge: Cambridge University Press, 1970), 45.

44. G. W. F. Hegel, *Philosophy of Right* (London: George Bell, 1896), 302 (§294) (translation amended).

45. Karl vom und zum Stein, "Nassauer Denkschrift," in *Briefe und amtliche Schriften,* ed. Walter Hubatsch and Erich Botzenhart (Stuttgart: Kohlhammer, 1960), II/2: 394.

46. Bernhard Dotzler, *Papiermaschinen* (Munich: Fink, 1996), 474.

47. Michael Stolleis, *Geschichte des öffentlichen Rechts* (Munich: C. H. Beck, 1992), 2: 405.

48. Reinhart Koselleck, *Preußen zwischen Reform und Revolution: Allgemeines Landrecht, Verwaltung und soziale Bewegung von 1791 bis 1848* (Stuttgart: Klett, 1967), 666.

49. Instruction to high-ranking officials of October 23, 1817.

50. Vom Stein, *Briefe und amtliche Schriften*, ed. Walter Hubatsch and Erich Botzenhard (Stuttgart: Kohlhammer), 5.

51. Ibid., 632.

52. Ibid., 381 (letter to Heinrich von Gagern of August 24, 1821).

53. *Translator's note: Schreibmaschine*, the German word for "typewriter," literally translates as "writing machine."

54. Koep, *Das himmlische Buch*, 49.

55. Johann Caspar Lavater, *Secret Journal of a Self-Observer; Or, Confessions and Familiar Letters of the Rev. J. C. Lavater*, trans. Rev. Peter Will (London: Cadell and Davies, 1795), 1: 4.

56. Hans Haussherr, "Die Lücke in den Denkwürdigkeiten des Staatskanzlers Fürsten von Hardenberg," in *Archivar und Historiker: Studien zur Archiv- und Geschichtswissenschaft zum 65. Geburtstag von Heinrich Otto Meisner* (Berlin: Rütten and Loenning, 1956), 501.

57. Wunder, *Geschichte der Bürokratie*, 14.

58. Haussherr, "Die Lücke," 502–3, 508.

59. Edict of November 24, 1776, quoted in Hellmuth Heyden, "Ludwig Wilhelm Brüggemann 1745–1817," *Pommersche Geistliche vom Mittelalter bis zum 19. Jahrhundert* (Cologne: Böhlau, 1965), 201.

60. After the writer Maximilian Samson Friedrich Schöll, whom Hardenberg had appointed as his literary executor, was removed, the files remained untreated. See further Haussherr, "Die Lücke," 509.

61. Leopold von Ranke, ed., "Vorrede" (Preface), *Denkwürdigkeiten des Staatskanzlers Fürsten von Hardenberg* (Leipzig: Duncker & Humblot, 1877), 2: vi.

62. According to an account by the physician and philosopher Johann Georg Zimmermann (1728–95), who visited Goethe's parents in Frankfurt in September 1775, "Goethe brought out a sack filled with little scraps of paper. He emptied it on the table and said: 'Voilà mon Faust!'" Quoted in Ernst Robert Curtius, "Goethe as Administrator," *Essays on European Literature*, trans. Michael Kowal (Princeton, NJ: Princeton University Press, 1973), 58.

63. Johann Wolfgang von Goethe, *Goethes Werke* (Weimar: Herausgegeben im Auftrage der Grossherzogin Sophie von Sachsen, 1903), second division, vol. 41.2: 402.

64. Goethe, *Werke*, ed. Erich Trunz (Munich: C. H. Beck, 1976), 10: 531.

65. Ibid., 532–34.

66. Goethe, *Goethes Werke* (1903), 400.

67. Goethe, *Werke*, ed. Trunz, 10: 535.

68. Ibid., 533f.

69. Ibid., 529.

70. Ibid., 533f.

71. C. Vogel, *Goethe in amtlichen Verhältnissen: Aus den Acten bes. durch Correspondenzen zwischen ihm und dem Großherzoge Carl August. Geh Rat Voigt u. a.* (Jena: Frommann, 1834), 38.

72. Ibid., vi–vii

73. Ibid., 34–35.

74. Quoted in Curtius, "Goethe as Administrator," 59.

75. Quoted in ibid., 63.

76. Quoted in ibid., 71.

77. Curtius, "Goethe," 68.

78. Quoted in ibid., 68 (translation amended).

79. Frank M. Bischoff and Axel Koppetsch, "Das archivische Menschenrecht," *Frankfurter Allgemeine Zeitung*, 7 July 1994, 34.

80. Pomian, "Les Archives," 182.

81. Ibid., 183.

82. Michael Bakunin, *Selected Writings*, ed. Arthur Lehning (London: Jonathan Cape, 1973), 168ff.

83. Weber, *Economy and Society*, 988 (emphasis in the original).

84. Ibid., 988–89.

85. Meta Kohnke, "Zur Geschichte des Generaldirektoriums 1712/1822," *Aus der Arbeit des Geheimen Staatsarchivs Preußischer Kulturbesitz*, ed. Jürgen Kloosterhuis (Berlin: Selbstverlag des Geheimen Staatsarchivs PK, 1996), 70.

86. Kohnke, "Zur Geschichte des Generaldirektoriums," 70.

87. Pütter, *Anleitung*, 267f.

88. Johann Gustav Droysen, *Historik*, ed. Peter Leyh (Stuttgart: Oldenbourg, 1977), 1: 70.

89. Quoted in Gerhard Zimmermann, "Hardenberg: Versuch einer preußischen Archivverwaltung und deren weiterer Entwicklung bis 1933," *Jahrbuch Stiftung Preußischer Kulturbesitz* (1966): 72.

90. Moser, "Preface," 114.

91. Ranke, "Vorrede zur ersten Ausgabe," *Preussische Geschichte*, ed. Willy Andreas (Wiesbaden: Vollmer, 1957), 48.

92. Lorenz von Stein, *Handbuch der Verwaltungslehre* (Wien: 1888), 5.

93. Adolf Brennecke, *Archivkunde: Ein Beitrag zur Geschichte und Theorie des europäischen Archivwesens*, ed. Wolfgang Leesch (Leipzig: Koehler & Amelang, 1953), 372.

94. Latour, "Visualization," 28.

95. Cosmar, *Geschichte*, 139.

Chapter 5

1. Quoted in Siegfried Schöne, *Von der Reichskanzlei zum Bundeskanzleramt* (Berlin: Duncker & Humblot, 1968), 60.

2. Arnold Brecht, *Aus nächster Nähe: Lebenserinnerungen 1884–1927* (Stuttgart: Deutsche Verlagsanstalt, 1966), 208.

3. Ibid., 515.

4. See Aly and Roth, *Nazi Census*, 43ff., 64ff., 84.

5. Raul Hilberg, *Sources of Holocaust Research: An Analysis* (Chicago: Ivan R. Dee, 2001), 51–52.

6. Instruction issued February 14, 1874, *Zusammenstellung von Vorschriften, die für den Dienstgebrauch im Reichsamt des Inneren von allgemeiner Bedeutung sind* [Compilation of regulations of general importance for office use in the Ministry of Interior] (Berlin, 1912), 179.

7. Preisigke, *Die Inschrift*, 31.

8. See Wilhelm Rohr, "Das Aktenwesen der preußischen Regierungen," *Archivalische Zeitschrift* 45 (1939): 60–63.

9. Bess Glenn, "The Taft Commission and the Government's Record Practices," *American Archivist* 21 (1958): 301.

10. See Raul Hilberg, *The Destruction of the European Jews, Volume I* (New Haven, CT: Yale University Press, 2004), 70; Aly and Roth, *The Nazi Census*, 73–74.

11. Alfred von Schlieffen, "War Today, 1909," in *Alfred von Schlieffen's Military Writings*, trans. Robert T. Foley (London: Frank Cass, 2003), 198–99.

12. Weber, *Economy and Society*, 1393.

13. Ibid., 219.

14. Ibid.

15. Schatz, *Behördenschriftgut*, 28.

16. Bill Drews, *Grundzüge einer Verwaltungsreform* (Berlin, 1919), 177.

17. Johannes Papritz, "Organisationsformen der Schriftgutbewahrung in der öffentlichen Verwaltung," *Der Archivar* 10 (1957): 286.

18. Rohr, "Aktenwesen," 54.

19. Wolfram Werner, "Quantität und Qualität moderner Sachakten: Erfahrungen aus dem Bundesarchiv," *Der Archivar* 45 (1992): 39.

20. Weber, *Economy and Society*, 973–74.

21. Arnold Brecht and Comstock Glaser, *The Art and Technique of Administration in German Ministries* (Westport: Greenwood Press, 1971), 32.

22. C. A. H. Burckhardt, "Die Archive-Geschäftsakten und der Shannon-Registrator," *Archivalische Zeitschrift* 13 (1988): 267–68.

23. Hans-Joachim de Wall, "Leitz," *Neue Deutsche Biographie* (Berlin: Duncker & Humblot, 1985), 14: 175–76.

24. Adolf Reitz, *Ein Rundgang durch die Fabrikanlage der Firma Louis Leitz* (Feuerbach: n.d.).

25. De Wall, "Leitz," 175 (emphasis added).

26. Ibid.

27. Adolf Reitz, *Ein Rundgang*.

28. Leitz, *Firmenschrift*, Deutsches Museum für Technik, Historisches Archiv, Berlin.

29. See further Goody, *The Logic of Writing*, 87ff.

30. JoAnne Yates, *Control through Communication: The Rise of System in American Management* (Baltimore, MD: Johns Hopkins University Press, 1989), 56–57; see also the illustration on p. 60.

31. Glenn, "Taft Commission," 287, 291.

32. See further Howard T. Senzel, "Looseleafing the Flow: An Anecdotal History of One Technology for Updating," *American Journal of Legal History* 44 (2000): 115–97, esp. 119–20. Senzel offers an excellent survey of the American innovations in office technology (especially looseleafing) from the mechanical to the electronic era, as well as of their legal implications. I am indebted to Miloš Vec for this reference.

33. Senzel, "Looseleafing the Flow," 120.

34. E. Demtröder, *Die Aktenführung: Ein Leitfaden für die Einrichtung, Führung und Aufbewahrung der Akten nach älteren und neuzeitlichen Formen nebst Aktenführungsplan and Aktenverzeichnis* (Berlin, 1921), 44.

35. Nerlich, "Zur Reform der Inneren Verwaltung," *Preußisches Verwaltungsblatt* 13 (1910): 236.

36. Schatz, *Behördengutschrift*, 45.

37. Willy Paulyn, "Registraturloser Geschäftsgang," in *Einzelne Büroprobleme* (Berlin, 1927), 27.

38. Quoted in Schatz, *Behördengutschrift*, 335.

39. Drews, *Grundzüge*, 194, 176.

40. Nerlich, "Zur Reform," 233.

41. Wilhelm Dilthey, "Friedrich der Große und die deutsche Aufklärung," *Gesammelte Schriften* (Stuttgart: Vandenhoeck & Ruprecht, 1979), 3: 197.

42. Arnold Brecht, *Die Geschäftsordnung der Reichsministerien: Ihre staatsrecht-liche und geschäftstechnische Bedeutung. Zugleich ein Lehrbuch der Büroreform* (Berlin, 1927), 29.

43. Brecht and Glaser, *Art and Technique*, 1.

44. Ibid., 35–36. See also the more extensive calculations in Brecht, *Geschäftsordnung*, 32–33.

45. Niklas Luhmannn, *Funktionen und Folgen formaler Organisationen* (Berlin: Duncker & Humblot, 1976), 193.

46. Wilhelm Günther, *Die praktische Durchführung der Büroreform bei den Behörden* (Berlin, 1930), 105.

47. Drews, *Grundzüge*, 197.

48. Schatz, *Behördenschriftgut*, 31.

49. Quoted in Hans-Joachim Fritz, "Der Weg zum modernen Büro—Vom Sekretär zur Sekretärin," *Vom Sekretär zur Sekretärin: Eine Ausstellung der Schreibmaschine und ihrer Bedeutung für den Beruf der Frau im Büro* (Mainz, 1985), 50.

50. Cf. J. M. Witte, *Amerikanische Büroorganisation* (Munich, 1925), 48.

51. Wilhelm Triebel, *Geschäftsvereinfachungen in der Preußischen Allgemeinen Verwaltung* (Cologne, 1931), 32.

52. Paulyn, "Registraturloser Geschäftsgang," 24.

53. Quoted in Glenn, "The Taft Commission," 297.

54. Günther, *Die praktische Durchführung*, 58.

55. Schatz, *Behördenschriftgut*, 132.

56. Ibid., 24.

57. Ibid., 25.

58. Otto Frank, *Aktenordnung* (Stuttgart, 1957), 44.

59. Burckhardt, "Shannon-Registrator," 269.

60. The Dadaist poet and painter Kurt Schwitters (1887–1948), who for a time worked as a graphic designer for Pelikan, a German manufacturer of writing utensils located in Hanover, claimed that the sound combinations in his "Ursonata" were "in part unconsciously stimulated by abbreviated printed labels or inscriptions on nameplates." See Schwitters, *Anna Blume und andere Literatur und Graphik* (Berlin: Volk und Welt, 1985), 391.

61. Cf. Mills, "White Collar," quoted in Delgado, *The Enormous File*, 5.

62. Brecht, *Geschäftsordnung*, 8.

63. Delgado, *The Enormous File*, 68.

64. Instruction of the state secretary of the Ministry of the Interior of September 28, 1909, quoted in *Zusammenstellung von Vorschriften*, 16. *Translator's note:* Both addresses are located in Berlin. Wilhelmstrasse 74 once housed the Ministry of the Interior, Luisenstrasse 33/34 the Patent Office.

65. Luhmann, *Funktionen und Folgen*, 194.

66. Ibid., 113–14.

67. Thomas-Michael Seibert, *Aktenanalysen: Zur Schriftform juristischer Deutungen* (Tübingen: Narr, 1981), 34.

68. Hitler's notorious preference for oral commands makes use of this tactic, though not with absolute success. Oral orders, too, leave traces, especially in the file-obsessed Nazi administration. Further see Hilberg, *Sources of Holocaust Research*, 34–38.

69. Weber, *Economy and Society*, 992.

70. Hans Magnus Enzensberger, "Toward a Theory of Treason," *Critical Essays*, ed. Reinhold Grimm and Bruce Armstrong (New York: Continuum, 1982), 91.

71. Stanton Wheeler, "Problems and Issues in Record-Keeping," in *On Record: Files and Dossiers in American Life* (New Brunswick, NJ: Transaction Books, 1969), 6, 14.

72. *BVerfGE* (Decisions of the Supreme Constitutional Court) 12, 296, 303.

73. Wheeler, "Problems and Issues," 9.

74. Spiros Simitis, "Bundesdatenschutzgesetz—Ende der Diskussion oder Neubeginn" *Neue Juristische Wochenschrift* 30 (1977): 731.

75. *BVerfGE* [Decisions of the Federal Constitutional Court] 65, 1, 42.

76. *BDSG* [German Federal Data Protection Act, January 14, 2003], article 46, section 1, sentences 1 and 2.

77. "First activity report of the Federal Commissioner for the Records of the State Security Service," 35.

78. Karl Wilhelm Fricke, *MfS intern. Macht, Strukturen, Auflösung der DDR-Staatssicherheit* (Cologne: Wissenschaft und Politik, 1991), 73 (emphasis added).

79. "First activity report of the Federal Commissioner," 5.

80. "Third activity report of the Federal Commissioner for the Records of the State Security Service," 38ff.

81. Ulla Jelpke, Albrecht Maurer, and Helmut Schröder, *Die Eroberung der Akten. Das Stasi-Unterlagen-Gesetz: Entstehung / Folgen / Analysen / Dokumente* (Mainz: Pahl-Rugenstein, 1992), 36.

82. Maren Brandenburger, "Stasi-Unterlagen-Gesetz und Rechtsstaat," *Kritische Justiz* 28 (1995): 356.

83. Klaus Stoltenberg, *Stasi-Unterlagen Gesetz: Kommentar* (Baden-Baden: Nomos, 1992), § 6, marginal note 32.

84. Quoted in Jelpke et al., *Die Eroberung der Akten*, 73.

85. Schatz, *Behördenschriftgut*, 79.

86. Pierre Legendre, *L'Inestimable objet de la transmission: Étude sur le principe généalogique en Occident* (Paris: Fayard, 1985), 56.

87. "First activity report," 53.

88. Brandenburger, "Stasi-Unterlagen-Gesetz," 368.

89. Wolfram Runkel, "Deutschstunde bei Gauck," *ZEIT-Magazin* (June 21, 1996): 11.

90. Legendre, *Empire de la vérité*, 37.

91. Timothy Garton Ash, *The File: A Personal History* (London: Flamingo, 1997), 10.

92. Wolf Biermann, *Nachlass (1)* (Cologne: Kiepenheuer & Witsch, 1977), 445.

93. Joachim Gauck, "Von der Würde der Unterdrückten," in *Aktenkundig,* ed. Hans Joachim Schädlich (Reinbek: Rowohlt, 1992), 270.

94. Gauck, quoted in Ilse Staff, "Wiedervereinigung unter Rechtsgesetzen: Ein Beitrag zur Verfassungskonformität des Stasi-Unterlagen-Gesetzes," *Zeitschrift für Rechtspolitik* 25 (1992): 467.

95. "First activity report," 53; "Third activity report," 19–20.

96. Hans Blumenberg, *Ein mögliches Selbstverständnis: Aus dem Nachlass* (Stuttgart: Reclam, 1997), 40.

97. Heiner Müller, "Volokolamsk Highway," *Explosion of a Memory,* ed. and trans. Carl Weber (New York: PAJ, 1989), 137–41.

Chapter 6

1. Thomas, *Oral Tradition,* 82–83.

2. *Translator's note*: In German, Kiefer's composition is called *Zweistromland,* which literally translates as "two-stream land," a reference to the Tigris and Euphrates Rivers that bounded ancient Mesopotamia.

3. Armin Zweite, "The High Priestess: Observations on a Sculpture by Anselm Kiefer," in *Anselm Kiefer: The High Priestess* (London: Thames and Hudson, 1989), 69.

4. Cf. Zweite, "The High Priestess," 90.

5. Weber, *Economy and Society,* 973.

6. Hans J. Nissen, Peter Damerow, and Robert K. Englund, *Archaic Bookkeeping: Early Writing and Techniques of Economic Administration in the Ancient Near East,* trans. Paul Larsen (Chicago: University of Chicago Press, 1993), 153.

7. Nissen et al., *Archaic Bookkeeping,* x.

8. Menne-Haritz, *Akten,* 109–10.

Crossing Aesthetics

Jean-Luc Nancy, *Being Singular Plural*

Maurice Blanchot / Jacques Derrida, *The Instant of My Death / Demeure: Fiction and Testimony*

Niklas Luhmann, *Art as a Social System*

Emmanual Levinas, *God, Death, and Time*

Ernst Bloch, *The Spirit of Utopia*

Giorgio Agamben, *Potentialities: Collected Essays in Philosophy*

Ellen S. Burt, *Poetry's Appeal: French Nineteenth-Century Lyric and the Political Space*

Jacques Derrida, *Adieu to Emmanuel Levinas*

Werner Hamacher, *Premises: Essays on Philosophy and Literature from Kant to Celan*

Aris Fioretos, *The Gray Book*

Deborah Esch, *In the Event: Reading Journalism, Reading Theory*

Winfried Menninghaus, *In Praise of Nonsense: Kant and Bluebeard*

Giorgio Agamben, *The Man Without Content*

Giorgio Agamben, *The End of the Poem: Studies in Poetics*

Theodor W. Adorno, *Sound Figures*

Louis Marin, *Sublime Poussin*

Philippe Lacoue-Labarthe, *Poetry as Experience*

Ernst Bloch, *Literary Essays*

Jacques Derrida, *Resistances of Psychoanalysis*

Marc Froment-Meurice, *That Is to Say: Heidegger's Poetics*

Francis Ponge, *Soap*

Philippe Lacoue-Labarthe, *Typography: Mimesis, Philosophy, Politics*

Giorgio Agamben, *Homo Sacer: Sovereign Power and Bare Life*